The Darkened Sky

THE

DARKENED

SKY

NINETEENTH-CENTURY AMERICAN NOVELISTS
AND RELIGION

John T.  Frederick

UNIVERSITY OF NOTRE DAME PRESS

NOTRE DAME   LONDON

Library of Congress Catalog Card Number: 69-14811

Manufactured in the United States of America

For Lucy

Acknowledgments

FOR THE YEAR 1963–1964 I WAS THE RECIPIENT OF A RESEARCH fellowship granted by the American Council of Learned Societies and a travel grant from the American Philosophical Society. These enabled me to work in libraries far from my home, and to devote time and effort to this book. I wish to express my deep and lasting appreciation of this assistance.

No one proceeds far in an undertaking of this kind without incurring heavy obligations to librarians. My own indebtedness in this respect began with the help of Mr. Paul Byrne and Miss Eileen Conley of the University of Notre Dame Library nearly twenty years ago. Later I incurred specific obligations for valued help to Mr. Robert W. Hill, Keeper of Manuscripts at the New York Public Library; to Mr. Watt P. Marchman, Director, and Mrs. Ballenger of the Rutherford B. Hayes Library at Fremont, Ohio; and to members of the staffs of the Barrett Library of the University of Virginia, the Cornell University Library, the New York State Library, the Columbia University Library, and the Library of Congress.

I am especially indebted to Mr. Frederick P. Adams, Director of the Morgan Library, New York, for permission to quote briefly from the unpublished notebooks of Nathaniel Hawthorne.

During the period of the inception and early development of my work on this book, I had the profound privilege and help of the encouragement and advice of two truly great men who are no longer living: Rev. Leo L. Ward, C.S.C., of the University of Notre Dame; and Dr. Frank Luther Mott of the University of Missouri. Their generous confidence in the project and in me, expressed in many letters and conversations, was decisive in my commitment to the undertaking. To name all of my colleagues at the University of Notre Dame with whom I discussed the project at various times would be to list almost all of my fellow teachers in the English Department there from 1950 to 1962. I hope that each of these will accept this general acknowledgment as a personal expression of thanks. At the University of Iowa I have been especially grateful to Professor John C. Gerber and Professor W. R. Irwin for warm encouragement, and to Professor Paul Baender for helpful suggestions. Dr. John L. Tuckey of Purdue University has given me especially valued advice.

Finally, this study would not have been undertaken but for the interest and encouragement of Esther P. Frederick; it would never have been completed without the help and support of Lucy G. Frederick.

John T. Frederick

Contents

Introduction

IN THE SEVENTH DECADE OF THE TWENTIETH CENTURY INTEREST in and concern for religious matters of various kinds is markedly more widespread and acute than it was in the earlier 1900's. This circumstance makes appropriate a fresh look at the religious attitudes and experiences of American writers of the preceding century, particularly the six great novelists who underwent, each in fashion different from all the others, the religious ordeal of the nineteenth century. The rediscovery and reappraisal of the work of Cooper, Hawthorne, Melville, Howells, Twain, and James which has been so prominent a feature of American literary study in the last forty years has been generally deficient in attention to and understanding of the importance of the responses of these writers to the religious tensions of their times. Notable exceptions to this broad indictment have tended to be offset by eccentric and distorted readings, rising from the ideas and preconceptions of twentieth-century readers. Many critics have failed to recognize clearly the concrete terms in which religious problems confronted the individual writers and the intensity and urgency of their responses.

Working back from the specific expression of religious attitudes in the writings of the six novelists, we can recognize three major factors which contributed to the tensions all underwent. One of these is the fragmentation of sects and the attending dissension and often acrimonious debate which were especially characteristic of the first half of the nineteenth century. This became a part of American experience well back in the eighteenth century, with the division of colonial Congregationalism accentuated by the emergence and growth of Unitarianism, the invasion of the colonies by Methodism and other evangelical

xi

sects, and—though more especially in the first half of the nine-teenth century—the immigration of national and ethnic groups who brought with them their own religious institutions.

A second major factor was the "higher criticism" of the Bible, which also had its origins in the eighteenth century in the work of German scholars but gained small notice in America until well into the nineteenth. Strauss's *Das Leben Jesu,* pub-lished in 1835–36, was promptly reviewed in *The Christian Ex-aminer* by Theodore Parker, but it did not claim wide attention until the appearance of George Eliot's translation ten years later. William Cooper Howells, the father of the novelist, read the translation aloud to his family, and the general effect of this and similar works—notably Renan's *Life of Jesus* later in the century—became a significant part of the religious environ-ment of all six novelists.

Overshadowing both of these factors in importance was the impact of evolutionary science. In the eighteenth century and even before, the Mosaic account of creation had been ques-tioned, chiefly on geological grounds. However the major effects of evolutionary science were limited to the nineteenth century and focused in the doctrine of evolution itself. As twentieth-century readers, we tend to assume that the evolutionary hypo-thesis began with Charles Darwin and found its first expression in his *The Origin of Species* (1859) and *The Descent of Man* (1871). It startles us, therefore, to find James Fenimore Cooper referring to "the great animated chain . . . in which man is thought to be so familiarly complicated with the monkey" in *The Prairie* in 1826. In the best account of the rise of the evo-lutionary theory which I have found, Loren C. Eiseley's *Dar-win's Century,* the accumulation of scientific discoveries and the emergence of theories anticipatory of Darwin's in their reli-gious bearings are shown as marking almost the whole first half of the century. The full impact of evolutionism was not felt in America, however, until after the publication of Darwin's books and particularly after the visits of Thomas Huxley to America. Its effect on our writers was compounded, especially in the case of Mark Twain, by the new findings in astronomy which became known in the 1850's and 1860's. Thus the point of greatest intensity in the religious ordeal of the nineteenth century appears to have been reached almost precisely one hundred years ago and is most fully expressed in the recorded experience of Melville, Mark Twain, and Howells.

For each of the six major American novelists of the nineteenth century, these three major sources of tension and doubt were important, though in terms and to degrees differing in each case as affected by individual factors. An inquiry into those terms and degrees should illuminate for us both the works and the lives of the six men, often essentially, and may contribute to our understanding not only of their century but of our own.

I

James Fenimore Cooper

IN STUDYING THE LIFE AND WORK OF JAMES FENIMORE COOPER IN relation to the religious tensions of the nineteenth century, we are confronted by special problems. Donald A. Ringe is entirely right in stating, in his admirable recent study of Cooper, that "he was always a deeply religious man" and that "he always affirmed the fundamental values of religious belief."[1] But beneath this sound general assertion lies an anomaly: although throughout his adult life Cooper helped to support the Episcopal mission church his father had established in Cooperstown, and even served it as a lay official, he did not make a public profession of faith and become a communicant until the last weeks of his life.

No one who can claim real knowledge of Cooper and his work will suppose that this action at the end of his life was induced by fear of death or the wishes of his family, or by anything except personal conviction. I believe that this circumstance reveals in Cooper a prolonged and highly personal quest for a definitely Christian faith. In some aspects his quest was similar to those of succeeding writers. From a first position essentially deistic, he moved—influenced in significant degree by his European experiences—through prolonged and sometimes painful self-examination to the positive conviction expressed by his ultimate religious action.

1

THE DARKENED SKY

Cooper's parents were former Quakers. The precise reasons and occasion for their alienation from the Society of Friends are not clear. They retained to the ends of their lives the "thee" and "thou" of Quaker speech and in some measure other attitudes identifiable with Quakerism. Such evidence as can be found suggests that in his rise from poverty and obscurity to affluence and influence William Cooper, the novelist's father, adopted the broadly liberal deistic views of the eighteenth century held by many of the aristocrats with whom he aspired to be numbered. At any rate, it is clear that for his youngest son, James, born in 1789, the early years were not marked by any rigorous religious influences.

William Cooper had begun as a land agent hired by others, but during and after the Revolutionary War, he and a partner acquired title to a vast region in southern New York state formerly known as the Croghan Tract: some 40,000 acres of forests, lakes, and potentially productive agricultural land. Cooper started sales to settlers in 1786 and met with immediate success. His policy in attracting settlement was different from that of most other proprietors of comparable tracts: he sold land outright, under mortgages which he interpreted liberally, and he took active measures to aid and encourage his settlers in periods of adversity. Before the end of his career he was able to say that he had been the agent of establishing more permanent and prosperous settlements than any other person in the nation. In addition he had become wealthy and broadly influential as a judge, member of the state legislature, and congressman.

The fact that William Cooper married an heiress no doubt helped to make possible his success as a land speculator, and encourager of settlement. But his own energy and keen intelligence and his genuine interest in the welfare of the settlers were primarily responsible for his achievement. His "Letter to William Sampson" states in detail the principles underlying his policy, notes especially his recognition of the fact that "he who comes to better his condition . . . will look for some religious institution," and describes concretely the practical effect of his

2

effort to supply this desirable element in the settlement at Cooperstown:

> The first settlement at Cooperstown was made by the poorer class of men; they labored hard all the week, but on Sunday they either went hunting, or fishing, or else collected in taverns, and loitered away the day, careless of their dress or actions. The sons caught the manners of the fathers, and for the first ten years, or before any religious establishment was formed, the want of it was manifest. We then turned our attention to remedy the evil, and our pains were rewarded; for, since that time, new and better morals and manners have prevailed, and it has now become a matter of honest pride, and as it were a fashion, to be orderly and correct. If any still follow the ancient practice of fishing and hunting on Sunday, they no longer go openly and publicly, but privately and unseen. The people now appear in decent clothing; they are taught to love each other, and the pastor moving among them, promotes by his influence and persuasion a happy spirit of union and good will. . . . they listen to him not as to a master, but as a friend, and pay him a willing obedience, beyond what the authority of the magistrates, or the power of the government ever could enforce. . . .[2]

The steps taken by Judge Cooper "to remedy the evil" were to obtain funds for the establishment of an Episcopalian mission church at Cooperstown and to support the parish substantially from his own funds.

William Cooper's choice of an Episcopalian mission as a religious institution to foster is an indication of the underlying motive of his life: the desire for respectability, for position, for acceptance by the aristocracy of New York. There were abundant and vigorous religious institutions on the frontier and in the village of Cooperstown: Methodist, Presbyterian, Baptist, Universalist, including groups who belonged to what one of Cooper's characters called the "standing orders"—those who refused to kneel for prayers. No doubt these denominational groups were actually more attractive to the settlers than the Episcopalian, and the credit which William Cooper takes for the good effects of his "establishment of religion" should be shared. But having his own family participate in Episcopalian services was for Cooper socially advantageous. In *The Story of Cooperstown*, Rev. Ralph Birdsall has recognized the effect of William Cooper's social ambitiousness in differentiating Cooperstown from most frontier communities:

> From the time of the first settlement, apparently, an aristocratic group was formed in the orbit of the Cooper nucleus, and social climbing began before the wolves and bears had been quite driven from the forests of Otsego.[3]

The most concrete evidence of Cooper's social ambition is perhaps the fact that the mansion which he erected when his wealth permitted it, Otsego Hall, was a duplicate of the Van Rensselaer manor house.

The same ambition no doubt had a part in his decision to remove his youngest son, then nine years old, from the local "academy" at Cooperstown and send him to the highly exclusive private school of the Reverend Ellison, an Episcopalian clergyman, at Albany, where his fellow students included two Van Rensselaers, a Livingston, and a Jay. How far the portrayal of the Episcopalian rector who is Corny Littlepage's tutor in *Satanstoe* is a sketch of Rev. Ellison—in his fondness for good food and drink, his interest in cockfights and horse races, and his personal timidity—is not clear. However, Cooper's later comment on the Albany experience includes the fact that the Reverend Ellison was living with a woman not his wife and suggests that the atmosphere of the establishment was more worldly than religious.

James Cooper's experience of college, at Yale, where he was sent at the age of fourteen after the death of Ellison, seems to have been even more worldly. In later years Cooper referred to his associations at Yale as marked by extreme wickedness. However, he did not specify the nature of this wickedness. All that is certain is that he was expelled in his third year, as the result, tradition has it, of a scientific experiment involving gunpowder, the lock on a fellow student's room, and a flint attached to the key or some other means of ignition. An older brother had previously been expelled from Princeton for setting fire to a building. The reaction of William Cooper was to send his youngest son to sea as a common sailor on a merchant vessel. Judge Cooper planned a career as a naval officer for James, and in the absence of a naval academy in those days, a year as a sailor before the mast was prerequisite for admission to cadetship.

It seems probable that this year at sea, which involved a thrilling voyage, was the turning point in James Cooper's career. For the first time in his life he had to submit to harsh discipline, work for plain fare, and achieve by his own conduct a satisfactory footing with his fellows. It was during the following two years while he was serving as a naval cadet, first at New York and later on Lake Ontario, that he met the young woman, Susan De Lancey, whom he married soon after obtaining his release from the Navy.

It was during this period, too, that Judge William Cooper died, the victim of a blow on the head from behind by a political opponent. The estate seemed huge, and also Susan De Lancey had prospect of an inheritance. But five years later James Cooper's five older brothers were all dead, having succeeded in dissipating the whole estate and leaving only debts. It was in part because of the resulting financial responsibilities that James became a writer.

The De Lanceys were loyal Episcopalians. One of Susan's brothers later became the Episcopalian bishop of western New York. No doubt it was with his wife's warm approval that Cooper assumed his father's obligations toward support of the Episcopalian mission at Cooperstown and continued that support as long as he lived. Cooper's wife and Cooper himself participated actively in church affairs, both during their residence in the De Lancey neighborhood and at Cooperstown. It was not until after his return from Europe, however, that (in 1834) Cooper became a lay officer of the Cooperstown parish. It was not until the year of his death, as noted above, that he became a communicant.

THE DARKENED SKY

II

Cooper's clergymen are among the most interesting of his fictional creations. They are numerous, widely varied, sharply individualized. Among some thirty "full-length" studies of clergymen are some of his most powerful and memorable characterizations. In the eight earlier novels, however, clergymen have relatively little importance. Men of the cloth are missing from the pages of *The Pilot, The Last of the Mohicans,* and *The Prairie*. The unnamed British divine of *The Spy* and Dr. Liturgy of *Lionel Lincoln* are treated briefly and satirically— the latter harshly so. In the Reverend Meek Wolfe of *The Wept of Wish-ton-Wish,* we have one of Cooper's characteristically vigorous and characteristically fair-minded dramatic attacks on Puritanism. Though Wolfe is a busybody and is bloodthirsty in his view of the Indians, he is not a coward.

Of all these clergymen of the earlier books, only the Reverend Grant, the Episcopalian missionary priest of *The Pioneers,* is treated kindly. He is shown as sincere, sensitive, unselfish— and also as largely ineffective. Some of the characters in *The Pioneers* are clearly portrayals of actual Cooperstown people of Cooper's boyhood, in spite of his and his daughter's denials (the actual name of one, Le Quoi, is used). However, the figure of Grant is sharply modified. The real first Episcopalian priest at Cooperstown, Father Nash, was colorful, widely admired, notably effective in his missionary endeavors. There is mild and kindly satire in Rev. Grant's delight that the young hunter of the story is an Episcopalian: "Bless me! to think that he has arrived at manhood in this country, without entering a dissenting meeting-house!"[4] He is frustrated in his attempts to secure from "John Mohegan" more substantial evidence of conversion than attending services, and "the proud consciousness of the Indian sounded a little heterodox" to him.[5] In short he fails completely to understand Mohegan's true religious attitude as implied by Cooper. He is even less successful in finding common ground with the aging Natty Bumppo, who states in *The Pioneers* his observation: "I never knowed preaching come into a settlement but it made game scarce, and raised the price of gunpowder."[6]

Henry Seidel Canby has called Cooper "the best Quaker among American authors."[7] He has argued that Cooper's religious views were derived primarily from those of his father and were essentially those of the Society of Friends. This view is tenable only insofar as we can identify Cooper's own religious position with that of Natty Bumppo as portrayed in the Leatherstocking Tales. It is largely accurate for the years before the European sojourn but not thereafter.

The preliminary sketch of Natty in *The Pioneers* is meager in religious details. He attends a service conducted by the Reverend Grant, but when Grant tries to urge him to "attend places of public worship" regularly and to prepare for "eternity,"[8] he is negative and evasive. Cooper comments later in the novel: "Although the faith of the old hunter was by no means clear, yet the fruits of early instruction had not entirely fallen in the wilderness. He believed in one God, and one heaven. . . ."[9] The religious nature of Hawkeye is much more fully shown in *The Last of the Mohicans,* and his views are more precisely defined. In more than thirty passages he refers to a Supreme Being, or to a future life. He argues with David Gamut over the latter's doctrine of predestination, on which Cooper makes one of the few author's comments on religious matters to be found in the earlier novels:

> David . . . was deeply tinctured with the subtle distinctions which, in his time, and more especially in his province, had been drawn around the beautiful simplicity of revelation, by endeavoring to penetrate the awful mystery of the divine nature, supplying faith by self-sufficiency, and by consequence, involving those who reasoned from such human dogmas in absurdities and doubts. . . .[10]

When David challenges the scout's denial of literal predestination, demanding to know "in which of the holy books do you find language to support you?" Hawkeye replies:

> "Book! . . . I never read in but one, and the words that are written there are too simple and plain to need much schooling. . . ."
> "What call you the volume? . . ."
> " 'Tis open before your eyes . . . and he who owns it is not a niggard of its use. I have heard it said that there are men who read in books to convince themselves there is a God. I know not but man may so deform his works in the settlement, as to leave that which is so clear in the wilderness a matter of doubt among traders and priests. If any such there be and he will follow me from sun to sun, through the windings of the forest, he shall see enough to teach him that he is a fool, and that the greatest of his folly lies in striving to rise to the level of One he can never equal, be it in goodness, or be it in power."[11]

Cooper comments that "The instant David discovered that he battled with a disputant who imbibed his faith from the lights of nature,"[12] he abandoned the controversy.

This incident illustrates one of the functions of David Gamut in the novel. In his rather narrow doctrinal views he serves as a foil to Hawkeye, emphasizing by contrast the scout's simple faith. The characterization of David is one of Cooper's best. From clownish eccentricity and incapacity he rises gradually and believably to dignity and heroism. The sole important reference to specifically Christian convictions in the novel occurs when Hawkeye promises David that his death will be avenged:

> "Hold!" said David . . . "I am an unworthy and humble follower of One who taught not the damnable principle of revenge. Should I fall, therefore, seek no victims to my manes, but rather forgive my destroyers. . . ."
> The scout hesitated, and appeared to muse. "There is a principle in that . . . different from the law of the woods; and yet it is fair and noble to reflect upon. . . . It is what I would wish to practice myself, as one without a cross of blood, though it is not always easy to deal with an Indian as you would with a fellow Christian. God bless you, friend!

I do believe your scent is not wholly wrong, when the matter is duly considered and keeping eternity before the eyes, though much depends on the natural gifts, and the force of temptation."[13]

Hawkeye places much emphasis on "gifts" as a form of Providential influence in human affairs, insisting that his "natural turn with a rifle . . . must have been handed down from generation to generation, as, our holy commandments tell us, all good and evil gifts are bestowed."[14] The white man's "gifts" make him accountable for his conduct in ways not applicable to the Indian: ". . . what might be right and proper in a redskin, may be sinful in a man who has not even a cross in blood to plead for his ignorance."[15] Hawkeye insists, however, upon the equality of red men and white before the eyes of God, and the validity of the Indians' religious faith: "Even the Mingo adores but the true and living God."[16]

Speculating on the question whether "the heaven of a redskin and of us whites will be one and the same," Natty concludes:

"I believe that paradise is ordained for happiness; and that men will be indulged in it according to their dispositions and gifts. . . . I have heard preachers say . . . that heaven was a place of rest. Now men's minds differ as to their ideas of enjoyment. For myself, and I say it with reverence to the ordering of Providence, it would be no great indulgence to be kept shut up in those mansions of which they preach, having a natural longing for motion and the chase. . . . But it is a comfort to know we serve a merciful Master, though we do it each after his fashion. . . ."[17]

The religious element in the character of Natty Bumppo is much more fully developed in *The Prairie* than in the preceding treatments. In this novel, as contrast to Natty's simple faith, the narrow doctrinal views of David Gamut are replaced by the pretentious scientific ideas of Dr. Obed Battius. The crux of their recurring disputes is reached when Battius asserts:

"Man may be degraded to the very margin of the line which separates him from the brute, by ignorance; or he may be elevated to a communion with the great Master Spirit of all, by knowledge; nay, I know not, if time and opportunity were given him, but he might become the master of all learning, and consequently equal to the great moving principle."[18]

Natty's eloquent rejoinder is representative of Cooper's lifelong attitude toward the pretensions of science in relation to religion:

"This is neither more nor less than mortal wickedness. . . . Your l'arnin', though it is man's boast, is folly in the eyes of Him who sits in the clouds, and looks down in sorrow at the pride and vanity of his creatur's. . . . Knowledge! It is his plaything."[19]

In an author's comment on Battius' mistaken identification of his donkey as a new species, Cooper reveals his knowledge of the ideas already becoming current in nineteenth-century science and expresses his attitude toward them:

From that moment the world has heard no more of the Vespertilio horribilis Americanus, and the natural sciences have irretrievably lost an important link in the great animated chain which is said to connect earth and heaven, and in which man is thought to be so familiarly complicated with the monkey.[20]

It is highly interesting to recognize here Cooper's familiarity with ideas usually associated with Darwinism, thirty years before the publication of *The Origin of Species*.

In *The Prairie,* as befits his greater age and deeper understanding, Natty's religious position is expressed more impressively and with greater dignity and emphasis than in the earlier treatments of his character. Representative of their quality is his rebuke of Ishmael Bush early in the novel:

"I hold but little discourse except with One, and then chiefly of my own affairs . . . a Judge; and Judge of all. Little does He need knowledge from my hands, and little will your wish to keep anything secret from Him profit you, even in this desert."[21]

There is a deeply religious tone in the impressive account of the death of Hawkeye at the end of the novel. Natty repeatedly refers to himself as a "Christian man," but reasserts his faith in the unity of religions as stated in *The Last of the Mohicans* and expresses his hope that he will see his "Indian son," the Pawnee Hard Heart, "before the face of your Wahcondah, who will then be no other than my God."[22] Significantly, both for the characterization of Hawkeye and for indication of Cooper's religious position at this time, there is no reference in this scene (or elsewhere in the novel) to the Trinity or to the mediation of Christ.

When after fifteen years Cooper returned to the characterization of Natty Bumppo in *The Pathfinder* and *The Deerslayer*, he was conscientious in following the lines laid down in the earlier novels, in religious matters as in other aspects. Natty's independent position is stated more explicitly in *The Pathfinder* than in any of the preceding Leatherstocking Tales when he replies to Cap's question:

> "What sect do you hold out for?—What particular church do you fetch up in?"
> "Look about you and judge for yourself. I'm in church now. I eat in church, drink in church, sleep in church. The 'arth is the temple of the Lord, and I wait on him hourly, daily, without ceasing, I humbly hope. No—no—I'll not deny my blood and color, but am Christian born, and shall die in the same faith. The Moravians tried me hard; and one of the king's chaplains has had his say too, though that's a class no ways strenuous on such matters; and a missionary sent from Rome talked much with me as I guided him through the forest during the last peace; but I've had one answer for them all—I'm a Christian already and want to be neither Moravian, nor Churchman, nor Papist."[23]

This conviction is echoed in *The Deerslayer* when the scout tells Judith: ". . . the whole 'arth is a temple of the Lord to such as have the right mind. Neither forts nor churches make people happier of themselves."[24] Later in the same novel he observes: "An open spot on a mountain side, where a wide look can be had at the heavens and the 'arth, is a most judicious place for a man to get a just idee of the power of the Manitou, and of his own littleness."25

Cooper's impatience with doctrinal differentiations at this time is amusingly expressed in a brief comment on a minor character in *The Pathfinder,* when Sergeant Dunham is quizzing a sailor:

> "Are you a Roman Catholic?" demanded the sergeant, sharply.
> "No sir, nor anything else. I'm a generalizer about religion, never troubling that which don't trouble me."
> "Hum! a generalizer; that is, no doubt, one of the new sects that afflict the country!" muttered Mr. Dunham, whose grandfather had been a New Jersey Quaker, his father a Presbyterian, and who had joined the Church of England himself after he entered the army.26

In *The Deerslayer* Natty wonders, wistfully, whether there will be woods in heaven, and in *The Pathfinder* Cooper identifies his own belief with Natty's conception of the unity of faiths in an author's comment on the moving scenes in which the widowed Indian woman, Dew of June, prays all night at the grave of her husband:

> Humble and degraded as she would have seemed in the eyes of the sophisticated and unreflecting, the image of God was on her soul, and it vindicated its divine origin by aspirations and feelings that would have surprised those who, feigning more, feel less.27

Although the presentation of Hawkeye's religious convictions in the final novels of the Leatherstocking series is generally consistent with the character as established in the earlier books, there is a single brief incident in *The Pathfinder* which betrays the altering religious views of the author. Here Natty is introduced to the problem which assumes increasing proportions in Cooper's later work and gains major emphasis in his last years. Sergeant Dunham is dying, and his friends, including Hawkeye, reassure him on the ground that he has "done his duty in life." Dunham is inclined to a comfortable confidence on this ground. But his daughter, Mable, beseeches him:

" . . . rely on nothing you have done yourself, for mercy and salvation; trust altogether in the blessed mediation of the Son of God! . . . Have you not often felt your own insufficiency to effect your own wishes in the commonest things, and how can you imagine yourself, by your own acts, equal to raise up a frail and sinful nature sufficiently to be received into the presence of perfect purity? There is no hope for any, but in the mediation of Christ!"

"This is what the Moravians used to tell us," said Pathfinder to Cap in a low voice; ". . . Mabel is right."[28]

With this single exception, the mind of Hawkeye is untroubled by the religious problems which confront many of Cooper's major characters in his later work. Natty's religion is deistic in its origin "from the lights of nature," Quaker in its sincere humility, its acceptance of Providence, and its denial of the importance of religious buildings, forms, and elaborate creeds. It seems fair to assume that this position was largely Cooper's own in his earlier maturity, before his experience of Europe. Certainly there is nothing in the other earlier novels to disprove this assumption.

Tom Coffin of *The Pilot* (1823) is very like a Quaker himself, for he prays "standing, and in silence."[29] His religious convictions are drawn from his experience of the sea, as those of Natty from the forest; his speech is replete with references to the "One who can see the winds of heaven"[30] and to "He who rules the tempests."[31] Apart from the characterization of Tom Coffin, the religious content of *The Pilot* is negligible. That of *The Spy* (1821) is almost wholly so, as is that of *The Water Witch* (1831), the last of the novels of Cooper's first period. In Job Pray, the religious fanatic of *Lionel Lincoln* (1825), and in the Reverend Meek Wolfe and his fellow Puritans of *The Wept of Wish-ton-Wish* (1829) we have candid but not wholly unsympathetic portrayals of religious sects and attitudes of which Cooper was always critical. These books hold no significant indication of the author's own convictions. *The Red Rover* (1828) gives more space and emphasis to religious matters than the books just mentioned, but this is solely related to development of the principal characters and throws no light on Cooper's own thinking.

The impression that Cooper's concern with religion in these years was largely external and incidental is borne out by his treatment of the matter in *Notions of the Americans; Picked up by a Travelling Bachelor,* which was published in the same year with *The Red Rover.* The "bachelor's" letter "To the Abbate Giromachi" on the state of religion in the United States is wholly descriptive and historical, with no manifestation of Cooper's own views except for his approval of religious institutions in general.

In his concern to defend and champion the United States in contradiction of the defaming reports of British writers, which was the chief purpose of this book, Cooper asserts that—for example—"New York is rich in churches. . . . But in a country where the state does not meddle with religion, one is not to look for much splendour in its religious edifices."[32] He notes that the British commonly think there is no religion in America, but he believes this is due to the fact that the United States has no established church. On the contrary the "travelling bachelor" asserts, on the basis of what he claims to be wide observation, that there is a strong religious tone in American life:

> So far as the human eye can judge, there is *at least* as much respect paid to religion in the northern and middle States, as in any part of the world I have ever visited. Were the religion of Europe to be stripped of its externals . . . I am persuaded it would be found that there is vastly more. There is much cant, and much abuse of cant, in America, just as elsewhere; but . . .I should not know where to turn to find a population more uniform in their devotions, more guarded in their discourse, or more consistent in all their practices.[33]

In the same passage the bachelor states that "men who wish to stand well in popular favour are compelled to feign" religious attitudes at least. Two public men whom Cooper personally admired greatly—John Jay, a personal friend, and Washington, always one of Cooper's heroes—are praised for their sincere religious faith.

Two incidental references to religious matters in *Notions of the Americans* are of especial interest. Cooper's treatment of New England in this work has been generally ignored in the contention of critics that Cooper was ruled by a violently intolerant attitude toward Yankees. Actually the whole specific treatment of New England in the *Notions* is one of almost unmixed though discriminating praise, with no discoverable irony.[34] Further, the bachelor's friend Cadwallader accounts for the simple and sincere manners of Americans—which he finds admirable —by Puritan background and influence:

> After the mind is imbued with healthful moral truths, it admits the blandishments and exaggerations of conventional politeness with great distrust, and not infrequently with distaste. When the principle is pushed into extremes, men become Trappists, and Puritans, and Quakers. Now, in this respect, every American, taken of course with the necessary allowances, is, more or less, a Puritan. He will not tell you he is enchanted to see you, when in truth, he is perfectly indifferent to the matter. . . . The native of New-England has certainly more of this peculiar exterior than the native of any other part of our country. This difference is unquestionably a result of the manners of the Puritans.[35]

A second noteworthy point in regard to religion in the *Notions* is Cooper's claim that Catholicism is respected in America and his pride in this fact. In describing the reception given to Lafayette at Philadelphia, on his visit to the United States, he notes that a procession of some sixty clergymen was led by:

> ". . . the Bishop of the Protestant Episcopal Church, with the Bishop of the Roman Catholic Church at his side. The former, who is a native of the country, and one of its oldest divines, delivered the sentiments of his brethren; but had the latter, who is a foreigner, been of a greater age, and of longer service, he would, undoubtedly, have been selected to per-

form the same ceremony." The "bachelor" concludes: ". . . no country in the world . . . is more decidedly Protestant than this, and yet, I do believe, it would give scandal to the whole nation, to learn that a slight, or an offence of any nature, were given to a priest, merely because he happened to belong to the Roman Catholic communion."[36]

This point is reiterated in the general letter on religion in America "To the Abbate Giromachi," in which Cooper claims good relations between religious sects in the United States, noting especially the support of needy churches by members of other denominations.[37]

The attitude expressed here is an interesting and important aspect of Cooper's work throughout his career. In a period of furious intolerance in the United States—an attitude illustrated in extreme degree by Cooper's friend, Samuel F. B. Morse, who became the patron of the author of *The Awful Disclosures of Maria Monk*—Cooper remained open-minded and was attracted by some aspects of Catholicism. This is clearly illustrated in the three European historical novels which he wrote in Europe and in his travel books, particularly *Italy*. In his later fiction he dealt in two instances with material which demanded treatment of Catholicism. In *Mercedes of Castile* (1840) the attitude toward Catholicism is objective, as in the European novels, but respectful. This book is rightly adjudged to be, as a whole, one of Cooper's feeblest works of fiction. As in the case of others of his novels, however, the general fatuousness of the story is entirely absent from one major portion. The account of Columbus' first voyage, from the actual embarkation to the landfall, is a powerful narrative of action and emotion, and its mainspring is the unfaltering religious faith of Columbus himself, treated with complete sympathy and realized with genuine power. Again in an almost utterly neglected novel of real merit, Cooper dramatized his conception of Catholic faith with sympathy and understanding. This is *The Wing-and-Wing* (1845), also published as the *Jack-O-Lantern*. The central characters are a French privateersman of 1799, Raoul Evart, who is an avowed atheist, and the Italian girl, Ghita, whom he loves and who loves him. Her final decision to remain true to her faith is dramatized by Cooper with insight and sympathy.

The fragmentation of sects and the accompanying antagonisms and dissensions so prevalent in the United States in the first half of the nineteenth century had relatively little impact on Cooper. He reacted to religious bickering with irritation, or even exasperation, and a degree of wry amusement. Related to Cooper's disapproval of intolerance and his respect for Catholicism is his frequent acidulous comment on religious controversy in general, throughout his career, and his critical attitude toward the denominations marked by emotionalism and rejection of formal worship. In *The Pioneers,* "the good taste" of Marmaduke Temple (clearly a character closely related to Cooper's father) "revolted at the familiar colloquies which the leaders of the conferences of dissenting sects held with the Deity, in their nightly meetings;"[38] and we have noted in that novel his reference to the Episcopalian priest's delight in the young man who had never entered a dissenting meetinghouse. Along with its other extravagant denouncements of American society, *Home As Found* (1838) places emphasis on the prevalence of religious controversy. Aristabulus Bragg points out with pride that the small town of Templeton has "seven hostile denominations,"[39] but concedes that the Presbyterians have a slight advantage because theirs is the biggest bell. He asserts that the abundance of churches is a business asset: ". . . any man would be more likely to invest in a place that has five churches than in a place with but one."[40] In *Homeward Bound,* Steadfast Dodge has boasted: "Our people get their idea of manliness early; and as for kneeling in churches, we have some superstitious sects—I do not mention them; but, on the whole, no nation can treat the house of God more rationally than we do in America."[41]

In his later years, and especially after his wife's brother, William H. De Lancey, became the Episcopalian bishop of western New York, Cooper took a considerable interest in denominational politics, attended Episcopalian conclaves, and wrote his wife detailed accounts of the accompanying intrigues and occasional scandals. One of the later of his many full-length characterizations of clergymen, that of the Reverend Worden in *Satanstoe* (1845), shows us a worldly cleric who does not deny betting on horse races and cockfights, relishes good liquor, and is central in a farcical incident: too timorous to risk crossing the frozen Hudson at Albany in a loaded sleigh, he insists upon walking across the ice alone. As a result he is pursued by various sleighs intent on offering the foot-traveler a ride and is compelled—in his view of the matter—to run for his life.

A comment in *The Crater* (1847) rather fairly sums up Cooper's critical attitude toward denominational controversy, including that of the denomination he himself was supporting. In the thriving community which has risen on the volcanic island of that novel, Cooper tells us:

> The birds sang as sweetly as ever, and their morning and evening songs hymned the praise of their Creator as of old; but, not so was it with the morning and evening devotions of men. These last began to pray *at* each other, and if Mr. Hornblower [Episcopalian rector] was an exception, it was because his admirable liturgy did not furnish him with the means of making these forays into the enemy's camp.[42]

III

Cooper's years in Europe were decisive for him in matters of religion, as in other ways. His travel books contain abundant evidence of his interest in religious buildings and in all aspects of religious life and practice. Early in his transatlantic experience he was favorably impressed by St. Paul's in London:

> There is something glorious and appropriate in beholding the temple of God rearing its walls above all similar things, which puts the shallow and pettifogging sophistry of closet-edifices and whittling sectarianism to manifest shame.[43]

But he was sharply critical of some of the churchmen he

observed, not at all deterred by the fact that they were Episcopalian:

> Our visit happened to be made during the season of festi-
> vals, and more than a usual number of the officials were
> loitering about the church. Who they were, I cannot say, but
> several of them had the sleek, pampered air of well-fed
> coach-horses; animals that did nothing but draw the family
> to church on Sundays, and enjoy their stalls. There was
> one fellow, especially, who had an unpleasantly greasy look.
> He was in orders, but sadly out of his place, nature having
> intended him for a cook.[44]

The books of travel in France, Switzerland, and Italy are
equally candid and concrete in their comments.

The major significance of Cooper's European experience,
however, with the exception of a single incident, lies in his
treatment of religious matters in the three European novels he
wrote during his later years abroad.

The general critical judgment that these novels were written
primarily as commentaries, by means of historical example and
parallel, on social and economic aspects of the American scene
of his own time is justified. But the fact that his materials
required Cooper to give close attention to Catholicism, and to
religious factors in general as aspects of society, seems to me
significant in relation to his own religious experience. In *The
Bravo* (1831), a novel of Venice during the Renaissance, religious characters and institutions are in the background and are
not treated extensively. I am in agreement, however, with the
judgment of George Hillard, expressed as early as 1862, that
the incident in which the central character is granted confession and absolution by a Carmelite monk, "in his boat, under
the midnight moon, upon the Lagoons, is one of the finest . . .
in the whole range of the literature of fiction, leaving upon the
mind a lasting impression of solemn and pathetic beauty."[45]

In *The Heidenmauer* (1832) Cooper undertook to deal with
the central drama of sixteenth-century Europe, the rise of Lu-
theranism. Marius Bewley has pointed out that in this novel

Cooper anticipated in 1832 the analysis of the forces involved in the Reformation later recognized by Brooks Adams in *The Law of Civilization and Decay* (1895) and R. H. Tawney in *Religion and the Rise of Capitalism* (1926).[46]

Evidence of Cooper's effort to treat impartially the religious crisis of Luther's time is clear in his presentation of the churchmen who figure dramatically in *The Heidenmauer*. Approximately equal treatment, in terms of dramatic incidents and number of pages, is given to two of the Benedictines of Limburg: Bonifacius, the abbot of the monastery, and Arnolph, the prior. Bonifacius is shown in the first fully developed action of the novel as engaged with Count Emich, the local nobleman, in a drinking bout to decide the sole ownership of an annual tribute of one hundred casks of Duerckheimer wine, which in the past has been equally divided between the abbey and the castle. Later Bonifacius is established as a sagacious clerical politician, quite willing to employ subterfuge and to play upon the superstition of the times in his defense of the existing order against an attack which he clearly measures. In balance to this negative portrayal of sixteenth-century Catholicism is Cooper's full and richly sympathetic treatment of Father Arnolph. A major character throughout the book, he is shown as truly devout, a man of great capacities but free of pride and self-seeking (he has thrice refused the mitre). He is the object of the wholehearted affection and respect of the people. To Bonifacius he is a puzzle.

In *The Headsman* (1833), the third of Cooper's novels of European history and a work much inferior to *The Heidenmauer,* the economic and the specifically social themes overshadow religious issues and materials. The actual villain of the story is a professed Catholic, a trafficker in bogus indulgences. He is counterbalanced by an Augustinian monk who plays an important part in the story and is presented in an entirely favorable light.

That his period of intense occupation with European history, including—especially in *The Heidenmauer*—its religious aspects, had an effect on Cooper's own religious thinking seems to me suggested by some changes he made in his journals of European travels when he revised these for book publication. Indeed, one of these changes seems of cardinal importance. The crux of the problem of Cooper's religious experience is his transition from the essentially deistic position, roughly Unitarian in spite of his support of the Episcopalian parish, to the Trinitarian conviction—of Christ as God—which enabled him to become an Episcopalian communicant in the last year of his life. The incident which, I believe, suggests a beginning in this prolonged and painful transition occurred at the shrine of Einsiedeln, in Switzerland.

In the late summer and early fall of 1828, Cooper took his wife, daughters, and nephew on extensive journeys in Switzerland and later into Italy. They traveled in two carriages, with abundant luggage. After establishing temporary headquarters at Berne, Cooper made four expeditions in Switzerland, two of these on foot accompanied only by a guide. On the visit to Einsiedeln, on Thursday, September 11, 1828, Cooper first established the party at an inn and then, after dinner, went alone to visit the shrine. In the journal which Cooper wrote during this expedition, he mentions certain legends concerning the shrine at Einsiedeln as "too strong for the 19th century."[47] His account of his evening visit to the shrine itself is as follows:

> Entered the church after dinner. It was touching to hear the prayers and to see bodies of pilgrims arriving and placing themselves before the shrine, with their packs on their backs, to pray for an hour without ceasing. Some with outstretched arms and some in silence. The whole business was prayer. I was the only human being who did not seem to pray. As twilight thickened the interior of the chapel was well suited to excite the awe of the worshippers. Its casing of dark stone, its insulated position, the light of three or four lamps so disposed as to fall on the mysterious looking countenances (black) of mother and child, surrounded by their glitter of gold. It is uncharitable to think any who knelt there were

21

idolaters, but it is not difficult to conceive how easily they might become so.[48]

When he revised the journal for book publication, seven years later, Cooper noted at the beginning of the account: "As I can scarcely recall a day of stronger or more varied sensations than this, it may be well to give you a brief history of the causes which have brought the shrine of Einsiedeln into such repute."[49] And he has elaborated on his original description of his visit:

> The shrine is of marble, and it stands quite near the great doors. Iron gratings in front, and on parts of the two sides, permit views of the interior, where the bronzed images of the Mother and Child are so placed as to receive the rays of a single but strong lamp. Their habiliments resembled pure gold.
> When I entered, hundreds of pilgrims were kneeling on the pavement around the grates, keeping their eyes riveted, without exception, on the dark, mysterious faces within. Many maintained this position for hours, and all appeared to be absorbed in subdued devotion. The light of the church was growing dim with the decline of day, and I walked stealthily around the groups, and through the vaulted aisles, with feelings of reverence, pity, admiration, and awe, so blended, that I find it difficult to describe them. I knew that the temple was God's, and that his Spirit was present; I felt persuaded that much devout reliance on his mercy was blended with the superstition I witnessed; and, while my reason showed how fearfully near idolatry these poor people had approached, the mystery of the incarnation never seemed so sublime, and, if I may so express it, so palpable, as at that moment.[50]

The difference between the two versions of the same experience is striking. By rearrangement and addition of details and by stylistic changes Cooper has greatly enriched and intensified the reader's vicarious experience. Beyond this, he has introduced into the final sentence an element of emphasized personal significance which justifies the impression that the visit to Einsiedeln may have had lasting importance for Cooper:

the "mystery of the incarnation" is precisely that aspect of Trinitarian Christianity which Cooper continued to debate with himself almost to the time of his death.

Whatever import the experience of Einsiedeln may have held for Cooper, it was in the year following the revision just noted that the name of Christ and the theme of Christ's mediation for sinful men first found extended dramatic expression in Cooper's fiction, in the novel *Homeward Bound* (1837). *Homeward Bound* has been too often undiscriminatingly linked with the work which followed it immediately, *Home as Found,* rightly condemned for its stridency in denunciation of American society and for the artificiality and exaggeration of its characterization. These defects do appear in the early chapters of *Homeward Bound,* but once the *Montauk* is fairly launched on the voyage across the Atlantic, the book becomes one of Cooper's better stories of adventure at sea and is marked by sound and interesting development of characters. In the course of the voyage an Englishman, Monday, becomes gravely ill and realizes that he is about to die. He is cared for and counseled by John Effingham, who is clearly in some substantial measure a self-portrait of Cooper.

Effingham appeals to Monday to place no hope on his admittedly faulty performance of Christian duties but to rely wholly on the love and mercy of Christ and on his mediation. Here we find the first example of the recurring dialogue with himself which Cooper was to place in his fiction henceforth, rising to a final urgency in his last fully considered novels. That dialogue is echoed in *The Pathfinder* in 1840, in the passage previously noted. It is present in *Miles Wallingford* and *Afloat and Ashore* (1844), the neglected novels in which Cooper gives his most generous portrayal of a clergyman in Rev. Harding. It finds its fullest expression and sharpest intensity in *The Oak Openings* (1848) and *The Sea Lions* (1849), the last two novels which Cooper wrote while still possessed of his characteristic powers. (Evidence of these powers is absent in his final novel, *The Ways of the Hour,* written in 1850.)

THE DARKENED SKY

The Oak Openings contains one of Cooper's most powerfully drawn characters in Parson Amen. This man is a self-appointed missionary to the Indians of western Michigan, in the troubled years about the time of the War of 1812. His peculiar conviction is that the Indians are Jews—the descendants of the Lost Tribes of Israel—and hence especially deserving of missionary attention. This belief arose from the effort to explain the existence of the Indian race in a manner harmonious with the Old Testament. The theory was first suggested in very early colonial times and was still being urged in Cooper's day.

It would be easy for Parson Amen to be merely ridiculous, and Cooper has drawn him realistically. His preaching fails to convince the Indians. They reject vigorously the suggestion that their ancestors would have killed the son of the Great Spirit. Innocently he becomes involved in a general conspiracy, led by a tribeless Indian called Onoah or Scalping Peter, to massacre all the whites in the region and regain it for the red race. Amen is given a dramatic trial by the assembled warriors and chiefs, and condemned to death. Upon hearing the sentence, the parson asks for a few minutes' time and spends it in a fervent prayer for God's forgiveness to these who are about to kill him. Peter, who knows English, listens to the prayer and is profoundly moved by it. I agree with James Grossman that this is one of Cooper's finest incidents:

> Past and present become confused and one in Peter's mind as he watches the missionary pray for him, and the martyr's death becomes the living proof of the great atonement on which the dying man places all of his hopes. Peter, denying by silence the truth that is being revealed to him, is for the moment at the Crucifixion, of which every martyrdom is in a sense a part.[51]

Peter is converted by this experience and saves the lives of the other white characters of the novel. In this work Cooper succeeded in dramatizing, powerfully and concisely, the conception of the atonement as central in Christianity. In his remaining

novel of religious significance he realized this theme more fully
but less effectively.

I believe that finally in *The Sea Lions* Cooper came to grips
with and externalized his great religious difficulty, that of
accepting fully the doctrine of the Trinity. Grossman points
out two virtues of this novel: its forceful and merciless portrayal of pious greed personified in Deacon Pratt—an extended
genre painting, as Grossman calls it, one of the most detailed
and effective in all Cooper—and its brilliant action sequences
in the Antarctic. Grossman sees only as a defect the third
major aspect of this novel, its religious problem, and I must
grant that insofar as we look at the novel as a work of art, he
is right. As in *Wing-and-Wing,* we have a man and a girl separated by religious differences. Roswell Gardiner is no atheist
like Raoul Evart of *Wing-and-Wing;* he is, in effect, a Unitarian: a devout worshipper and a man of high standards in every
way. But to Mary Pratt, whom he loves and who loves him, his
refusal to accept the doctrine of the Trinity—on the ground
that he can't understand it, doesn't find it rational—is a form
of idolatry, a worship of his own reason above the word of
God. Roswell's experiences in the South Seas, his frequent
approaches close to death, his nights under the icy stars, are
enough to convert him to a more humble view of God and to
dissuade him from his reliance on his own powers. But Cooper
has to provide him with a companion who preaches Trini-
tarianism to him through the long watches of the Antarctic
night, to the very considerable distress of the reader and dam-
age to the book. *The Sea Lions* ends happily with Roswell's
admission of the error of his previous thinking, his marriage
to Mary, and the discomfiture of the Deacon. As Herman Melville commented in his review of *The Sea Lions* in *The Literary World,* "the moist, rosy hand of our Mary is the reward of
his orthodoxy."[52]

I am not sure that Cooper's fiction reflects his religious experience so fully as the fiction of his great successors in America
reflects theirs; but it does so directly and clearly. From a com-

paratively unreflective deism of his early years, he moved slowly
and painfully to a humble acceptance of the tenets of orthodox Christianity. Along the way he confronted the religious
dilemma of his age in the same terms in which it was confronted by Hawthorne, Melville, Twain, Howells, and in a
measure by James. He was alone among them in the final resolution he found. But his work shows that he did not find it
easily, or without pain and struggle. No less than those who
followed, he was a man of the century.

2

Nathaniel Hawthorne

HAWTHORNE'S WRITINGS SHOW LESS OF OVERT RESPONSE TO THE
special religious tensions of the nineteenth century than do
those of any of the other writers considered in this book except
Henry James. Yet, somewhat paradoxically, Hawthorne's religious views and their effect on and expression in his work have
been the occasion of more extended discussion and conflicting
interpretation than those of the other five writers—except that
one with whom Hawthorne often discussed these very matters,
Herman Melville.

Hawthorne lived through the age of Lyell and Asa Gray and
into that of Darwin and Huxley, but science remained for him
a matter related to magic and alchemy, not to be taken seriously
—rather to be condemned. As late as 1862 he declared: ". . . and
even heroism—so deadly a gripe is Science laying on our noble
possibilities—will become a matter of very minor importance."[1]
There is no positive evidence that he was even aware of the
existence of the new critical study of the Bible. The interest
in spiritualism—of his friends the Brownings, for example—
aroused in him only a profound indifference.[2] At Bowdoin he
was exposed to the fiercely intolerant religious controversy of
the early nineteenth century, and this experience had a lasting
effect on his attitude toward institutional religion. But Haw-

thorne's personal religious experience and position were only remotely affected by contemporary movements and attitudes. He did treat these matters in his work, however, often very clearly and candidly; and in his penetration of the New England past in his greatest fiction he achieved a grasp and understanding of the religious dimension of the life of that past in a measure unapproached by any other writer. Emphasis on religious matters is very marked in his fiction—an emphasis resulting from subject matter and intention, and thus widely divergent in effect. This divergence has occasioned an astonishing conflict in interpretations of Hawthorne's own religious position.

A tabulation of some of the conclusions of thoughtful readers will serve to demonstrate the range of this conflict:

> First critic: "Hawthorne was essentially a Unitarian."
> Second critic: "It is patently impossible to call Hawthorne a Unitarian."
> Third critic: "Hawthorne was a Puritan of the Puritans."
> Fourth critic: "Hawthorne's religion is wholly existential."
> Fifth critic: "Hawthorne's whole attitude is one of quiet affirmation."
> Sixth critic: "Hawthorne was the most consistent of skeptics."

Admittedly, I have heightened the divergences in these interpretations by omitting the reservations and qualifications which in most cases accompany them. But the fact of disagreement is obvious and its range is not exaggerated by these brief summaries. In the face of this degree of inconsistency, the only practicable course is to turn to Hawthorne's work itself. In Hawthorne's case we have fuller documentation for the nature and development of his personal religious attitudes than we possess for any other of the six writers. In addition to the published writings, there are letters, the testimony of many contemporaries, and—most important of all, and unique—the personal notebooks which extend to hundreds of thousands of words. By use of all these resources we may be able to clarify if not wholly resolve the conflict.

28

Nathaniel Hawthorne

The importance of an understanding of Hawthorne's religious views to the thoughtful reader of his work is emphasized by the degree of disagreement just demonstrated. It may be appropriate, therefore, to outline in advance the general views which will be developed in the discussion of specific works.

On the one hand, throughout his productive career Hawthorne was a consistent theist. Primary in his thinking was unquestioned belief in God—in the reality of an Omnipotent and Omniscient One who is also a God of Love, with whom the human spirit possesses a permanent personal relationship. Since references to Christ are relatively infrequent in Hawthorne and generally ambiguous as to Christ's divine nature, and since there is no clearly identifiable reference in his work to the third person of the Trinity, it seems fair to name Hawthorne's faith as Unitarian, the position shared by most members of his family and most of his friends. However, Hawthorne's Unitarianism was conservative. He vigorously rejected the assumptions of liberal Unitarianism as preached by Channing and others, notably the doctrines of the natural goodness of man and the perfectibility of man through his own efforts; and he saw in the transcendentalist refinements of Unitarianism a deadly danger to the human soul.

During the decades of Hawthorne's youth and early development Calvinism was undergoing a strenuous renewal in New England. It was led by such pulpit orators as Lyman Beecher and marked by the emergence of new denominations. Hawthorne was at a center of intense religious controversy during his four years at Bowdoin College. His own searching study of human nature in succeeding years led him to recognize an operative validity in certain convictions then usually associated with Calvinism. No reader of Hawthorne has ever recognized the resulting element in his writing more perceptively or described it more precisely than did Herman Melville, in his review of *Mosses from an Old Manse,* written before he had met Hawthorne and published in *The Literary World* in 1850.

For spite of all the Indian-summer sunlight on the hither side of Hawthorne's soul, the other side—like the dark half of the physical sphere—is shrouded in a blackness, ten times black. . . . Whether Hawthorne has simply availed himself of this mystical blackness as a means to the wonderful effects he makes it to produce in his lights and shades; or whether there really lurks in him, perhaps unknown to himself, a touch of Puritanic gloom,—this, I cannot altogether tell. Certain it is, however, that this great power of blackness in him derives its force from its appeals to that Calvinistic sense of Innate Depravity and Original Sin, from whose visitations, in some shape or other, no deeply thinking mind is always and wholly free. For, in certain moods, no man can weigh this world without throwing in something, somehow like Original Sin, to strike the uneven balance. At all events, perhaps no writer has ever wielded this terrific thought with greater terror than this same harmless Hawthorne. Still more: this black conceit pervades him through and through. You may be witched by his sunlight—transported by the bright gildings in the skies he builds over you; but there is the blackness of darkness beyond. . . .[3]

Yet Hawthorne clearly was not a Calvinist in any precise sense. He believed in the reality of evil and in the pervasive and permanent effect of sin. But so far as the record shows he was never able to embrace wholeheartedly, as a concomitant doctrine, the redemptive sacrifice of Christ. In his later years he felt his way toward a conception of the educative value of sin, or at least of the vision of evil; but his findings in this direction were apparently inconclusive for himself, as is his expression of those findings for most readers.

The crux of the problem of faith seems to have been for Hawthorne, as it was for many men and women of the nineteenth century, the question of personal immortality. Throughout most of Hawthorne's life, his assertion of faith in life after death was positive and constant, both in writings for publication and in letters and journals. Indeed, it seems so frequent, and so often relatively gratuitous or even irrelevant, as to suggest a fundamental though less than conscious uncertainty and anxiety. In Hawthorne's last years that anxiety became conscious and dominant, and the problem of immortality obsessive.

II

Much more seriously than in the case of any other of our six writers, understanding of Hawthorne has been hampered by false views of his personal life. A pervasive legend arose, of abnormality and eccentricity, which resulted in large part from the virtual pre-emption of the field of Hawthorne biography by members of his immediate family—his wife, his son and daughter, his son-in-law—for a generation after his death. According to this legend the circumstances of Hawthorne's life were in the highest degree exceptional and abnormal in the direction of repression, isolation, and gloom, up to the time of his marriage, and everything he wrote, both in these earlier years and thereafter, must be interpreted in the light of this period. Fortunately this legend has been effectively, though belatedly, exploded in recent years: notably through the finely rounded biographical studies of Mark Van Doren, Randall Stewart, and Hubert J. Hoeltje, as well as by the contributions of Robert Cantwell and many others.[4] Yet the legend has been so prominent in the work of critics who accepted the seemingly authoritative testimony of nineteenth-century biographers that it is still difficult to escape its influence completely. In regard to Hawthorne's religious experience and convictions, the influence of the legend has been especially pernicious and misleading.

It has been a frequent attitude in criticism of Hawthorne, for example, to view his conviction concerning the reality and seriousness of sin as symptomatic of a morbidity and gloominess of temperament, and to account for this assumed quality on biographical grounds. Both the biographical assumption and the interpretative deduction are fallacious. At no period was Hawthorne's life excessively unhappy, or eccentric to the point of abnormality. The only tenable impression to be drawn from the total body of his writings and the full record of his conduct, fairly considered, is that of a robust, well-rounded, and essentially healthy personality.

According to the legend, Hawthorne's boyhood was cruelly shadowed and distorted by his mother's excessive grieving, and consequent alienation from her three children, following the death of her husband at sea when Nathaniel was four years old. This view is invalidated by the evidence of a normal and affectionate relationship between mother and son which we find in his earliest letters, as well as by the recollections of his older sister, Elizabeth. Another item in the legend of gloom has it that an injury to his foot at the age of nine, which kept Nathaniel from participating in games with other boys, resulted in excessive isolation and introversion. But contemporary sources indicate only that because of the injury, the boy had unlimited leisure for reading, which was used to the fullest degree, and that he was even more petted and indulged than he would have been in any case, as the only man-child in a household of women, unmarried uncles, and small girls.

There is no doubt that Hawthorne enjoyed the comparatively lonely life of the family when Mrs. Hawthorne moved to Maine. But he seems to have had good companions there, and the story of his acquiring during the Maine years of his boyhood a dominating taste for solitude is a bit shaken by a letter which he sent from Salem in the summer he was fourteen. His mother and her family were visiting there and Hawthorne's uncle Robert Manning was in Maine. He told his uncle, ". . . I think I would rather go to dancing school a little longer before I come to Raymond." As Manning Hawthorne remarks, "The fact that he enjoyed the dancing school is somewhat at variance with the picture of a morbid, lonely boy, who loved to be alone."[5]

Very little can be deduced from the actual records of these early years as to religious impressions which may have been part of the boy's experience. Apparently he attended services at the

East Church of Salem with his mother and sisters, though not regularly. Two successive issues of *The Spectator,* the hand-written newspaper with which Hawthorne amused himself briefly while preparing for college, give praise to sermons he had heard, and in its few issues the "newspaper" has three references to pastors' calls to churches.[6] His mother established and taught a Sunday school during the years of her residence in Maine, and no doubt Nathaniel attended it. It is possible that (like many mothers of the time and place) Mrs. Hawthorne would have liked to have her only son become a minister. In two letters to his mother written at the age of seventeen, after the decision had been made that he should go to college and while he was actively engaged in preparation, Nathaniel raised the question of his future occupation, and in both he made it clear that he was unwilling to consider the ministry. But what the tone of these and other letters of the young Hawthorne to his mother and sisters makes most clear is a mutual relation of rather exceptional frankness and affection.[7]

Adherents to the legend of gloom have been rather hard put to find evidences of the abnormal in the records of Hawthorne's four years at Bowdoin College. About all they have to go on are his complaints about not having enough money and its not coming on time; and anyone who interprets these as exceptional must have forgotten his own student days. Actually Hawthorne's college career was depressingly average, even to the point of his graduating just above the middle of his class (eighteenth in a class of thirty-eight). Like that of most of his fellow students, his conduct was in frequent violation of the stringent rules of the little frontier college. He incurred fines for gambling, for drinking, for being seen at the local tavern on Saturday night, and repeatedly for absence from religious services, especially on Sunday evenings.

His closest friend, Horatio Bridge, recalled being fined twenty-five cents for "unnecessary walking on the Sabbath," and was sure that Hawthorne was likewise guilty of "taking a

stroll after our compulsory attendance at morning and after-
noon services."[8]

I think it is clear that certain attitudes related to religious
matters which marked Hawthorne's whole later life had their
origins at Bowdoin. One of these was a decided aversion to
attendance at religious services of any kind. The boys at Bowdoin were subjected to a regimen which could lead to such an
attitude. They were routed out at six daily, all through the long
Maine winters, for morning prayers and were required to
attend another service on weekday evenings and three services
on Sundays. Hawthorne's recurring "Sunday sickness," which
he mentioned in letters as preventing church attendance, is not
exceptional for college students. But Hawthorne never recovered from it, and his college letters show how irksome he found
these requirements.

Also possibly related to Bowdoin experience was his subsequent hostility toward the species clergyman—though he was
occasionally warm in his approval of an individual representative of the cloth. The minister whose church Bowdoin students
were required to attend, Rev. Mead, was a zealous Calvinist; he
and the college president, Rev. Allen, were thought to be in
league to resist the advances of Unitarianism, of which some
of the younger faculty members were suspected. Also, the Reverend Mead was deficient in tact, or in mercy. When, at the
beginning of Hawthorne's sophomore year, a student was taken
sick during the evening service—presumably from overindul-
gence in wine—and had to be led vomiting from the room,
Rev. Mead switched his discourse to a violent attack on drinking. This exasperated the students, who retaliated by shuffling
their feet and thumping the floor so that the sermon could not
be heard. The disorder led to various fines, suspensions, and one
expulsion. President Allen refused the petition of some of the
students to be permitted to attend services conducted by another minister. Feeling rose so high that the offending Parson
Mead was hung in effigy in the course of a minor riot. Though
Hawthorne seems to have played no prominent role in the agita-

tion, it is a fair guess that Bowdoin experiences account in large measure for both his nearly unbroken record of nonattendance at religious services during the rest of his life and his persistent distrust and dislike of the clerical profession in general.

The college years also yielded, on the other hand, positive and permanent enrichment in at least two ways. The first of these was the result of his good fortune in at least two of his teachers. Samuel P. Newman began teaching "rhetoric and oratory" at Bowdoin in 1823. He required fortnightly compositions of substantial length, which were handed in for criticism, returned for revision, and again submitted. The best of these, or portions of them, were then read to the class without identifying the author. There is no better way of teaching composition; and since Professor Newman maintained "a strict rule of Punctuality,"[9] his influence on Hawthorne as a potential writer was of practical importance. Although Hawthorne was occasionally fined for "tardiness in themes," the requirement of regular writing must have been beneficial.

Quite possibly the influence of Thomas Cogswell Upham was even more important. This young man, formerly a Congregational minister (and not to be confused with the Reverend Upham who was later Hawthorne's false friend at Salem), came to Bowdoin in 1824 as Professor of Moral and Mental Philosophy. Five years earlier he had published a small volume of poems, *American Sketches,* and in its preface had urged the use of native themes and materials by native writers. This was, of course, a common note of the day, but it had an impact on such students as Hawthorne and his classmate Henry Longfellow because Upham became their friend. Longfellow wrote to his mother:

. . . no one of our government . . . is so universally admired in college, as he is. His "sayings and doings" are altogether different from anything we have hitherto met with from our instructors and officers of college. He associates with us as if he were one of us—he visits us at our rooms and we visit him at his.[10]

Horatio Bridge also testified as to Upham's relation to his students: "He was young, scholarly, gentle, and kind to the students, by all of whom he was much beloved."[11]

There is no way of proving that the ideas Upham expressed ten years later in his *Philosophical and Practical Treatise on the Will* (1834), and formulated at fuller length in the two thick volumes of his *Elements of Mental Philosophy*, first published in 1840, were present, at least in embryo, in the lectures Hawthorne attended in 1824 and 1825. However, some of Upham's teachings show such striking resemblance to ideas expressed by Hawthorne during his early years as a writer that the hypothesis is attractive. For example, Upham insists on the primary importance of the study of the sensibilities:

> . . . a knowledge of the springs of action, back of the intellect, which, in the shape of the emotions and passions, give an impulse and a character to the conduct both of individuals and of communities. In other words, a knowledge of human nature is essentially a knowledge of the *Heart;* a term by which men commonly distinguish the sensitive from the intellectual nature.[12]

"A knowledge of human nature is essentially a knowledge of the *Heart*"—one is not quite sure whether the words are Upham's or Hawthorne's. Upham uses a figure which would be at home in Hawthorne, in speaking of death and immortality: "Death . . . only lifts up the veil which conceals from our eyes the invisible world."[13] He shares Hawthorne's view as to the spiritual meaning of nature:

> The soul, considered in its relationship to external nature, may be compared to a stringed instrument. . . . The nerves, the eye, and the senses generally are the chords and artificial framework which God has woven round its unseen and unsearchable essence.[14]

What could have been most important to Hawthorne was Upham's eloquent demand—contrary to much of the teaching of the day—that the imagination be respected and cultivated.

This point receives so much emphasis in the professor's note-book discussions that it is scarcely possible to think it was not present very early in his teaching. And Upham's defense of the imagination on a broad front, religious and moral as well as utilitarian, could well have given needed encouragement to a young man contemplating the unconventional and unpromising career of a writer. Though positive documentation is wanting, a comparative study of Hawthorne's fiction and Upham's psychological writings offers many parallels, some very striking.

Of even greater significance, indeed of major effect in the events of Hawthorne's life, were his college friendships. The closest of these was with Horatio Bridge, and it was renewed and reinforced in almost every year after their graduation. Bridge was the only person to whom Hawthorne confided his determination, formed well before he left college, to become a writer. It was probably Bridge's ardent encouragement that carried Hawthorne through a period of acute depression ten years later; it was certainly Bridge's intervention, in advancing a considerable sum of money to a publisher without his friend's knowledge, which made possible the publication of *Twice-Told Tales* in 1837 and the beginning of Hawthorne's public career as a writer. Though Longfellow and Hawthorne had been classmates at Bowdoin and had common interests in literature, they were not closely associated in their student days. But Longfellow, already highly popular and influential, reviewed *Twice-Told Tales* in glowing terms that contributed substantially to its critical success and resulted in a close, sometimes intimate, relationship much valued by Hawthorne for the rest of his life. Finally, Franklin Pierce was a close friend at college, asked Hawthorne to write the campaign biography during his candidacy for the presidency, gave Hawthorne the appointment as consul at Liverpool which meant the first financial independence he had ever known, and was with him at his death. Few college careers can have been so fruitful in terms of lifelong friendships.

THE DARKENED SKY

III

Hawthorne came back to Salem in the summer of 1825 after his graduation from Bowdoin. In January, 1839, he began work at the Boston Custom House. Except for relatively brief intervals, for the intervening thirteen and a half years his home was with his mother and her family at Salem. This is the period about which the legend of seclusion, alienation, isolation grows thickest. It appears to have its beginnings in information furnished by Elizabeth Peabody to Hawthorne's son Julian for his biography, *Nathaniel Hawthorne and His Wife,* which was published fifty years after the events in question. Miss Peabody was the older sister of the Sophia Peabody whom Hawthorne married. According to this story, Elizabeth, having recognized the merit of *Twice-Told Tales,* achieved single-handedly the rescue of Hawthorne from nearly ironclad isolation. As a professional lion hunter for many years, she had no other trophy quite so splendid or so deserving of a good story. And it lost nothing in the fumbling, sentimental handling of Julian. Moreover, Hawthorne himself contributed substantially to the legend in his love letters to Sophia, which were also a source for Julian. "Life was a desert until I met you" is a universal staple of love letters. Hawthorne devoted his best talents to elaboration of this theme—with, of course, complete sincerity.

And, to be sure, with factual basis. The years *were* lean years, so acutely so that what Hawthorne might have chosen as a social life was literally beyond his means. Hawthorne's total income for the entire thirteen and one-half years, from writing (and he had no other, except for a small inheritance), appears to have been not much more than one thousand dollars. Whether he was contributing toward the family's bills for food, fuel, and the like, is not certain, but his extreme punctiliousness in matters of personal obligation, in later years, suggests that he did contribute whenever he had money in his pocket. He had to buy paper and ink, at least; he borrowed books from a rental library as well as from the library of the Salem Athenaeum.

Clothes and shoes undoubtedly had to last a long time, and lack of money for these and other needs must have been galling. They were years of bitterly hard work, too, with only the most tardy and grudging recognition. It is no wonder that Hawthorne looked back to them, in the new happiness of his engagement to Sophia Peabody, as a dark time.

Yet in this period there is far more of variety, of brightness, of sheer normality of conduct and attitude than the legend allows; the morbid gloom is a fallacy. Hawthorne kept in close touch with his friends, particularly Bridge. He belonged to a card club. He attended dances. He traveled repeatedly and extensively in New England and farther west, with little money but with obvious enjoyment. He thought himself in love at least twice, indulged in sundry flirtations, appears to have been preposterously involved by a famous and fickle beauty of Salem in some vague affair which led to his challenging an acquaintance to a duel. He was always to be seen at fires, or wherever a crowd gathered. He contributed reports of sensational events to the local newspaper. He frequented taverns where fishermen and laborers gathered. All this in addition to the inveterate walking which even Elizabeth Peabody admitted. Perhaps the strongest body of evidence in this matter is that presented by Edward B. Hungerford, in "Hawthorne Gossips About Salem."[15]

In short, once we allow for the fact that Hawthorne had undertaken the all but impossible task, in the America of his time, of living by his pen, and recognize the actual difficulty and hardship which this inevitably involved for one in his financial situation, the impression which must emerge from any candid contemplation of the record is that of a young man of quite extraordinary dedication to a purpose and pertinacity in its pursuit, who still managed to live a fairly wholesome and well-rounded life. As Norman Holmes Pearson succinctly expressed it, "Hawthorne's silent years were silent only to us."[16] For our present purpose, the details of these years and indeed the whole legend of gloom are not of primary importance except for the persistent and still imperfectly recognized effect of the legend on the assessment of Hawthorne's writing, both in these years and during its whole course.[17] Of a piece with the fallacy of the gloomy years is the fallacy of the gloomy Hawthorne: a writer abnormally preoccupied by sin and sorrow. And the exorcism of that fallacy is essential if we are to understand the nature and penetrate the depth of Hawthorne's religious commitment.

The *Notebooks* and the fiction of his early years provide much testimony to Hawthorne's perennial reflection on religious matters and particularly on immortality. Somewhat curiously, there is also a wealth of allusion to these matters in his contributions to *The American Magazine of Useful and Entertaining Knowledge*, 1836. Arlin Turner's selections in his useful *Hawthorne as Editor* afford many examples. Characteristic is this comment, from "An Ontario Steamboat," on steerage passengers who excited Hawthorne's interest:

> As we had all our destined port, and the skill of the steersman would suffice to bring us thither, so had each of these poor wanderers a home in futurity, and the God above them knew where to find it.[18]

Especially interesting, in view of Hawthorne's concern with the possibility of earthly immortality in his last romances, is another passage in the *American Magazine*:

> We desire to give mortality its own. . . . We have no yearnings for the grossness of this earthly immortality. If somewhat of our soul and intellect might live in the memory of men, we should be glad. It would be an image of the ethereal and indestructible. But what belongs to earth, let the earth take it.[19]

Considering the insistent piousness of most contemporary books for children, it is perhaps surprising that *Grandfather's Chair* (1841) is almost entirely free from such intrusions. It does offer one example of a frankly fanciful conception of the future life, in portraying the welcome given Eliot, the apostle to the Indians, on his arrival at "the celestial abodes," by "those

40

earliest apostles and evangelists who had drawn their inspiration from the immediate presence of the Saviour."[20] Again, in the *Biographical Stories* for young readers we find Hawthorne opining that Sir Isaac Newton "is still searching out the infinite wisdom and goodness of the Creator as earnestly, and with even greater success, than while his spirit animated a mortal body."[21] Hawthorne was to use the same concept in reference to Delia Bacon, in *Our Old Home,* when he imagined Shakespeare welcoming her to heaven.[22] The memoir of Thomas Green Fessenden, who died in 1838, ends with a forthright expression of faith in a future life: "Dark would have been the hour, if, when we closed the door of the tomb upon his perishing mortality, we had believed that our friend was there."[23]

IV

Hawthorne's writing career of some forty years (if we accept the view that it began at Bowdoin) was punctuated by three periods in which he was "gainfully employed" and did little or no writing. The first of these interruptions occurred in 1839 and 1840, when Hawthorne held a minor post at the Boston Custom House, followed by a few months in 1841 at Brook Farm. During this time he was trying to accumulate a financial backlog which would justify marriage to Sophia Peabody. The second came with Hawthorne's appointment, in April of 1846, as surveyor at the Salem Custom House and lasted a little more than three years, until Hawthorne's dismissal in June of 1849. The third interruption, lasting nearly five years, was occasioned by Hawthorne's service as United States consul at Liverpool.

After we deduct these years of nonproduction, we see that approximately one-half of Hawthorne's actual writing lifetime belongs to the first period of some fourteen years, beginning at Bowdoin and ending when he started work at the Boston Custom House in 1839. We have no way of knowing how much Hawthorne wrote in this period. To it belong the short novel,

Fanshawe, which Hawthorne tried to suppress shortly after its publication in 1828, and some seventy stories, tales, and sketches, most of them published anonymously or under assumed names. There may be other published pieces not yet identified, and we have Hawthorne's word for it that he burned many of his early productions. In addition there is the very substantial body of writing in Hawthorne's *American Notebooks*—mutilated and bowdlerized by Sophia Hawthorne in her *Selections from the American Notebooks* and restored insofar as possible to their original character and completeness by Randall Stewart in *The American Notebooks of Nathaniel Hawthorne.*

The range of Hawthorne's religious thought during this period is clearly evidenced in the published work and even more clearly in the *American Notebooks.* In the sketch "Sunday at Home," published in 1837, we find one of his very few references to personal religious doubts. The writer describes his thoughts as (overtaken presumably by "Sunday sickness") he listens from his window to the church bells and watches the people going to church. The sunshine, he says, has a special quality on Sunday.

> . . . still I recognize the Sunday sunshine. And ever let me recognize it! Some illusions, and this among them, are the shadows of great truths. Doubts may flit around me, or seem to close their evil wings, and settle down; but so long as I imagine that the earth is hallowed, and the light of heaven retains its sanctity, on the Sabbath—while that blessed sunshine lives within me—never can my soul have lost the instinct of its faith. If it have gone astray, it will return again.[24]

The religious references in some of these stories strongly suggest the pious platitudes characteristic of the annuals and gift-books which provided the chief market for Hawthorne's fiction in this early period. An extreme example is the ending of "Night Sketches," published in 1838. In the darkness of a stormy night, the writer observes a man with a lantern and comments:

This figure shall supply me with a moral. . . . He fears not to

42

tread the dreary path before him, because his lantern, which was kindled at the fireside of his home, will light him back to that same fireside again. And thus we, night wanderers through a stormy and dismal world, if we bear the lamp of Faith, enkindled at a celestial fire, it will surely lead us home to that heaven whence its radiance was borrowed.[25]

It is not necessary to conclude, however, that such pietistic passages were consciously inserted in the interest of salability; the notebooks of this period yield many comments similar in tone and content.

The *American Notebooks* show that Hawthorne was not averse to frank discussion of religious problems or intolerant of views in conflict with his own. Though the Frenchman with whom he became acquainted while visiting Bridge in 1837 was "an infidel" and "damnably perverted as to religion," Hawthorne recorded with evident relish an evening spent in talking with him, "after Bridge is abed . . . of Christianity and Deism . . . all deep matters of this world and the next."[26] In similar vein, he recounts with gusto his listening, at a country inn on one of his solitary expeditions into New England, to an indecorous debate on religious matters:

> In the evening there was a strange fellow in the barroom—a sort of mock-Methodist—a cattle drover. . . . All his talk turned on religion. . . . A group of universalists, and no religionists sat round him, making him their butt, and holding wild argument against him; and he strangely mingled humor with his enthusiasm, and enthusiasm with his humor, so that it was almost impossible to tell whether he were in jest or earnest.[27]

Although there is, then, ample evidence in the early writings of positive religious faith, we also encounter very early in the Hawthorne canon equally clear expression of something far from a comfortable Unitarian belief: recognition of evil as a reality, of sin and its penalties. A letter of January 19, 1830, from Samuel Goodrich, who as editor of an annual giftbook called *The Token* published some of Hawthorne's early work, shows that he had already received three of the greatest of these stories: "Roger Malvin's Burial," "The Gentle Boy," and "My Kinsman, Major Molineux," which is called here "My Uncle Molineux." Also to the very early period belong those shorter masterpieces of style and mood, "The Hollow of the Three Hills," "The Wives of the Dead," and probably "Young Goodman Brown." Seymour L. Gross and Alfred J. Levy have shown that the imperfect but powerful story "Alice Doane's Appeal" is probably earlier than most or all of these.[28] It is hard to avoid the conclusion that there was a relatively brief period before or about 1830 when Hawthorne reached a level of quality and intensity he was to attain only once again: in the six or eight months in which he wrote *The Scarlet Letter*. It may be observed, further, that only in these two periods did Hawthorne succeed in rendering his vision of evil as wholly realized experience, not as partially dramatized idea; and that in both cases, in the stories mentioned and in *The Scarlet Letter,* the material is historical.

Hawthorne's conception of the possibility of high significance in historical fiction is clearly stated in his review of William Gilmore Simms's *Views and Reviews*. After complaining that "The themes, suggested by him, viewed as he views them," would produce only more examples of an already "worn-out mould," he defines Simms's primary deficiency in terms which indicate his own ideal: "he possesses nothing of the magic touch that should cause new intellectual and moral shapes to spring up in the reader's mind, peopling with varied life what had been a barren waste."[29]

Hawthorne's early imaginative saturation in the life of Puritan New England can be easily documented in his preoccupation with family history, his voracious reading of colonial materials in the collection of the Salem Athenaeum, his project for collected "Tales of My Native Land." Something in him responded profoundly to the experience of men and women who lived with witchcraft and the darker aspects of Calvinism, and he made that experience his own. His reading and his reflection upon it enabled him to recreate imaginatively the shape and texture of that experience with extreme completeness and vitality of historical detail. But beyond this, operating within the realized historical nexus and taking it for granted, building upon it, is a second, a psychological realization—an unfaltering grasp of the individual consciousness as it functions within the historical context. It is this twofold vision, at once historical and psychological, which is the heart of Hawthorne's greatness, and in the relatively small portion of his work in which it is operative lies the justification for counting him among the masters.

In "Young Goodman Brown" the historical situation is defined at the outset, yet every detail thereafter enriches it. Young Goodman Brown has already given himself to sin— although he is not, as the story opens, beyond the reach of redemption. He knows perfectly well who it is that he has engaged to meet in the forest and what the meeting portends. But he is proud, self-confident. He rejects the pleadings of his wife and his own conscience. Willingly and knowingly he enters into commerce with Evil. Nor, the commerce achieved, does he repent. His is a classic example of what the theologians may call formal sin, since it is conscious and voluntary; and it is unrepented. Through the twofold vision of Hawthorne's realism, the historical field centered in the individual mind, Young Goodman Brown becomes Everyman and the story achieves the rank of one of literature's great paradigms of evil.

Since it is in his fictions of colonial New England that Hawthorne's vision of evil reaches its most adequate expression, it might be thought that the vision so rendered is itself a historical achievement—merely a part of Hawthorne's realization of what it was like to be a New Englander of Puritan times. If this idea were not immediately controverted by the evidence of practically the whole body of Hawthorne's work, the contradiction between his Unitarian belief and his recognition of evil would be resolved. We would be left free to admire the historical achievement in itself and for its own sake. But of course there is no such easy solution. The problem of evil is everywhere in Hawthorne. It is only that in the best of the historical writing it is most powerfully projected. Two other relatively early stories may be noted, almost at random, as examples of Hawthorne's treatment of sin in other than colonial contexts. "Fancy's Show Box" (1837) is devoted to exposition, rather than actual dramatization, of the view that sin contemplated, enacted in imagination, incurs guilt equally with sin actually committed. "The Minister's Black Veil" (1835) suggests in purely dramatic terms the universality of sin, the kinship of human beings resulting from their common sinfulness, and also the irremediable aspect of sin, its effects as lasting and immitigable this side the grave.

V

Hawthorne's religious position had become clear in his mind and had been forcibly, if not always unequivocally, expressed in his fiction before he met Sophia Peabody. Both before and after she became Sophia Hawthorne he successfully resisted any pressure toward change. The three Peabody sisters were ardent transcendentalists. They idolized Emerson (Sophia thought him the greatest man who ever lived) and were avid readers of the *Dial* and admirers of Alcott and Margaret Fuller. No doubt it was assumed, when Hawthorne's love for Sophia became clear, that the quiet young man could be made over in the Peabody image. The assumption was false, however. When early in the engagement Sophia adjured Hawthorne, in Boston, to hear sermons of the famous Father Taylor, his refusal was a model of gentleness and firmness. When Elizabeth Peabody proclaimed her discovery that Sophia's famous headaches could be cured by mesmeric treatment, Hawthorne intervened, with less gentleness and equal finality.

Hawthorne was thirty-four when he met Sophia, thirty-eight when they were married. The interval included two years of active physical labor at the Boston Custom House and another half-year at Brook Farm. During these periods and until after his marriage he wrote little fiction. His letters to Sophia constitute the larger part of his writing for the time, and in these the positive elements of his religious attitudes find frequent and eloquent expression. He is grateful to God for Sophia and for their love, and he is confident of an immortality of happiness in that love. This confidence is asserted in nearly every letter.

When Hawthorne returned to his writing, he encountered, as might be expected, great difficulty in "settling down." He enjoyed gardening, working about the grounds of the Old Manse, gathering the abundant fruit. The Hawthorne home was hospitable, and many friends were visitors. The beautiful countryside around Concord was a constant invitation for walking. It is perhaps surprising that many stories can be assigned to this period. They include "A Virtuoso's Collection," "The Hall of Fantasy," "The Celestial Railroad," "Earth's Holocaust," "The New Adam and Eve," "The Birthmark," "Egotism —The Bosom Serpent," "The Artist of the Beautiful," "Rappaccini's Daughter," and a few others.

The difference between even the best of these stories and the best of a dozen years before—such stories as "Roger Malvin's Burial," "My Kinsman, Major Molineux," "Young Goodman Brown"—is palpable in the mere act of reading and is open to easy analysis. These stories of the 1840's are intellectual in their origin rather than emotional. They are fabrications rather than creations. Not only is the intellectual purpose and meaning of each story perfectly obvious, but all too often it is overtly stated, to the reader's embarrassment and distress, as at the ending of "Rappaccini's Daughter." The great stories of the early period are essentially experiential: Hawthorne (and with him the reader) becomes first a naturalized citizen of primitive New England, and then Young Goodman Brown himself meeting the Black Man in the forest, or Robin on the streets of Boston. There is nothing approaching this intensity of concrete vicarious experience, this emotional total immersion, in the stories written at the Old Manse. They came from the head, not from the heart, as Hawthorne himself must have been well aware.

This means, of course, that in their relation to Hawthorne's value structures, including the religious, these stories are more readily accessible in terms of specific meaning and implication than are the earlier ones. Many are overtly didactic. "The Celestial Railroad" is so definite and so devastating in its dissection of fashionable religious liberalism that advocates of more rigorous systems pirated the tale and circulated it in pamphlet form as a tract. If his Peabody in-laws and his Concord neighbors had hope of pushing Hawthorne in the direction of liberal Unitarianism, we may guess that they abandoned the effort after this story appeared. It borrows its pattern from Bunyan, of course: *The Pilgrim's Progress* seems to have been for Hawthorne a favored and frequently read book, from the age of six to the end of his life. The modern pilgrim follows Christian's progress almost step by step, and at each phase Hawthorne portrays the smugness, the materialism, the selfishness, the insincerity of contemporary "liberal" religion. His chronic dislike for clergymen is pointedly expressed in the names of those who preside at the churches of Vanity Fair, from Rev. Mr. Shallow-deep to Rev. Dr. Wind-of-Doctrine. Almost too late— at the end of the journey—the narrator and the reader realize together that the amiable companion of the journey, Mr. Smooth-it-away, is the Devil himself or his emissary.

Religious implications are present also in "Earth's Holocaust," one of the more interesting and effective of a group of stories similar in pattern. With its "once upon a time" beginning, this story describes a "general bonfire" by means of which the inhabitants of earth propose to rid themselves of "an accumulation of wornout trumpery." Published in *Graham's Magazine* in 1844, "Earth's Holocaust" may have drawn part of its inspiration from the Millerite excitement of the preceding year, when the end of the world was confidently awaited by thousands of Americans. But its principal targets were the Fourierists who had taken over Brook Farm, the abolitionists, the temperance advocates, the transcendentalists: all the advocates of and believers in an imminent Great Leap Forward. In the religious application of the idea, which occupies the position of climax, religious emblems and sacramental vessels are thrown into the flames and consumed, even "the humble communion tables and undecorated pulpits which I recognized as having been torn from the meeting-houses of New England."[30] The narrating witness comforts himself, feeling that the externals of religion can be spared.

> But the Titan of innovation . . . at first shaking down only the old and rotten shapes of things, had now, as it appeared, laid his terrible hand upon the main pillars which supported the whole edifice of our moral and spiritual state. The inhabitants of the earth had grown too enlightened to define their faith within a form of words, or to limit the spiritual by any analogy to our material existence. Truths which the heavens trembled at were now but a fable of the world's infancy. Therefore, as the final sacrifice of human error, what else remained to be thrown upon the embers of that awful pile except the book which, though a celestial revelation to past ages, was but a voice from a lower sphere as regarded the present race of man? It was done![31]

But the Bible refuses to burn; its pages "only assumed a more dazzling whiteness as the finger marks of human imperfection were purified away. Certain marginal notes and commentaries,"[32] however, burned readily enough. Whether Hawthorne in this passage is offering oblique comment on contemporary criticism of the Bible (Strauss's *Das Leben Jesu* had appeared in 1835–36 and had been reviewed in America) does not seem to me perfectly evident. His target may have been merely the recurring one of ultraliberal Unitarianism and related positions.

But there is no ambiguity about the ending of the story. When the hangman, the last thief, the last murderer, and the last toper are mourning together because there will be no place for them in "the purified world," they are reassured by a bystander whose "complexion was indeed fearfully dark, and his eyes glowed with a redder light than that of the bonfire."

". . . There's one thing that these wiseacres have forgotten to throw into the fire, and without which all the rest of the conflagration is just nothing at all. . . ."[33]

"And what may that be?" eagerly demanded the last murderer.

"What but the human heart itself?" said the dark-visaged stranger, with a portentous grin. "And, unless they hit upon some method of purifying that foul cavern, forth from it will reissue all the shapes of wrong and misery—the same old shapes or worse ones—which they have taken such a vast deal of trouble to consume to ashes. . . ."[34]

Reflecting, the narrator agrees: "if we go no deeper than the intellect, and strive, with merely that feeble instrument, to discern and rectify what is wrong, our whole accomplishment will be a dream. . . ."[35] Here, simply stated, is not only a theme of *The Blithedale Romance* but a cardinal conviction of Hawthorne's which is closely tied to his religious outlook.

VI

Though Hawthorne produced more writing in the years at the Old Manse than might have been expected, his income was painfully inadequate. The appointment as surveyor at the Salem Custom House, therefore, seemed a great good fortune and his dismissal from the post in 1849, following a change in national administration, a grievous calamity. But the loss of the Custom House job proved most fortunate for Hawthorne and for literature. Out of the immediate necessity of earning money by writing and out of the emotional excitement which had shaken to the roots a nature that had developed no small capacity for self-indulgence and rationalized procrastination during the preceding six years came the writing of *The Scarlet Letter*. Hawthorne himself came to see the dismissal clearly as a blessing. When in 1853 he repaid the money which George Hillard and others had advanced in his time of great need following the dismissal, he wrote to Hillard from Liverpool:

This act of kindness did me an unspeakable amount of good;

for it came at a time when I most needed to be assured that anybody thought it worth while to keep me from sinking. And it did me even greater good than this, in making me sensible of the need of sterner efforts than my former ones, in order to establish a right for myself to live and be comfortable.[36]

The Scarlet Letter has been closely examined from almost every conceivable critical standpoint. Its value as revelation of Hawthorne's own views on social and religious matters has sometimes been exaggerated, for *The Scarlet Letter* is first and last a historical novel. It illustrates in supreme degree that two-fold vision, that psychological truth integrated with historical truth which I have suggested as the peculiar achievement of the great stories of Hawthorne's first period. Fittingly, this quality is supremely illustrated in the climax of the novel's action, the final scene on the scaffold—the scene which has been the subject of the most extreme and conflicting critical interpretations.

The gift of grace is granted Dimmesdale only at the foot of the scaffold. The frequent reading which assigns his "conversion" to the time of the writing of the new Election Sermon seems to me mistaken. Nothing in what precedes his final confrontation of Hester, Pearl—and Chillingworth—at the foot of the scaffold has indicated a purpose of clear public confession, essential in the Calvinist view for salvation. His repulse of Chillingworth in Chapter 20 is merely the logical result of his opened vision—cleared by Hester's aid in the interview in the forest—as to the physician's true motive and character. Hawthorne's account of the rewriting of the Election Sermon, in the final paragraph of that chapter, carries suggestions of the wild and reckless mood in which he had returned from the forest: "flinging the already written pages of the Election Sermon into the fire, he forthwith began another, which he wrote with such impulsive flow of thought and emotion, that he fancied himself inspired."[37] The words "impulsive" and, especially, "fancied" call for careful attention here. The implication of "fancied" is that the impression is false, as well as that the minister exults in his achievement; according to Calvin's own teaching, when one is most pleased with himself in religious matters he is in greatest danger:

> . . . there is no way of salvation till we have laid aside all pride, and attained sincere humility . . . as far as any man is satisfied with himself, so far he raises an impediment to the exercise of the grace of God.[38]

Dimmesdale's manner and appearance as he walks in the procession (which exert a "dreary influence"[39] over Hester) give no sign of repentance. The occult vision of Mistress Hibbins still recognizes Dimmesdale as one of her own. In regard to its effect upon his audience, the Election Sermon itself differs from his earlier sermons only in intensity. There is no indication that to his congregation he speaks now with a difference of kind, but only of degree. "The complaint of a human heart . . . telling its secret"[40] in the Election Sermon is of a piece with Dimmesdale's speaking "the black secret of his soul"[41] as described in Chapter 11. Now as then the people "but reverence him the more,"[42] this time to the point of "rapture."[43]

The extreme physical exhaustion (he is, indeed, almost at the point of death) which Hawthorne stresses so strongly in his description of Dimmesdale's emergence from the church to his sudden confrontation with Hester, Pearl, and Chillingworth beside the scaffold gives psychological probability to what the minister does and says. His condition, a state of extreme depletion of human strength, makes fitting and probable, in the Puritan view, the instantaneous influx of saving grace, dramatized first in the invitation to Hester and Pearl and then by public confession. Then there is a moment, as he "made a pause,"[44] when his eternal salvation depends upon a single step toward the scaffold or away from it. It is the instantaneous operation of God's grace—in full conformity with Puritan belief[45]— which determines that step. The suggestion of a miracle at this point of crisis is of great significance: ". . . nor would it have

seemed a miracle too high to be wrought for one so holy, had
he ascended before their eyes, waxing dimmer and brighter,
and fading at last into the light of heaven."[46] A miracle does
occur, the miracle of grace, and Dimmesdale does ascend,
though not in the manner imagined. For the following sentence
portrays the action which determines Dimmesdale's eternal
fate: "He turned towards the scaffold, and stretched forth his
arms."[47]

This scene is the supreme illustration of Hawthorne's highest
reach—for the psychological truth of Dimmesdale's action,
in view of all that has preceded, is correlative with its historical
truth according to Puritan belief. The same thing may be said
of the subsequent conversation between Dimmesdale and Hester on the scaffold: it is wholly consistent both with the tenor
of Dimmesdale's seventeenth-century faith and with the action
of his mind as previously developed in the story. Those who
have quarreled with this much-discussed passage have failed
to give due allowance to one or the other of these factors.

Woodberry complained that "There is no Christ in this
book,"[48] and of course he is right. In another comment made
early in this century, W. C. Brownell defended the omission:

> The story . . . is real and true. If it is thought to show a bias
> in pushing too far the doom of evil, to ignore the whole New
> Testament point of view . . . the answer is that though in
> this way it may lose in typical value, it gains in imaginative
> realism, since it is a story of that Puritan New England
> where it sometimes seems as if the New Testament had been
> either suspect or unknown.[49]

The omission of the role of Christ as Redeemer in *The Scarlet
Letter* has significance beyond its historical realism, however.
There is salvation in Hawthorne, most pointedly illustrated in
"Egotism, or the Bosom Serpent," a story of the *Mosses* period.
But Roderick of that story is saved by the love and self-giving
of his wife, and in this life. As I suggested early in this study,
the vicarious atonement is not a part of Hawthorne's theology.

THE DARKENED SKY

The most remarkable fact about Hawthorne's writing in the period between the end of his employment at the Salem Custom House and the beginning of his work as American consul at Liverpool is the volume of his production. Within the less than forty-eight months between the time he is known to have begun *The Scarlet Letter* and the day he and his family sailed for Liverpool he completed not only *The Scarlet Letter* and his second and third major novels, *The House of the Seven Gables* and *The Blithedale Romance,* but also his two fine books of Greek myths for children, *A Wonder Book* and *Tanglewood Tales,* a biography of his friend Franklin Pierce to be used in his presidential campaign, and a few stories.

Beyond the fact that both *The House of the Seven Gables* and *The Blithedale Romance* are parables of sin and punishment, their contribution to our understanding of Hawthorne's religious posture is incidental rather than central. In *The Blithedale Romance* the focus—on the sin of intellectual pride, the most heinous of all in Hawthorne's view—is clear and firm; and the retribution visited upon Zenobia and Hollingsworth—the latter an extreme example of the intellectually motivated reformer Hawthorne particularly detested—is total, without relief or promise. In contrast, the factor of sin in *The House of the Seven Gables,* though powerfully dramatized in Judge Pyncheon, is otherwise clouded by the hocus-pocus of an ancestral curse and various other standard props of the Gothic novel. The reformer of this book is not permitted to destroy the curse (that is accomplished very neatly by a timely stroke of apoplexy) but is instead chastened and developed to become a partner in the only happy ending of Hawthorne's novels. The book has power and charm in its evocation of place and in its feminine characters.

In the obviously hasty putting together in 1848 of "Ethan Brand," Hawthorne had first indulged to an extravagant degree in the expedient of fleshing out a new fiction by thrusting into it large undigested lumps of material from his notebooks. In writing *The Blithedale Romance* he used this expedient freely in the treatment of experience at Brook Farm, in the hotel scenes in Boston, in the narrative of the finding of Zenobia's body after her suicide, and elsewhere. These passages have such solidity of specification, such vigor as realized experience, that all the rest of the book is quickly seen to be the rather feeble and flimsy tissue of invention which it is. It is obvious that neither *The House of Seven Gables* nor *The Blithedale Romance* has the structural symmetry or the thematic unity which distinguish *The Scarlet Letter*. But since the historical dimension is removed, in these studies of his contemporary New England, such overtly religious elements as do appear in the two later novels may justly be regarded as expressions of Hawthorne's personal position.

Emphasis on human imperfection is present in *The House of the Seven Gables,* as generally in Hawthorne, but in this "sunny" book it is regularly relieved by reference to God's goodness, as in the following passage:

> Nevertheless, if we look through all the heroic fortunes of mankind, we shall find this same entanglement of something mean and trivial with whatever is noblest in joy and sorrow. Life is made up of marble and mud. And, without all the deeper trust in a comprehensive sympathy above us, we might hence be led to suspect the insult of a sneer, as well as an immitigable frown, on the iron countenance of fate.[50]

In this novel the evil actions which were responsible for the ancestral curse have been compounded, in Hawthorne's eyes, by the sin of willful isolation from humanity—a sin also treated in some of his stories, perhaps most definitely in "The Man of Adamant" (1837).

> In her grief and wounded pride, Hepzibah had spent her life in divesting herself of friends;—she had wilfully cast off the support which God has ordained his creatures to need from one another;—and it was now her punishment, that Clifford and herself would fall the easier victims to their kindred enemy.[51]

THE DARKENED SKY

One of the most characteristic and frequently recurring positive religious elements in Hawthorne's work is his sense of holiness in nature. This element is expressed repeatedly throughout the novel:

> . . . a bird, in whose small strain of music we recognize the voice of the Creator, as distinctly as in the loudest accents of His thunder.[52]

> It was the Sabbath morning; one of those bright, calm Sabbaths, with its own hallowed atmosphere, when Heaven seems to diffuse itself over the earth's face in a solemn smile, no less sweet than solemn. On such a Sabbath morn, were we pure enough to be its medium, we should be conscious of the earth's natural worship ascending through our frames, on whatever spot of ground we stood.[53]

The daguerreotypist, Holgrave, of *The House of the Seven Gables,* stands alone among Hawthorne's reformers in being treated kindly—thanks to the demands of the novel's approaching happy ending. However, Hawthorne is careful to qualify his approval explicitly:

> He had that sense, or inward prophecy—which a young man had better never have been born, than not to have, and a mature man had better die at once, than utterly to relinquish —that we are not doomed to creep on forever in the old, bad way, but that, this very now, there are the harbingers abroad of a golden era, to be accomplished in his own life-time. It seemed to Holgrave—as doubtless it has seemed to the hopeful of every century, since the epoch of Adam's grandchildren—that in this age, more than ever before, the moss-grown and rotten Past is to be torn down, and lifeless institutions to be thrust out of the way, and their dead corpses buried, and everything to begin anew.
> As to the main point,—may we never live to doubt it!— as to the better centuries that are coming, the artist was surely right. His error lay, in supposing that this age, more than any past or future one, is to see the tattered garments of Antiquity exchanged for a new suit, instead of gradually renewing themselves by patchwork; in applying his own little life-span as the measure of an interminable achievement;

and, more than all, in fancying that it mattered anything to the great end in view, whether he himself should contend for it or against it.[54]

The "sunny" quality of *The House of the Seven Gables* (and it was Hawthorne's avowed intention to write a "happy" book) rests in part on a generous display of the author's notable capacity for humor—in his portrayal of Hepzibah's first customer, of Uncle Venner, of the Pyncheon poultry—but chiefly on his characterization of Phoebe. That characterization has been less than satisfying to many modern readers, including some of Hawthorne's ablest critics.[55] They allege that she is shown as "too good to be true." We note that salvation in this novel is achieved by human love, unaided by supernatural intervention except insofar as human love itself is an expression of God's love.

The Blithedale Romance is again a story of sin and retribution. Unlike *The House of Seven Gables,* however, it lacks the outward look, the admission of potential recompense for suffering and the possibility of salvation through human love—except, perhaps, in the attenuated and ambiguous suggestion of what Priscilla's love may do for Hollingsworth. The reason for the difference may lie in the nature of the sin: in *The Blithedale Romance* it is clearly that of intellectual pride, whereas *The House of Seven Gables* dramatizes the comparatively venial sin of greed. It is noteworthy that in this novel Hawthorne (and the reader) feel little of that involved sympathy for the sinners which is such an important quality of *The Scarlet Letter.* Chillingworth, in the earlier novel, holds the reader's understanding even when his actions are most diabolical, while the corresponding sinner in *The Blithedale Romance,* Westervelt, is utterly abominable. Again, both Dimmesdale and Hester gain a hold on the reader's sympathy far beyond anything felt for Hollingsworth and Zenobia. *The Blithedale Romance* is the fullest and most unsparing of Hawthorne's many indictments of the arrogance of self-appointed reformers. As F. O. Matthiessen expressed it, Hollingsworth "became an incarnation of the terrible egotism that mistakes its own will for the promptings of God."[56] The religious implications of the attitude revealed by Hawthorne in this novel are not trivial, as Austin Warren has pointed out:

> Hawthorne had little or no belief in man's own power to add a cubit to his stature. In theological language, he was not a Pelagian but an Augustinian. Man is ignorant and impotent, and his most zealous efforts at mending the world but damage it the more. We are not to thrust ourselves in to the place of Providence or attempt to hasten the slow, inscrutable processes of the Divine working. . . . Fine theories will not save men: nor will legislation. The heart must undergo regeneration, and God (who alone can effect that) bides his own time.[57]

A factor in the understanding of *The Blithedale Romance* which has been too often overlooked, and one which applies especially to some of its statements on religious matters, is well developed by Frederick C. Crews in his article, "A New Reading of *The Blithedale Romance.*" Crews says that we must remember to view the book as a romance written by Coverdale. He suggests that *Blithedale* "belongs to a tradition that includes *Gulliver's Travels* and *Ulysses*—books whose greatness lies in the author's ability to express his deepest judgments through a narrator who is himself a subject of judgment. . . . Hawthorne is attempting what few writers have dared: a surface plot, an imaginative reconstruction of that plot by a narrator, and a symbolic commentary on both."[58]

This means that for our present purpose we cannot take for granted that the religious views and attitudes expressed in the novel are Hawthorne's own. For example, Coverdale's opinion of Hollingsworth's morning prayers may not be precisely that of Hawthorne:

> It is so rare, in these times, to meet with a man of prayerful habits, (except, of course, in the pulpit), that such an one is decidedly marked out by a light of transfiguration, shed upon him in the divine interview from which he passes into his daily life.[59]

Nathaniel Hawthorne

The reader may judge for himself, I should think, how far Coverdale's excuse for giving Moodie liquor to "thaw him out" carries Hawthorne's approbation.

> What else could possibly be done for him? How else could he be imbued with energy enough to hope for a happier state, hereafter? How else be inspirited to say his prayers? For there are states of our spiritual system, when the throb of the soul's life is too faint and weak to render us capable of religious aspiration.[60]

Since there is no immediate occasion for Coverdale's seeking to arouse Moodie's "religious aspiration," the passage seems a stroke of characterization somewhat playfully intended.

A more serious problem arises concerning the passages which relate to Zenobia's death by drowning. Not infrequently they are cited as evidence of Hawthorne's positive religious faith. While there are three of these passages in the narrative, only the last is usually quoted. Of the river:

> So obscure, however, so awfully mysterious, was that dark stream, that—and the thought made me shiver like a leaf—I might as well have tried to look into the enigma of the eternal world, to discover what had become of Zenobia's soul, as into the river's depths, to find her body.[61]

Of a sunken log hauled up by Hollingsworth:

> "That looked ugly!" quoth Silas. "I half thought it was the Evil One on the same errand as ourselves—searching for Zenobia."
> "He shall never get her," said I, giving the boat a strong impulse.
> "That's not for you to say, my boy," retorted the yeoman. "Pray God he never has, and never may! . . ."[62]

Of the discovered body:

> Her arms had grown rigid in the act of struggling, and were bent before her, with clenched hands; her knees, too, were bent, and—thank God for it!—in the attitude of prayer. Ah, that rigidity! It is impossible to bear the terror of it. It

seemed—I must needs impart so much of my own miserable idea—it seemed as if her body must keep the same position in the coffin, and that her skeleton would keep it in the grave, and that when Zenobia rose, at the Day of Judgment, it would be in just the same attitude as now!

One hope I had; and that too was mingled half with fear. She knelt, as if in prayer. With the last, choking consciousness, her soul, bubbling out through her lips, it may be, had given itself up to the Father, reconciled and penitent. But her arms! They were bent before her, as if she struggled against Providence in never-ending hostility. Her hands! They were clenched in immitigable defiance. Away with the hideous thought. The flitting moment, after Zenobia sank into the dark pool—when her breath was gone, and her soul at her lips—was as long, in its capacity of God's infinite forgiveness, as the lifetime of the world![63]

How much of this is Coverdale, how much is Hawthorne? The passages are sufficiently enigmatic to allow of variant interpretations. Since there is no positive evidence of belief in hell or eternal punishment elsewhere in Hawthorne's writings, it seems to me that Silas Foster's remark about the "Evil One" is merely an element in the characterization of Foster—the thought is natural enough for him—rather than a seriously intended suggestion on Hawthorne's part. Further, in view of Hawthorne's seemingly unshaken belief in personal immortality at this period in his life and his recurring emphasis on God's mercy, I feel that the concluding reflection is Hawthorne's as well as Coverdale's.

VIII

The English Notebooks of Nathaniel Hawthorne, the product of diligent journal-writing throughout his residence in England, are by far the longest of Hawthorne's works (300,000 words) but eminently worth reading. These notebooks cover the interval between the appearance of *The House of the Seven Gables* and the writing of his last completed novel, *The Marble*

Faun. As with the earlier *American Notebooks,* they contain numerous references to religious matters and I shall take up the most important of these entries later, when considering the changes he made in them for *Our Old Home.* Apart from these, we find largely familiar or predictable expressions of attitude. Hawthorne criticizes clergymen for being perfunctory or unfeeling in the performance of their duties. He is also critical of the emphasis placed on ritual and ceremonial, in contrast to the usual simplicity of religious exercises in America. Moreover, he charges that, in general, religious beliefs in England are more superficial than those in America. However, he gives much attention to cathedrals and their contribution to religious feeling—strengthening in Hawthorne as he visited them repeatedly. More than once Hawthorne sees in church or cathedral windows—dull and colorless from without, richly brilliant when viewed from within—a significant analogy to religious faith itself as seen by the unbeliever and the believer.

Most numerous among the religious references are those which touch on the matter of personal immortality. This is the more impressive because the *English Notebooks* contain very few of the ideas for stories and the reflections on life and experience which hold so large a place in the *American Notebooks.* The English journals are almost wholly confined to straightforward accounts of daily activities and observations. Yet more than a score of times Hawthorne finds occasion to refer to the future life.

One such reference is notably positive and explicit. After recounting his meeting with Harriet Martineau, whom he liked and admired, Hawthorne writes:

> And this woman is an Atheist, and thinks, I believe, that the principle of life will become extinct, when her great, fat, well-to-do body is laid in the grave. I will not think so, were it only for her sake;—only a few weeds to spring out of her fat mortality, instead of her intellect and sympathies flowering and fruiting forever![64]

THE DARKENED SKY

Hawthorne's humor is richly exhibited in the *English Notebooks,* perhaps more fully than in any other of his books. One passage is worth quoting here despite its obviously less than serious intention. It appears in the entry for September 9, 1855, following a family excursion to the London Zoological Gardens:

> In a future state of being, I think it will be one of my inquiries, in reference to the mysteries of this present state, why monkies [sic] were made. The Creator could not surely have meant to ridicule his own work. It might rather be supposed that Satan had perpetrated monkies [sic], with a malicious purpose of parodying the masterpiece of creation.[65]

If Hawthorne meant *The House of the Seven Gables* to be his "happy" book, it may well be that he intended *The Marble Faun* to be his "religious" book. Certainly its theme is a matter of the highest theological significance. I believe Hawthorne may have decided he must come to grips at last with a problem that he had repeatedly touched in peripheral fashion, and one that, granted his nature and experience, he could hardly have escaped: the reason for the existence of sin and evil in a world created by an omnipotent and beneficent God. The conception of *The Marble Faun* as an exploration of this problem is, as W. C. Brownell observed long ago, "one of the noblest in literature;"[66] and I think we can be sure that Hawthorne put into it the best effort that circumstances permitted. Yet many modern readers have found *The Marble Faun* less satisfying than any other of Hawthorne's completed novels.

There appear to be several explanations for his lack of success. In the first place, the circumstances of writing were unpropitious. The labor of composition came not long after the exacting ordeal of his daughter Una's illness in Rome, and the work was carried on under pressure of the family's eagerness to return to America; in fact, the actual rate of composition seems to have been considerably faster than for any of the preceding novels. Hawthorne had made preliminary drafts in Italy, but he composed the final text (150,000 words) in England, in the almost incredibly brief period of 105 days—July 26 through November 7, 1859.

A more important factor may have been the state of Hawthorne's health. I am convinced that Davidson is right in his suggestion: "The tentative reason I should like to assign for this weakness [of *The Marble Faun*] is that Hawthorne was already beginning to show the decline which becomes a precipitous descent to the romances of the last phase."[67] The final notebooks, written in France and Italy during and just preceding the composition of *The Marble Faun,* contain frequent complaints of fatigue, loss of interest and energy, near exhaustion. Perhaps the strongest is in the entry for June 11, 1859:

> Rest, rest, rest! There is nothing else so desirable; and I sometimes fancy, but only half in earnest, how pleasant it would be to be six feet underground, and let the grass grow over me.

A few days later Hawthorne returned to this feeling:

> . . . really I lack energy to visit places of interest, curiosity even so much as to glance at them, heart to enjoy them, intellect to profit by them. I deem it a grace of Providence when I have a decent excuse to my wife, and to my own conscience, for not seeing even the things that have helped to tempt me abroad. It may be disease; it may be age; it may be the effect of the lassitudinous Roman atmosphere; but such is the fact.[68]

Sophia Hawthorne did not include these entries in her *Passages from the French and Italian Notebooks.*

Whatever the cause of the weakness, its effects in the actual execution of the novel are not hard to identify. Even more than in *The Blithedale Romance,* Hawthorne borrowed heavily from his notebooks, and many of these passages lack dramatic justification in terms of their relation to the action. The novel is marred by factitious complications intended as adjuncts to plot, among them the childish mystification as to Donatello's ears (for which, to be sure, poor Hawthorne was adequately punished by contemporary readers) and the pointless confinement of Hilda near the end of the book. But the roots of the trouble are deeper than this. In an early evaluation, the very perceptive Edwin P. Whipple, that contemporary critic "for whom Hawthorne had the greatest respect,"[69] pointed out a central weakness:

> . . . all readers think that Donatello committed no sin at all; and the reason is, that Hawthorne has deprived the persecutor of Miriam of all human attributes, made him an allegorical representation of one of the most fiendish forms of unmixed evil, so that we welcome his destruction with something of the same feeling with which, in following the allegory of Spenser or Bunyan, we rejoice in the hero's victory over the Blatant Beast or Giant Despair.[70]

It may be added that by completely withholding the facts as to Miriam's background before she enters the story and as to her precise relationship with her persecutor, Hawthorne robs Miriam herself of firm reality. As to Donatello, Mark Van Doren has stated the fault succinctly:

> He [Hawthorne] contrived, rather than was possessed, to write this tale of an innocent creature educated by sin. The idea is valuable, but since there are no innocent creatures it cannot be stated in a novel. . . .[71]

In other words, the assumed Donatello, the Donatello of the earlier part of the story, is incredible; and in the degree to which the reader fails to accept his creator's assertions about him, the whole action of the central drama is weakened if not nullified—as it is by our hearty approval of his "sin."

Ultimately *The Marble Faun* fails, as I suppose ambitious works of fiction most often do, in its characters. We are left with Kenyon and Hilda. Kenyon is a clumsy and too voluble Coverdale, used inconsistently as a point-of-view character. As to Hilda (a necessary evil in relation to the quasi-happy ending), she may well be a medium for expressing Hawthorne's own uncertainties as to his theme or—I think more probably— a hedge against the clamor of those who would be outraged by the meaning of Donatello's experience as evaluated first by

Miriam and then—before his hasty retreat—by Kenyon. Perhaps she is Hawthorne's defense against the criticism of the wife he knew so well. Sophia's remark, in a letter she wrote on the date of the completion of *The Marble Faun*, is the most complete self-revelation she ever made: "Mr. Hawthorne has no idea of portraying me as Hilda. Whatever resemblance one sees is accidental."[72] At the least, it can hardly be denied that the "admirable little icicle existing for this express purpose,"[73] as Brownell called her, serves chiefly to blunt and place in question rather than to reinforce the theme of the educative function of sin.

That theme is most clearly stated in two speeches of Kenyon. One of these is to the despairing Donatello (who is not noticeably heartened by it):

". . . with its difficult steps, and the dark prison cells you speak of, your tower resembles the spiritual experience of many a sinful soul, which, nevertheless, may struggle upward into the pure air and light of Heaven at last!"[74]

The other is the speech to Hilda in which Kenyon restates the view Miriam has suggested to him—the speech in which the doctrine of *felix culpa* is explicitly stated—which causes Hilda to shrink from him with "an expression of horror":

"Sin has educated Donatello, and elevated him. Is sin, then,—which we deem such a dreadful blackness in the universe,—is it, like sorrow, merely an element of human education, through which we struggle to a higher and purer state than we could otherwise have attained? Did Adam fall, that we might ultimately rise to a far loftier paradise than his?"[75]

I believe that Kenyon speaks for Hawthorne here, rather than in his hasty retraction of the idea, and that we have in *The Marble Faun* the imperfectly achieved product of his effort to dramatize and illuminate the problem of the existence of evil in a divinely created and governed world.

Apart from its theme, the most interesting aspect of *The Marble Faun* from the religious standpoint is that it reveals

Hawthorne's conflicting feelings about Catholicism. His anti-
pathy toward clergymen is fully displayed in his comments
on priests and monks, even to the extreme of putting his
villain into monkish garb. Possibly this appalling example
of disparity between profession and practice owes something
to an experience in Liverpool: an American doctor of divinity
presented himself at the consulate, having come abroad on
money furnished by his parishioners. He returned a week later
so changed in appearance that Hawthorne did not recognize
him. On May 27, 1855, Hawthorne wrote to Ticknor:

> . . . I sent home by this steamer a Doctor of Divinity who has
> been out here on a spree, and who was brought to my office,
> destitute, after a week's residence in a brothel! He shook in
> his shoes, I can tell you. Not knowing whether I should ever
> have another opportunity of preaching to a Doctor of Divin-
> ity (an Orthodox man, too), I laid it on without mercy; and
> he promised never to forget it. I don't think he ever will.[76]

Apart from almost uniform disparagement of the clergy,
however, *The Marble Faun* offers numerous evidences of the
attractiveness which Hawthorne found in Catholicism. His recognition of value in the confessional—dramatized in Hilda's
recourse to it—and of the appropriateness of addressing petitions through a saint, his reflections on St. Peter's and the Pan-
theon (taken directly from the *Notebooks*), his appreciation
of wayside shrines—these and many other items testify to Hawthorne's responsiveness. Perhaps most important is his repeated
recognition of the ability of Catholicism to meet widely varied
human needs—a quality which, at least by implication, he
found lacking in the Protestant institutions he had known in
England and America. His ambivalent and ultimately suspended judgment is perhaps most clearly stated in a passage in
which Hawthorne speaks in his own right, as commentator:

> To do it justice, Catholicism is such a miracle of fitness
> for its own ends, many of which might seem to be admirable
> ones, that it is difficult to imagine it a contrivance of mere
> man. Its mighty machinery was forged and put together, not

on middle earth, but either above or below. If there were but angels to work it, instead of the very different class of engineers who now manage its cranks and safety-valves, the system would soon vindicate the dignity and holiness of its origin.[77]

IX

When Hawthorne took ship at Liverpool for the return voyage to America, on June 16, 1860, he had less than four years left to live. Even that brief span was heavily burdened. After the first joyful and satisfying renewal of relationships with friends and relatives and a somewhat fuller social life than Hawthorne had known before in his native land, there were problems of making arrangements for the children's education. More onerous and distressing was the inordinately prolonged and expensive remodeling, refurnishing, and decorating of the Wayside, the home at Concord which Hawthorne had bought before he went abroad. This process dragged on for almost two of the final four years. It cost so much that in spite of the savings accumulated at Liverpool (much depleted, of course, by the expenses of the years after this income ended) and the royalties from *The Marble Faun,* Hawthorne soon felt financial pressure to prepare work for publication. Doubtless more depressing than any of these was the outbreak of the Civil War—a painful time for Hawthorne as for every thoughtful American.

In spite of difficulties and distractions, Hawthorne persisted in the attempt to write, almost throughout this period. In fact, in number of words he turned out more during these years (if we except the *English Notebooks*) than in any preceding period of equal length except that just preceding his going to England in 1853. But the only work he completed was the redaction of the *English Notebooks,* published serially in *The Atlantic Monthly* and in book form as *Our Old Home* less than a year before his death, and the essay "Chiefly on War Matters," which appeared in the *Atlantic* in July, 1862.

During this period, however, Hawthorne wrote portions of four works of fiction. The thorough and extremely valuable study of the manuscripts by Edward Hutchins Davidson, in *Hawthorne's Last Phase,* enables us to understand both the author's intent and the works themselves in a measure wholly impossible before. They fall into two groups, in relation to their central themes. *The Ancestral Footstep* was begun in Rome, but quickly laid aside when Hawthorne became interested in *The Marble Faun. Doctor Grimshawe's Secret* (the title given by Julian Hawthorne when he "edited"[78] the work for publication in 1882) must have been begun soon after Hawthorne's return from England, for in spite of all distractions he had written many thousand words before he abandoned the project.[79] Both of these books undertook to explore the mystique of homecoming and the problem of Anglo-American relationships, a recurring theme in the *English Notebooks,* from which Hawthorne drew freely. He stated his purpose in what Davidson calls "Study B" for *Doctor Grimshawe's Secret:*

> The great gist of the story ought to be the natural hatred of men—and the particular hatred of Americans—to an Aristocracy; at the same time doing a good deal of justice to the aristocratic system by respecting its grand, beautiful, and noble characteristics.[80]

Although neither in the hasty and relatively feeble sketch, *The Ancestral Footstep,* nor in the more sustained effort of *Doctor Grimshawe's Secret* did Hawthorne effectively realize this purpose, he did create memorable characters in the later work. Hubert J. Hoeltje is fully justified in his comment that Doctor Grimshawe himself "emerges from the story with the breath of life in him, and the little boy and girl of the earlier chapters hauntingly suggest aspects of childhood. . . ."[81] Whether Davidson is correct in identifying Grimshawe and Elsie with Seymour Kirkup and his daughter,[82] whom Hawthorne had met at Florence, is uncertain. And how much of the successful characterization in this novel rests on Dr. Oliver and Dr. Peabody of Salem days, and how much comes, as Hoeltje suggests, from

Hawthorne's observation of his own children, may also be argued. The fact remains that, in spite of the unachieved plot and general form of the unfinished book, these characterizations are superior, in their appeal and as illustrating Hawthorne's most characteristic creative powers, to anything in *The Marble Faun*. A passage about the mystery of birth is, I feel, clearly from Hawthorne's own reflections as a father:

> Whence did you come? Whence did any of us come? Out of the darkness and mystery; out of nothingness; out of a kingdom of shadows; out of dust, clay, mud, I think, and to return to it again. . . . Out of a former life, of which the present one is the hell![83]

Also autobiographical, it seems to me, as reflecting the experience of a conscientious father faced by a child's need for religious guidance, is a passage which Julian printed in two versions, apparently from different parts of the manuscript. This is the first and fuller version:

> At first . . . the Doctor paid little attention to the moral and religious culture of his pupil; nor did he ever make a system of it. But by and by, though with a singular reluctance and kind of bashfulness, he began to extend his care to these matters; being drawn into them unawares, and possibly perceiving and learning what he taught as he went along. One evening, I know not how, he was betrayed into speaking on this point, and a sort of inspiration seized him. A vista opened before him: handling an immortal spirit, he began to know its requisitions. . . . His voice grew deep, and had a strange, impressive pathos in it. . . .[84]

Hawthorne's third and fourth unfinished romances are related in their subject matter, as were their immediate predecessors. Both deal primarily with the problem of personal immortality, and specifically with the idea of earthly immortality achieved through scientific research—a concept which may seem less farfetched today, when almost every month brings a new claim that the artificial production of living matter is just around the corner. In his boyhood Hawthorne read and enjoyed

THE DARKENED SKY

The Travels of St. Leon, by William Godwin, the story of a man who gains knowledge which enables him to live forever.[85] Possibly this was the beginning of Hawthorne's interest in the notion. At any rate, it recurs periodically in his work, as one facet of his preoccupation with the topic of immortality in general.

Thoreau had told Hawthorne of a man who had once lived in the Wayside, Hawthorne's house in Concord, who believed that he would never die. Shortly after he abandoned *Doctor Grimshawe's Secret* as hopeless, Hawthorne began work on the book we know as *Septimius Felton.* He persisted until he had written two long drafts and many fragmentary notes and studies, but finally gave up the project early in 1863, hardly more than a year before his death. An edition made by Una Hawthorne, with the aid of Robert Browning, was published in 1872.

Septimius Felton presents opposing views of the desirability of earthly immortality, and there is some indication of wavering in the author's own view. It is because the brevity and wasted opportunities of earthly life weigh heavily on Septimius Felton that he desires to live forever. He voices his motivation in a conversation with a minister:

> "May it not be possible," asked Septimius, "to have too profound a sense of the marvelous contrivance and adaptation of this material world to require or believe in anything spiritual? How wonderful it is to see it all alive on this spring day, all growing, budding! Do we exhaust it in our little life? Not so; not in a hundred or a thousand lives. The whole race of man, living from the beginning of time, have not, in all their number and multiplicity and in all their duration, come in the least to know the world they live in! And how is this rich world thrown away upon us, because we live in it such a moment! . . . No lesson is taught. We are snatched away from our study before we have learned the alphabet. . . ."
> "But the lesson is carried on in another state of being!"
> "Not the lesson that we begin here. . . ."[86]

A little later on, the author comments on Septimius and this idea of his:

> He was not a new beginner in doubt. . . . And now the new, strange thought of the sufficiency of the world for man, if man were only sufficient for that, kept recurring to him: and with it came a certain sense . . . that he . . . might never die. The feeling was not peculiar to Septimius. It is an instinct, the meaning of which is mistaken. We have strongly within us the sense of an undying principle, and we transfer that true sense to this life and to the body, instead of interpreting it justly as the promise of spiritual immortality.[87]

Septimius devotes himself to searching for the formula of an elixir of life, while the other spokesmen in the story—one can hardly call them characters—seek to dissuade him. After he believes he has found the elixir, Septimius comes to feel that he has isolated himself from humanity:

> It seemed to him, at that final moment, as if it were Death that linked together all; yes, and so gave the warmth to all . . . all that warm mysterious brotherhood that is between men; passing as they do from mystery to mystery in a little gleam of light; that wild, sweet charm of uncertainty and temporariness,—how lovely it made them all, how innocent, even the worst of them; how hard and prosaic was his own situation in comparison to them.[88]

In one of the later studies for *Septimius Felton,* Davidson's "Study H," Hawthorne suggests that the search for the elixir is to debase Septimius, depriving him of affection and sympathy, "at the same time that his intellect has acquired wonderful force and expression."[89] Later in the same study Hawthorne outlines his sought-for effect:

> The reader is made to see how all that is highest and holiest in this life depend [*sic*] on death and the expectation of it; how it immortalizes the love that, at first sight, it seems to blight and make a dream; how, without, man would be but an intellectual brute.[90]

In a still later fragment, Davidson's "Scenario K," Haw-

THE DARKENED SKY

thorne's thinking seems to veer toward his old target, the arrogant and self-centered reformer:

> Perhaps, the moral will turn out to be, the folly of man thinking that he can ever be of any importance to the welfare of the world; or that any settled plan of his, to be carried on through a length of time, could be successful. God wants short lives, because such carry on his purpose inevitably and involuntarily; while longer ones would thwart and interfere with his purpose, by carrying on their own.[91]

This "Scenario K," presumably written not long before Hawthorne abandoned *Septimius Felton* altogether, ends on what seems to me an autobiographical note of deep pathos:

> All through, represent Septimius as visited by frequent fits of despondency as to the pursuit he is engaged in, perceptions of its utter folly and impractibility [*sic*]; but after an interval, without any apparent reason why, he finds himself in full faith again—just as in writing a poem or romance. [92]

Septimius Felton is occasionally invaded by elements from the previously discarded *The Ancestral Footstep* and *Doctor Grimshawe's Secret*—the bloody footstep of the first, for example, and the English estate of both—compounding the confusion as a result. Though it contains occasional bits of powerful writing, and though it is fascinating and revealing as Hawthorne's dialogue with himself, as a work of fiction it is definitely inferior to its immediate predecessor. The inferiority lies chiefly in the characterization. The people of *Septimius Felton* are shadowy at best, if really developed at all. There is nothing here of the vitality which marks Doctor Grimshawe and his youthful charges.

Our Old Home, the last book Hawthorne completed and the last published in his lifetime, has received less critical recognition than it deserves. It is true that virtually its whole substance is to be found in the *English Notebooks,* and that generally this material is used with little change except that demanded by topical organization. However, Hawthorne's personal style in its easy richness of melody and imagery and his command of total form is displayed again and again in this book. Also, some of the most profound self-revelation in all Hawthorne is to be found in its pages. There are in *Our Old Home* a few additions to the journal text, and one of these seems to me so significant in relation to the problem of Hawthorne's religious position in his final years that it deserves detailed consideration.

The essays which make up *Our Old Home* were undertaken soon after the Hawthornes' return from Europe, at the request and with the encouragement of James T. Fields, for serial publication in the *Atlantic Monthly*. The first appeared in October, 1860, and others followed at irregular intervals. The essay titled "Outside Glimpses of English Poverty" was the last but one of the volume's twelve chapters to be serialized; it appeared in the *Atlantic* for July, 1863. Since Fields was using the articles promptly as they were submitted, it appears to have been written, or at least completed, within the final year of Hawthorne's life.

Following his usual method in assembling material for these essays, Hawthorne drew on many entries in his journal, especially those containing observations in the Liverpool slums. For the portion of the essay I wish to consider the notebook materials used include the entries for August 20th, 24th, and 25th, 1853. In the first of these the focus is on the gin-shops and their patrons; the second describes the women of the slums, including street vendors, and concludes: "My God, what dirty, dirty children! And the grown people are the flowers of these buds, physically and morally."[93] In the third the emphasis is on the cheap foods displayed in the shops and on children taking care of younger children. This entry ends with comparisons:

> The people are as numerous as maggots in cheese; you behold them, disgusting, and all moving about, as when you raise a plank or log that has long lain on the ground, and find many vivacious bugs and insects beneath it.[94]

Hawthorne also uses in this essay the long account of his visit to Liverpool's West Derby Workhouse, which appears as the

THE DARKENED SKY

Notebooks entry for February 28, 1856. This entry includes the frequently quoted account of the sickly child which "adopted" Hawthorne, to his horror, and also a detailed description of a diseased baby, "begotten by Sin upon Disease":

> I can by no means tell how horrible this baby was; neither ought I. And yet its pain and misery seemed to have given it a sort of intelligence. . . . Did God make this child? Has it a soul capable of immortality?—of immortal bliss? I am afraid not. At all events, it is quite beyond my conception and understanding.[95]

In "Outside Glimpses of English Poverty" Hawthorne used the notebook narrative of the visit to the workhouse almost in its entirety.[96] He did, however, change the first person in the account of the "adoption" to "one member of our party," and he omitted the reference to the soul of the diseased baby. Far from dropping that point, however, in his reworking he gave it a broader reference, to all slum children, and he amplified the street experiences recorded in 1853:

> The population of these dismal abodes seemed to consider the sidewalks and middle of the street as their common hall. . . . Whatever the disadvantages of the English climate, the only comfortable or wholesome part of life, for the city poor, must be spent in the open air. The stifled and squalid rooms where they lie down at night, whole families and neighborhoods together, or sulkily elbow one another in the daytime, when a settled rain drives them within doors, are worse horrors than it is worth while (without a practical object in mind) to admit into one's imagination. No wonder that they creep forth from the foul mystery of their interiors, stumble down from their garrets, or scramble up out of their cellars, on the upper step of which you may see the grimy housewife, before the shower is ended, letting the raindrops gutter down her visage; while her children (an impish progeny of cavernous recesses below the common sphere of humanity) swarm into the daylight and attain all that they know of personal purification in the nearest mud-puddle. It might almost make a man doubt the existence of his own soul, to observe how Nature has flung these little wretches into the

street and left them there, so evidently regarding them as
nothing worth, and how all mankind acquiesce in the great
mother's estimate of her offspring. For, if they are to have no
immortality, what superior claim can I assert for mine? And
how difficult to believe that anything so precious as a germ
of immortal growth can have been buried under this dirt-
heap, plunged into this cesspool of misery and vice! As often
as I beheld the scene, it affected me with surprise and loath-
some interest, much resembling, though in a far intenser degree, the feeling with which, when a boy, I used to turn over
a plank or an old log that had long lain on the damp ground,
and found a vivacious multitude of unclean and devilish-
looking insects scampering to and fro beneath it. Without
an infinite faith, there seemed as much prospect of a blessed
futurity for those hideous bugs and many-footed worms as
for these brethren of our humanity and co-heirs of all our
heavenly inheritance. Ah, what a mystery! Slowly, slowly,
as after groping at the bottom of a deep, noisome, stagnant
pool, my hope struggles upward to the surface, bearing the
half-drowned body of a child along with it, and heaving it
aloft for its life, and my own life, and all our lives. Unless
these slime-clogged nostrils can be made capable of inhaling
celestial air, I know not how the purest and most intellectual of us can reasonably expect ever to taste a breath of it.
The whole question of eternity is staked there. If a single one
of those helpless little ones be lost, the world is lost![97]

I am unable to find quiet affirmation here or indeed anything
but a cry of agony voiced by one whose cherished faith is at
the breaking-point. The passage seems to me to support the view
that his sustained and unfruitful effort to deal with the problem of immortality in *Septimius Felton* resulted from a weak-
ening of religious faith in that element which had been crucial
for Hawthorne almost from the beginning, belief in personal
immortality. Obviously, the question of immortality for the
diseased child had remained in Hawthorne's mind, for when
he relived the experience in the last year of his life, he broadened its application to all underprivileged children, as we have
seen, and gave it the emphasis and impact of the most powerful
image he ever created. Certainly there is nothing here of the

positive confidence so characteristic of the many earlier references to a future life. It seems a fair deduction that Hawthorne's keenly analytical intelligence had been working on the problem in his later years, without arriving at a completely satisfactory solution. I believe that this explains his preoccupation with the subject in his final attempts at fiction—even though in these attempts he approaches the question tangentially through the device of the elixir of life—and that it affords one of the reasons for his inability to bring those attempts to fruition.

All that we have of *The Dolliver Romance* was written within the last year of Hawthorne's life. He began work in October, 1863, and, either at his own or the editor's suggestion, he undertook to furnish regular installments of the projected book for serial publication in the *Atlantic Monthly,* perhaps hoping that the obligation to deliver sections of the manuscript at stated intervals would help him to keep at work. Further, he planned to provide a biographical sketch of Thoreau—who had given him the story of the man who thought he would never die—as a preface. But the undiagnosed disease which was to cause his death in May, 1864, was becoming so debilitating that he could work only at intervals. He had completed a first chapter by December, but wrote only two more and some exploratory studies before the end of his life.

The Dolliver Romance is generally and rightly regarded not only as the best of the four unfinished romances but also, even in its incompleteness, as one of Hawthorne's finest works of fiction. The figures of Doctor Dolliver and Pansie are obviously related to the earlier Doctor Grimshawe and his charges, but the portrayal is even more effective, vital, and deeply appealing in its tenderness and warmth. The theme of earthly immortality and the device of the elixir of life reappear from *Septimimus Felton,* but within the brief scope of the work as we have it, they do not seriously impair the memorable human convincingness and significance of Doctor Dolliver.

As Davidson remarks, "the mystery of *The Dolliver Romance*

will doubtless never be solved: either Hawthorne or one of the heirs destroyed a number of pages and various paragraphs have been deleted in the published version."[98] The eight studies for the work which Davidson has distinguished enable us to see that in this as in his work on the earlier romance of earthly immortality Hawthorne's intention wavered—that he entertained alternative motives for and effects of the discovery and use of the elixir of life. It would appear, however, that his latest intention was to posit the elixir as a reality and to show in contrasting characters the divergent effects resulting from different motives for its use: in the briefly established Colonel Dabney, whose motive is brutally selfish (and whom it kills), and in Dr. Dolliver, whose motive is human love and concern for the child, Pansie. This intention seems clear in the latest of the studies Davidson has found, his "Study H," which reads in part:

> The Apothecary and the Colonel must be specimens of two different modes of growing old; the former [*sic*; but the context shows that the reference is to the Colonel] fossilized, harshly defined, narrow, hard, selfish, with the humanity petrified out of him . . . so selfish that he would eat child broth. and have a daily child slaughtered to make it with, if he thought it would do him any good . . . the Doctor mild, gentle, getting worn away and defined by age, readily melting into tears, fading out, cackling into mild laughter. . . .[99]

If it was indeed Hawthorne's purpose to show earthly immortality as beneficent in the case of Dr. Dolliver, as seems probable both on the basis of the published text and the indications in the latest notes, Hawthorne was at the last developing a notebook entry of 1848, as Davidson has noted: "A man, arriving at the extreme point of old age, grows young again. . . ."[100]

Whatever may have been Hawthorne's ultimate intention for *The Dolliver Romance,* if, indeed, he ever thought it through completely, I believe the testimony of the work itself—its profound sympathy, its tenderness, its "sunniness"—shows that he had somehow reached an accommodation with the doubt which had tortured him when he revised his English notes for *Our*

Old Home. Perhaps he achieved at least that degree of acceptance which was expressed by his close friend Herman Melville
in the "Epilogue" to *Clarel,* the final poems, and—as I read the
story—in *Billy Budd.*

3

Herman Melville

THROUGHOUT THE MORE THAN FOUR DECADES OF MODERN CRITICAL study of the writings of Herman Melville there has been general agreement that his works afford major reflections and interpretations of the religious problems of the nineteenth century. Not one of his books lacks significant and substantial religious orientation and implication. There has been wide, even violent disagreement as to Melville's religious position and the meaning of some of his books as statements of that position. But the very fact of that disagreement underlines the major importance of Melville in relation to our present purpose.

William H. Gilman has shown, in what I feel to be one of the most perceptive and fruitful of the many books about Melville, *Melville's Early Life and Redburn,* that up to the time of his father's financial failure, when Herman was eleven, and his mental collapse and death in 1832, when Herman was thirteen, the boy's life was an exceptionally favored and happy one. He was the third of eight children of parents notably devoted to each other and to their four sons and four daughters. Allan Melville, the father, was during this period a rising young merchant in New York City. Twice within ten years he was able to move his increasing family to a new and better home. He provided for them luxuries as well as comforts and the best educational opportunities the city could offer. He was a somewhat pompous and sentimental gentleman, very proud of his distinguished Scottish ancestry, and fond of voicing pious platitudes. But there is ample evidence of his openhearted affection for his wife and children. Maria Gansevoort Melville had pride of ancestry even greater than her husband's, for she was the daughter of a distinguished soldier of Revolutionary days, General Peter Gansevoort, and was related to some of the most prominent New York families either by blood or through marriage. Her devotion to her husband, her home, and her children was, however, real and complete.

Naturally—perhaps inevitably, in marrying a Gansevoort—Allan Melville became a member of the Dutch Reformed Church, though his parents were Unitarians; and throughout Herman's childhood the family regularly attended services of Dutch Reformed churches, first at the South Church on Garden Street, later at a newly built church at Broome and Greene Streets; and the children went to Sunday school. Just at this time the authorities of the Dutch Reformed Church became disturbed by certain innovations in Sunday school teaching, especially in New York City. Some teachers were following the example of the Sunday schools of other denominations in using biblical history and "Bible stories" as the chief material for their lessons. After some spirited discussion, these innovations were condemned, and the teachers were enjoined to restore memorization of creed and catechism to their former primacy in Sunday school procedure.

Herman's Grandmother Gansevoort was a most rigid Calvinist; her home was filled with religious books, and the Sabbath was observed there with Puritanical austerity. But vacation visits with their maternal grandmother were balanced for the Melville children by vacations spent in the liberal atmosphere of the Melville grandparents in Boston. Though the Bible was reverenced and read in the home of Allan Melville, the atmosphere was quietly and moderately worldly rather than rigorously pious, with sufficient emphasis on good food, good drink, good social connections, and good business practice. The burden of Calvinist doctrine rested heavily on the youthful Herman only in the weekly hours of sermons and catechism—which may well have seemed endless to an active boy—and during the annual month-long visits to the Gansevoort mansion in Albany.

During his stays at Albany, even before his father's sudden business failure precipitated the family's removal there, the boy must have heard some of the sermons of the Reverend John Ludlow, pastor of the First Dutch Reformed Church, of which his grandmother Gansevoort was one of the most active and affluent parishioners. Certainly after the move to Albany and especially after his father's death when the Reverend Ludlow became his mother's close friend and advisor, Herman saw and heard much of this clergyman. Of Rev. Ludlow an historian of his denomination says:

> His most striking characteristic was "strength." . . . His voice was strong. With difficulty he restrained it from what in another would have been vociferousness; but when his earnest soul burst through such caution, its tones thundered through the largest edifice, commanding the most distant hearer, and often overpowering those who sat nearer to the pulpit.[1]

This was the clergyman who was almost a daily visitor at the Melville home in the months following the death of Herman's father.

The years in Albany from 1830 to 1836, from the time when he was eleven to the family's second bankruptcy, when he was seventeen—years of sufficient strain and difficulty for almost every boy—held for Herman Melville such exceptional tensions, such painful experiences beyond any power of his to control, as to affect his character and personality permanently. Knowledge of these years is crucial for understanding his lifelong preoccupation with religious problems—a preoccupation which informs his writing, in various ways and degrees, from his first book to his last.

The sudden breaking-up of the happy and seemingly stable home in New York was the first blow. Herman probably did not understand the details of the financial disaster, but he shared the full shock of the upheaval. His mother fled to Albany with the younger children, leaving her husband and two older sons, including Herman, alone in the house no longer theirs to pack or sell furniture and personal belongings. When the actual move occurred, an accident compelled Herman and his father to spend a dreary night without lodging on the docks.

A second experience of a kind that leaves its imprint on the mind of a sensitive child was the death, a few months after the Melvilles' arrival in Albany, of Herman's grandmother Gansevoort, with whom he had spent happy if somewhat repressed vacations in earlier years. Her funeral, as that of one of the wealthiest and most socially distinguished of Albany's citizens, was an event of great impressiveness, with some four hundred invited mourners.

His grandmother's death demanded of Herman a new effort to shape the boy's world he was trying to build for himself in Albany. No doubt a large factor in that world was afforded by the life of the school he and his older brother, Gansevoort, were attending, the Albany Academy. This was a private school, relatively expensive, for until Allan Melville's death the generous help of her mother and later of her brother Peter kept Maria Melville and her family in very comfortable circumstances. This school was rigorous and conservative, with heavy emphasis on religious training. Perhaps the sense of their father's failure stimulated in the Melville boys a determination to excel. At any rate, at the end of their first year at the academy Gansevoort won various honors and Herman was rewarded —by public presentation of a volume of literary selections— for leading his class in arithmetic!

The heavy emphasis on religious matters at the Albany Academy is illustrated by the contents of the book used for the study of literature, the *English Reader* of the American-born British grammarian Lindley Murray. More than one-third of the prose selections in the book are taken from the writings of the Reverend Hugh Blair, an eminent Scottish Calvinist, and the introductory "Observations on the Principles of Good Reading" (which fill eight pages of very small type) are based on Blair's *Lectures on Rhetoric and Belles Lettres,* 1783. Most of the selections from Blair and such other writers as Addison and Goldsmith (who rank second and third, respectively, to Blair in number of selections) are heavily pious. Some are sentimentally lachrymose.

Murray's *English Reader* offers one striking exception, however, to its heavily pious tone. The longest selection in the book is a dialogue by Lord Lyttleton, taken from his *Dialogues of the Dead* and entitled: "Locke and Bayle: Christianity defended against the cavils of skepticism." Although the avowed purpose of the selection is to support religious orthodoxy, and although Bayle says at one point, "You are very severe upon me," his side of the argument is given with astonishing adequacy. At the end, when Bayle defends his skeptical position by indicating that contemporary teachers of religion are at fault, Locke admits that "What you now say is too true!" leaving Bayle, in effect, master of the field.

Since Bayle was important to Melville at a crucial point in his career, that of the composition of *Moby Dick,* as has been generally recognized, it is interesting to note that he probably became aware of skepticism in general, and of Bayle's arguments in its defense, at this early age. If the words put into the mouth of Bayle by Lord Lyttleton are not actually repeated in Melville's writing, certainly far from strange to the reader of Melville will be the ideas and even the rhetoric of such passages as this:

> The mind is free; and it loves to exert its freedom. Any restraint upon it is a violence done to its nature, and a tyranny, against which it has a right to rebel.[2]

II

Herman Melville had less than two years of Murray's *English Reader* and the Albany Academy. His father made a courageous effort to recoup his fortunes, obtaining a position as manager of a small fur store in Albany. But the pressure of unpaid debts and uncertain income proved too much for him. In January of 1832, when Herman was not yet thirteen, Allan Melville's physical and then his mental health gave way. He became in his brother's words—possibly exaggerated—"a raging maniac," and after three weeks of such pains and terrors for his sensitive second son as can only be imagined, he died on January 28. Again, and with even greater immediacy, Herman experienced the austerity of a Calvinist funeral. In the changed financial situation caused by their father's death, the older Melville boys left the academy, Gansevoort to replace his father as manager of the fur store, Herman to become—at thirteen—a clerk in the New York State Bank and later a copyist, like Bartleby of his later fiction, in his uncle's law office.

It is not at all to impugn the justice of William H. Gilman's portrayal of Maria Melville as an exceptionally loving mother to suggest that in the months following her husband's death her heightened religiosity may have been something of a burden to her older sons. In less than three months after Allan Melville's death his widow became a member of the First Dutch Reformed Church of Albany—a step she had neglected to take earlier—and was followed by her daughter Helen in July and by Augusta in October. Though neither Gansevoort nor Herman became communicants, Gansevoort's journal of this time shows that they attended church services and Sunday school even more regularly than their mother and sisters.[3]

Two years as a bank clerk and copyist may have injured Herman's health. At any rate, he apparently spent much of his sixteenth year, 1834, at the farm of his uncle Thomas Melville near Pittsfield, Massachusetts, helping with the field work and the care of animals. Here he encountered religious attitudes quite different from those he experienced in Albany, for his uncle was an Episcopalian whose first wife had been a Frenchwoman and a Roman Catholic. When Herman returned to Albany early in 1835, perhaps with improved health and certainly with greater personal independence, he did not go back to the bank or the law office but became his brother Gansevoort's assistant in the fur business, which was, briefly, prospering. Also he entered the new Albany Classical School for his final months of formal education, and became a member of the Albany Young Men's Association, which gave him access to an excellent library of books chosen specifically for their appeal to young men. The literary allusions in his first writings, the "Scraps from a Writing Desk" published in a newspaper four years later,[4] indicate that he read especially Romantic poetry, including Byron, to whom he had been introduced by his prize volume in 1831.

When Herman returned to the services of his mother's church after his months at Pittsfield, he found that the Reverend Ludlow had been succeeded by a younger man of somewhat different type, the Reverend Thomas E. Vermilye. Vermilye was as thoroughgoing a Calvinist as his predecessor, as is made clear by the tenor of his sermons published in *The National Preacher* and other periodicals of the time.[5] But he was interested in young men and in their literary ambitions and activities, was influential in the Albany Young Men's Association, to which he delivered a series of lectures, and may well have afforded fatherless Herman Melville a significant friendship.

Whatever Herman's relation with his mother's new pastor, it is clear that the next two years were marked by rapid personal development along lines largely normal for a teenage boy. He was stimulated by wide if haphazard reading and by association with youths of his own age and interests. He carried on an elaborate war of charge and countercharge in the columns of the *Albany Microscope* with a rival for leadership in the Philo Logos Debating Society. He found increasing satisfaction in his daily work as chief assistant to Gansevoort in the family fur business. Just how important was Gansevoort's influence on his younger brother, or how close was their relationship at this time, is difficult to determine. But in the light of Herman's dependence on Gansevoort in the early phases of his literary career, a few years later, and the abundant evidence of their cordial relationship at that time, it seems probable that his widely read and intellectually independent if not already skeptical elder brother, in these two years of close daily association, had greater influence on Herman than has hitherto been suggested.

However, these relatively favorable and fruitful years, like earlier ones, came to a sudden end. The panic of 1836–37 caught Gansevoort's business with overextended credit. The market for furs collapsed, and on April 15, 1837, Gansevoort went into bankruptcy. His mother's credit was also involved. Uncle Peter Gansevoort, whose generous help to the Melvilles had depleted his own capital, could no longer sustain their financial burdens in addition to his own. Maria moved to a relatively humble residence in the nearby village of Lansingburgh, and eighteen-year-old Herman got a job—with the help of his uncle, Thomas Melville—as teacher of a rural school near Pittsfield.

Ten years later, at twenty-eight, Herman Melville was a successful novelist, with two widely sold books to his credit, with influential friends, and newly married to a daughter of the chief justice of Massachusetts. In the interval he had found school teaching unrewarding, both intellectually and financially; had tried his hand at writing for a newspaper; had studied engineering briefly in the vain hope of getting a construction job on the Erie Canal, and in 1839 had sailed on a merchant ship to Liverpool and back as a common hand before the mast. Then, after making his way as far west as Galena, Illinois (where his uncle Thomas Melville had moved) in an unsuccessful quest for work, he spent another three years (1841–44) in a voyage to the Pacific, sailing out on a whaler, serving on two others, and returning on a United States man-of-war. Within a year after his return he had completed the manuscript of *Typee,* which made him famous.

In these years Melville had experienced physical hardship and mental isolation such as were encountered by no other great writer of his century. He had seen much of the world's evil and suffering. He had been deprived of religious association and observance save for the perfunctory services on the man-of-war. He had accumulated abundant concrete evidence on which to base the questioning of church and creed which marked his work for the rest of his life.

For the student of Melville's religious thought, his first two novels, *Typee* (1846) and *Omoo* (1847), offer objective commentary rather than subjective revelation. It is sufficient here to say that in these books he treated the pagan religion of the Polynesians with sympathetic respect and had hostile criticism for the missionaries who tried to destroy that religion and substitute their varying versions of Christianity. The angry condemnation of these books by spokesmen for religious organizations and supporters of missionary enterprises probably contributed to their wide circulation rather than impaired it, and their general critical reception was favorable. The reason Melville's third novel, *Mardi* (1849), is vastly different from its predecessors lies less in the public response to the first two novels than in the circumstances of Melville's personal life: his marriage, his involvement in literary and political squabbles in New York, and above all his reading. Again in this period Melville was reading voraciously and voluminously—borrowing, buying, and reviewing books—and reading especially books of philosophical and related content: Shakespeare, Rabelais, Sir Thomas Browne, Plato, Milton, and Montaigne.

I have believed from my first reading of *Mardi* that Melville began the book with the conscious intention of producing a companion volume to *Typee* and *Omoo* and held to that intention for nearly forty chapters. Certainly in those chapters he wrote better than he had ever written before—with more verve, more change of pace and tone, more effective spotlighting of event and individual, more humor. But at this point he grew tired of what he had begun—or perhaps the pressure of ideas, from his reading and the world around him, simply overpowered his intention. From the entrance in the novel of the mysterious Yillah, whom the narrator rescues—murdering her guardian, the priest Aleema, in doing so—*Mardi* becomes the least controlled and for most readers the least rewarding of Melville's books.

Using a timeworn device—here a group of garrulous fellow travelers who join in a search for Yillah, who has disappeared as mysteriously as she came—Melville provides himself with all too fluent spokesmen for conflicting views of religion, government, poetry, philosophy, and things in general; and their travels afford opportunity for Gulliverlike description of societies and institutions. In the later chapters the group reaches the actual world, after extended exploration of the mythical archipelago of Mardi, and the satire—especially of "Vivenza" (the United States)—becomes primarily political.

In the course of this development, or more precisely, this extension of the novel, the definite and consistent first-person point of view of the earlier chapters ravels out and is lost, though some attempt is made to reestablish the narrator—now named "Taji" for an unknown reason—as the central figure in the remaining and major portions of the book. This device fails to bridge the sharp cleavage following the introduction of Yillah.

In relation to the whole range of Melville's work, *Mardi* is more significant as evidence of growing pains and indication of the direction of growth than as fictional achievement. The voyaging companions talk endlessly, but seldom very brilliantly. The book is burdened by the frequent irruption, without apparent relation to the current action, of three voluptuous "damsels" who bring to Taji messages from a mysterious Queen Hautia in "the language of flowers"—which is borrowed, literally, from a popular contemporary handbook on that sentimental subject![6] It is never very clear who Yillah and Hautia are, and the attempts of scholars to find definite meaning for them and for the book as a whole seem to me unsatisfying.

Inevitably the far-ranging dialogues of the Mardian pilgrims touch on the subject of religion—indeed they do so very frequently—and their explorations bring them to or near two places, islands of the fabulous Mardian archipelago, which have definite religious significance. The first of these, Maramma, objectifies in extreme form the adverse view of institutional religion which Melville had now come to hold. This "holy island" is approached with awe, and the vaguely central Taji (as Melville's representative and spokesman) is prepared to be open-minded about it. But its professional guides prove greedy and corrupt; its holy of holies is found to contain nothing at all; and the common people of the island are cruelly oppressed by their priestly masters. Some details suggest that Melville's immediate target is the Roman Catholic Church, though in his previous books he had treated Catholic missionaries less harshly than the Protestants.

It is on the island of Serenia that all the pilgrims—except, significantly, Taji himself—decide, at the end of their journeyings, to make their home. This is the island of brotherly love, a place where the teachings of Alma, a Polynesian Christ, are put into practice. Again, perhaps meaningfully, the pilgrims do not actually see Serenia. They are only told about it by one of its inhabitants. They have no actual experience of its reported peacefulness and happiness, whereas they have directly observed the venality, cruelty, and deception of Maramma.

Most of the extensive discussion of religious problems in *Mardi* is put into the mouth of Babbalanja, the philosopher of the group of pilgrims. An initial obstacle to taking *Mardi* seriously, after the first forty chapters, is the fantastic nomenclature Melville imposes on his shadowy characters. The other pilgrims are Mohi or Braidbeard, a historian; Yoomy, a poet of negligible talent so far as his recorded effusions show; and Media, a king of practical good intentions. Babbalanja is occasionally "possessed," for reasons not made clear, by a devil who is known as Azzageddi; and he quotes at length from an ancient sage called Bardianna. The most coherent statements of religious ideas in *Mardi* occur in speeches of Babbalanja and in his reading of passages from Bardianna. Newton Arvin has commented:

> . . . it is clear that Melville is struggling to avoid "a brutality of indiscriminate skepticism," as he calls it, and no doubt—divided and confused as he was, when he wrote the book, among a host of contradictory emotions and ideas—he came nearest to expressing his basic thought in a speech of Babbalanja's as he "discourses in the dark:" "Be it enough for us to know that Oro"—God—"indubitably is."[7]

In the lines just preceding the sentence quoted by Arvin, Babbalanja has voiced a protest against religious disputation and persecution, appealing:

> Ah! let us Mardians quit this insanity. Let us be content with the theology in the grass and the flower, in seed-time and harvest.[8]

Not surprisingly, *Mardi* fell far short of the popular and critical success of its predecessors. Under financial pressure to support his growing family—his first child was born just before *Mardi* was published, and his mother and sisters persisted in making his home theirs (on what financial basis is not known) —Melville produced in rapid succession in 1849 two novels in which he returned to his own actual experience for his basic material, *Redburn* and *White Jacket*. The narrative core of *Redburn* is largely the story of Melville's voyage to Liverpool and return on the *St. Lawrence* in 1839, that of *White Jacket* his experience as an enlisted sailor on the frigate *United States* in the voyage from Honolulu to Boston in 1843–44. In both books, however, as critics have amply demonstrated, the actual experience has been liberally amplified and embroidered by literary borrowings and the writer's imagination.

In regard to the development of Melville's religious thought, these novels are important chiefly for their positive humanitarianism. In *Redburn* the most powerful chapters are those which recount the youthful traveler's impressions and experiences in the Liverpool slums. There is no reason to doubt that the intensity of these chapters arises from Melville's own emotions under the circumstances narrated. He approves in this book the efforts of Christian ministers who enter the slums and the docks to preach to the sailors and rebukes the institutions calling themselves Christian which make no attempt to relate themselves to social realities. In *White Jacket,* in a detailed account of Sabbath services on a warship, he etches sharply the gulf between the services, especially the chaplain's sermon, and the sailors' needs. Repeatedly in this book the incompatibility between a real Christianity on the one hand and a warship, the Articles of War, and war itself on the other is driven home. The major target of Melville's humanitarian protest, however, is the practice of flogging as punishment for offences against Navy discipline—a practice which was soon to be abolished by act of Congress, possibly in some small part because of the impact of Melville's book. Both novels, and especially *White Jacket,* are written in what may be called a Christian idiom, with reference to God and appeals to the attention and concern of Christian readers.[9] It is not necessary to assume that this constitutes intentional device or conscious artifice on Melville's part. He is writing to and for professedly Christian readers. There can be no question of the sincerity of his humanitarian intentions, and it was wholly natural that he should use Christian terms in invoking Christian sanctions against undeniable evils. While Melville regarded the two novels as potboilers and inferior productions, they are in general remarkably sound and consistent works of fiction. However, they offer few clues as to what was really going on in his religious consciousness, in his quest for truth. That revelation had to wait for *Moby Dick.*

III

Moby Dick (1851) is of course generally and rightly regarded as the greatest of Melville's books and by many as the greatest achievement of American literature. For our present purpose it is of especial specific importance because it is the first effective presentation in Melville's work of an essentially religious theme as central and dominant—an emphasis which was to remain constant for the rest of his life.

Moby Dick is more nearly akin to *Mardi* than to any other of its predecessors, but the differences are greater than the resemblances. In the first place, the Mardian voyage is fanciful, in detail and in total conception—avowedly so. The whale-hunting voyage of *Moby Dick,* on the other hand, is firmly anchored to reality by wealth of concrete detail, by fully realized human characters, by deliberate preparation of the reader for the extraordinary. Even at its most theatrical moments, for most readers of *Moby Dick* the flow of acceptance, the illusion of actuality, remains unbroken.

The effect of a second difference, primarily structural, is far-reaching. In *Mardi* the romantic rebel, Taji, ostensibly the central figure whose adventures are being recounted, is also the point-of-view character, the "I," the registering consciousness so far as an ascertained point of view obtains in the book at all. But in *Moby Dick* the central figure of Ahab is *viewed,* revealed in his speeches and actions and only rarely by clearly identified passages of introspection. The whole vast complex of action and emotion is given to the reader chiefly through the consciousness of Ishmael, an initially appealing, constantly developing, and altogether firmly established character in his own right.

In every other aspect of fiction—in style, in organization, in the presentation of character and the realization of event, *Moby Dick* shows not only a shift in intention from that of *Mardi,* a focusing of purpose, but also a growth of artistic resourcefulness and power that is all but incredible within the space of two years. I ascribe this change in part to a clarification within Melville's mind of his religious position. Broadly speaking, he was to express in *Moby Dick* his assertion of the individual freedom of the human mind; in *Pierre* and *The Confidence Man* his conception of the failure of Christianity to meet the needs of the thoughtful man in the life of the actual world; and in *Clarel* and thereafter to seek a reconciliation and resolution of those needs.

Yet a basic parallelism between *Mardi* and *Moby Dick* remains, one which lies at the heart of their religious meaning. Both Taji and Ahab are rebels, wholehearted adherents of the view previously quoted from Lord Lyttleton's "Locke and Bayle," that "The mind is free. . . . restraint upon it is a violence done to its nature, and a tyranny, against which it has a right to rebel." Both defy God, and oppose their wills to His. Both sacrifice other human beings in the exercise of their own wills and are specifically conscious of guilt in so doing. Both persist in their courses to the point of suicide. But though parallel in general terms, these two literary creations are worlds apart as achieved experience for the reader. Taji is patently artificial, shadowy, relatively uninteresting, whereas Ahab, of course, is one of the most completely realized characters in all fiction. Perhaps the highest reach of Melville's creative power may be seen in those passages in which he reveals in Ahab a capacity for normal human feeling and suffering: his tenderness toward Pip, his confession and admonition to Starbuck, his thoughts of wife and child. In all literature, there is no other rebel equally great, equally human.

In addition to their artistic inequality, there is a crucial difference between *Mardi* and *Moby Dick* in their religious content and implications. Whereas *Mardi* makes an uneasy and partial accommodation with Christian teaching—at least with Christian ideals of conduct—no such attempt is made in *Moby Dick*. Christ is scarcely mentioned in its five hundred pages. It has its theology indeed—but it is a theology of the Old Testament, not of the New: the theology of the Book of Job. The God defied by Ahab is the God who permitted the Devil to afflict Job and then rebuked Job for complaining. Ahab is given ample opportunity to repent, to renounce his defiance, as is the Jonah of Father Mapple's sermon. But Ahab rejects appeals from without and from within his own heart. He remains the obdurate rebel and dies in his defiance.

THE DARKENED SKY

The fact that Christ and the Christian ethic are absent from *Moby Dick,* either as dramatic elements or as points of reference, suggests the important transition that was occurring in Melville's attitude. He is passing here from the relatively positive view of Christianity as a practicable pattern for human conduct to the violently negative view which will be apparent in *Pierre.*

The materials pertinent to Melville's religious attitudes in *Moby Dick* begin with the vivid accounts of Ishmael's acquaintance with the pagan harpooneer, Queequeg. Ishmael gradually comes to recognize the sincerity of Queequeg's religious observances and to find his initial fear and repulsion toward the tattooed cannibal replaced by admiration and love. Here are echoes of the recognition of elements of goodness in paganism in *Typee* and *Omoo.*

Father Mapple's sermon, though clearly indicated as a point of reference for the whole novel by its placing and detailed treatment, is scarcely a Christian utterance. Father Mapple preaches in the Old Testament context of the Book of Jonah, and the sins of Jonah, in consciously disobeying the commands of God and in consciously involving other human beings in the peril of punishment, are essentially the sins of Ahab in the body of the novel.

The only positively Christian character in *Moby Dick* is the first mate, Starbuck. But in his preliminary account of Starbuck in the first of the two chapters titled "Knights and Squires," Melville pointedly prepares for Starbuck's ultimate failure in his attempts to resist Ahab's domination:

> But were the coming narrative to reveal, in any instance, the complete abasement of poor Starbuck's fortitude, scarce might I have the heart to write it; for it is a thing most sorrowful, nay shocking, to expose the fall of valor in the soul.[10]

Seventy pages later Melville renews his assertion of "the incompetence of mere unaided virtue or right-mindedness in Starbuck."[11]

In addition to predicating the inadequacy of Christian virtues, in these comments and later dramatized in Starbuck's actions, Melville makes many unfavorable references to institutional Christianity. One of these is the reference in the chapter called "Fast-fish and Loose-fish" to "The Archbishop of Savesoul's income of £100,000 seized from the scant bread and cheese of hundreds of thousands of broken-backed laborers. . . ."[12] At the end of this chapter Melville suggests that "the principle of religious belief" in "all men's minds and opinions" is itself but "a Loose-Fish" (previously defined in the same chapter as "fair game for anybody who can soonest catch it").[13] In the brief sixty-ninth chapter, "The Funeral," Melville asserts that the sighting of a dead whale may cause a logbook entry of "shoals, rocks, and breakers hereabout," and comments:

> There's your law of precedents; there's your utility of traditions; there's the story of your obstinate survival of old beliefs never bottomed on the earth, and now not even hovering in the air! There's orthodoxy![14]

Finally, in the matter of the changing attitude toward Christ and Christianity revealed in *Moby Dick,* William Braswell noted that "Whereas in *White-Jacket,* published the year before, Christ is held up as a model for all men to imitate, in *Moby-Dick* Christ is barely mentioned, and the only very significant reference to Him is uncomplimentary."[15] Braswell then quotes from the passage which praises Michelangelo's depiction of strength in his painting of God the Father, which continues:

> And whatever they may reveal of the divine love in the Son, the soft curled hermaphroditical Italian pictures, in which his idea has been most successfully embodied; these pictures, so destitute as they are of all brawniness, hint nothing of any power, but the mere negative, feminine one of submission and endurance, which on all hands it is conceded, form the peculiar practical virtues of his teachings.[16]

But Melville's adverse references to Christ and Christianity, both overt and implicit, are of minor importance in comparison to the major achieved purpose: the powerful realization of the character of the rebellious Ahab. Two pertinent observations may be made regarding this achievement. The first is that although the whole fictional structure of the pact with Fedallah and the hocus-pocus of the stowaway Malay crew could have been spared without notable distress to some readers, the fact remains that Ahab's reliance on Fedallah's promises serves to humanize Ahab, to show him as less wholly committed to his own purpose of revenge than he would otherwise appear, and to validate the desperation of his action when Fedallah's promises prove to be false. But an even more significant aspect of this characterization, and one sometimes overlooked, is Ahab's recourse to fatalism in the later stages of the action as explanation and defense of his conduct. In the great chapter "The Symphony," in which Ahab makes the most profound and important self-revelation of the novel, he places the blame for his conduct on God:

> Is Ahab, Ahab? Is it I, God, or who, that lifts this arm? But if the great sun move not of himself; but is as an errand-boy in heaven; nor one single star can revolve, but by some invisible power; how then can this one small heart beat; this one small brain think thoughts; unless God does that beating, does that thinking, does that living, and not I. By heaven, man, we are turned round and round in this world, like yonder windless, and Fate is the handspike.[17]

In the penultimate chapter, again to Starbuck, Ahab repeats his disclaimer of personal responsibility. When Starbuck tells him that it is "Impiety and blasphemy to hunt him more!" Ahab's defense is that he cannot help doing what he does: "This whole act's immutably decreed. 'Twas rehearsed by thee and me a billion years before this ocean rolled. Fool! I am the Fates' lieutenant; I act under orders."[18]

One of the puzzling problems for the student of Melville's writings is the fact that the novel generally recognized as his greatest achievement, *Moby Dick,* was followed by the work many readers consider his least successful, the novel *Pierre* (1852). Major differences in the two works—in background, characterization, theme—are obvious. But the inferiority of *Pierre* is at least partially accounted for by the fact that it is the hurried work of a tired man. Melville allowed himself too little time for physical and mental recuperation after the immense and intense labor of the writing of *Moby Dick*. He was unable to send the final "closing sheets" of *Moby Dick* to his British publisher, Bentley, until July 29, 1851. The correspondence of the preceding and following months makes very clear his state of extreme fatigue and close approach to utter exhaustion. Yet he began *Pierre* before the end of the year. In Melville's famous letter to Hawthorne (in response to Hawthorne's now lost comment on *Moby Dick*), which was probably written in November, 1851, he said "Leviathan is not the biggest fish;— I have heard of Krakens."[19] This could conceivably be a reference to the work he had in hand in *Pierre*. However, the first unmistakable mention of the new book is in his letter to Mrs. Hawthorne of January 8, 1852, when he promises her "a rural bowl of milk"[20] as his next novel. It is hard to conclude that the actual writing of *Pierre* began before early November, 1851. This would mean that Melville produced an average of at least one thousand words for every day until the task was completed; the proofs of the whole novel of 165,000 words were sent to Bentley (who refused it) by April 15, 1852.

Certainly he wrote *Pierre* at a rate and with a degree of concentration which drew the attention of his friends and alarmed them. His Pittsfield neighbor and friend, Mrs. Morewood, wrote to Evert Duykinck on Christmas Day, 1851, that Mr. Melville "is now so engaged in a new work as frequently not to leave his room until quite dark in the evening—when he for the first time during the day partakes of solid food—he must therefore write under a state of morbid excitement which will soon injure his health."[21] The following March, Dr. Amos Nourse wrote to Judge Lemuel Shaw congratulating him on the recovery of his daughter Elizabeth (Melville's wife) and adding: "Her husband I fear is devoting himself to writing with an assiduity that will cost him dear by and by. . . ."[22]

THE DARKENED SKY

The circumstances of its composition make it less than surprising that *Pierre* is a hectic and uneven book, marked by a frenetic, even frantic quality not found in any other writing in all of Melville's work. If we assume that its elaborate and artificial style is deliberate—and in the light of the stylistic virtuosity displayed in *Moby Dick,* any other conclusion seems impossible—perhaps the most charitable surmise is that in parts of the story Melville was deliberately and savagely parodying the saccharine prose of those contemporary feminine authors of best-selling fiction whom Hawthorne denounced in a letter to his publisher as "a damned tribe of scribbling women."

In its essential technique, apart from the style and the preposterousness of much of the action, Melville's seventh novel displays much of the mastery he had gained through the writing of its predecessors. It opens with an idyllic account of young Pierre Glendinning, heir to the great estate of Saddle Meadows, the idol of his proud widowed mother, and betrothed to highborn and lovely Lucy Tartan. All of this is so high-flown in lush sentimentalism as to arouse the profound suspicions of any experienced reader of Melville. The suspicions are soon justified. Pierre discovers that his father, whose memory he has revered, has had an unacknowledged illegitimate daughter, Isabel, who is now in the neighborhood and appeals to Pierre for help. Sure that his mother will reject the girl and frustrated in his hope to get advice from the local clergyman, Pierre decides that it is his sacred duty to pretend to marry Isabel— thus concealing the blot on his father's memory. In carrying out this remarkable course of action, he nearly kills Lucy by the melodramatic announcement of his intention, and actually kills his mother by his conduct. He takes Isabel to the city, where he proposes to make a living for them by writing. They are joined by Lucy, who wants only to help them, and pursued by Lucy's indignant brother and Pierre's jealous cousin, who replaces Pierre as the heir to Saddle Meadows. Pierre's writing fails, and the book ends with a flurry of murders and suicides in which all the principal characters perish—an all but incredible mishmash of melodrama and bad writing, entirely lacking in the authority and dignity, the achieved catharsis, of the ending of *Moby Dick*.

In the account of Pierre's attempt at writing and his experience with publishers, Melville gave vent to some of his personal exasperations and disappointments, which are expressed savagely and—as one is compelled to admit if he looks at the practice of the day—with no great exaggeration. Apart from this element and from the book's possible value in suggesting unconscious psychological factors in Melville's career, the chief value of *Pierre* lies in revealing the point Melville had reached in 1851 and 1852 in the ordeal of religious uncertainty which marked his middle years: a point, it seems clear, that was close to despair.

For a third time Melville had composed a history of the heroic rebel, but there are profound differences from Taji and Ahab. Pierre tries to convince himself, and Melville seems bent on convincing the reader, that his conduct is in accordance with the will of God and the teachings of Christ and that what he is defying is the false convention, the selfishness and complacency, of a heartless world. In *Mardi,* as we have seen, though institutional religion was pilloried, the example of Christ himself was chosen by all the pilgrims save Taji—who wills himself to destruction—as man's best hope on earth. In *Moby Dick,* though Christ has no meaningful place in its pages, Christian virtues are sympathetically dramatized as counterweights to Ahab's self-centered rebellion, and the Church is given a worthy representative in Father Mapple. But in *Pierre* Father Mapple is replaced by the Reverend Falsgrave, a revolting example of clerical expediency and self-seeking, and Pierre's monstrous course of action is defended as an attempt to apply literally the teachings of Christ.

This point of the book is sharpened by Pierre's chance discovery and reading of a mutilated pamphlet called "Chronometricals and Horologicals," setting forth the doctrines of one Plotinus Plinlimmon. Plinlimmon appears in the book (though

Pierre never meets him) as a denizen of the cheap lodgings in which Pierre installs his entourage. This tenement is called the Church of the Apostles, with some irony and perhaps symbolically, for it is a disused church building. The Plinlimmon pamphlet likens the teachings of Christ to chronometrical time—that established by the chronometer at Greenwich—which is always the same in all parts of the world; while the actual, practical relations between human beings, the working principles by which they really live, are compared to horological time—that shown by clocks and watches on any given part of the earth's surface, and observed and accepted there. The conclusion is that to attempt to shape one's life in full accordance with Christ's teaching is as unwise and impracticable as it would be to try to regulate one's life in China by Greenwich time. What Pierre makes of the pamphlet does not appear. But repeatedly, not only in Pierre's thoughts but also in author's comments, Melville attempts to explain or defend Pierre's conduct as inspired by Christ's example.

In one highly significant aspect the case of Pierre is identical with that of one of his predecessors. Taji recognizes early an element of guilt in his ostensibly chivalrous rescue of Yillah and the murder by which he achieves it. He sees that his motive has been partly his desire for "the companionship of a beautiful maid."[23] In precisely the same way, Pierre recognizes early in his relation to Isabel the part played by her physical attractiveness. And much as Taji is pursued by accusing phantoms, Pierre recurringly confronts the selfish and physical elements in his motivation, until before the final catastrophe his relation to Isabel is recognized by both of them as incestuous love. Ahab too, on a loftier plane than either the phantasmal Taji or the frenetic Pierre, knows and names his own sins, not only toward God but toward men. All persist, and all are destroyed. Yet it is too easy to conclude that *Pierre* parallels *Mardi* and *Moby Dick* in its meaning and its religious implications. I am inclined to agree with Henry Murray's opinion: "Melville's moral is that there is *no* moral, no satisfactory solution: it is impossible for a man 'to reconcile this world with his own soul.' "[24] The psychological realist in Melville painted Pierre as the self-known sinner, like Taji and Ahab. But in his own tortured human heart Melville clung to the frustrated idealist he had created, despite Pierre's acknowledged impurities and shortcomings. The final spoken words of the novel, Isabel's dying comment on the already dead Pierre, are: "All's o'er, and ye know him not!" Coming from a writer who knew the Bible as Melville did, these words can have no other intention than to connect Pierre once more and finally with Christ.

In its implications as to Melville's religious experience and changing attitudes, *Pierre* reflects his final and painful abandonment of a Christian position: a change foreshadowed in *Moby Dick* and confirmed in more explicit dramatic terms a few years later in the opening chapters of *The Confidence-Man*. In the light of the Plinlimmon pamphlet, and in the obvious contrast between Pierre's ideals and the actual results of his conduct, this intention is clear. Its faulty realization at every level may be logically ascribed to Melville's imperfect recovery from the strain of producing *Moby Dick* and to the speed at which he wrote *Pierre*.

IV

A full eighteen months elapsed between the completion of *Pierre* and the appearance of Melville's next published work, the story "Bartleby the Scrivener" on November 1, 1853. This was a much longer interval than that between any two previous works since Melville had begun to write: the seven novels had appeared within less than six years. Melville had not absented himself from his desk for all this time. In the middle of July, 1852, he wrote to Hawthorne declining an invitation for a visit, declaring that he had been for the "last three months an utter idler, and a savage—out of doors all the time. So, the hour has come for me to sit down again."[25] The actual sitting down was delayed by an enjoyed excursion to Nantucket with his father-in-law, Judge Lemuel Shaw, and other expeditions. But before the end of the year he appears to have been at work on a fictional project which he had discussed with Hawthorne, offering his friend the idea: a novel based on the life of a whaler's wife. When Hawthorne decided not to undertake the project, Melville wrote him that he would write the work himself.

Nothing more is heard of this novel, however. For the first time in his life, Melville was finding it impossible to carry a long work to completion. A year later there was correspondence between Melville and Harper and Brothers about "a book on tortoises," on which he received an advance of three hundred dollars and about which he twice wrote apologizing for non-delivery of the manuscript. Fragments of this projected work may appear among the sketches of "The Encantadas." It was not until the summer of 1854 that Melville was again able to complete a long work, and this was *Israel Potter,* which Melville himself called—unjustly—no more than a rewriting of an auto-biographical volume which had been published in 1825.[26]

During this period of silence a vigorous attempt was made by Melville's family and friends to obtain for him a consular appointment, such as Hawthorne had received. Hawthorne himself, Uncle Peter Gansevoort, Judge Shaw and others pulled all the strings they could. The numerous letters of Peter Gansevoort and Judge Shaw in Melville's behalf invariably cite the danger to his health of continued close confinement in his occupation as a writer. There is no record as to any participation by Herman Melville himself in these efforts or what he thought of them. In any event, they were fruitless and he went on writing.

However, Melville's work when he did resume publication reveals profound changes in tone and temper, even in style, from anything he had produced before. The heroic rebel has disappeared from his pages. He would not reappear for more than twenty years and then (in *Clarel*) not as central figure but as part of a larger pattern. The single exception is the brief story "The Bell Tower," and in this the romantic rebel is speedily destroyed. A scalding indictment of institutional Christianity is expressed in "The Two Temples," which Charles Briggs refused for publication in *Putnam's Magazine* because Mr. Putnam thought it might "disturb" some of the magazine's readers. But in general this story is more an objective statement of things as they are than an appeal for improvement such as is at least latent in the parallel attacks in *Redburn* and *White Jacket*. Perhaps the most dependable indication of Melville's religious attitude and experience in the middle 1850's is to be found in Hawthorne's often-quoted comment in his *English Notebooks* for September 12, 1856. This entry was made the day after the two friends had conversed on the sand dunes near Liverpool when Melville visited Hawthorne on his way to the Mediterranean:

> Melville, as he always does, began to reason of Providence and futurity, and of everything that lies beyond human ken, and informed me that he had "pretty much made up his mind to be annihilated;" but still he does not seem to rest in that anticipation; and, I think, will never rest until he gets hold of a definite belief. It is strange how he persists—and has persisted ever since I knew him, and probably long before—in wandering to and fro over these deserts, as dismal and monotonous as the sand hills amid which we were sitting. He can neither believe, nor be comfortable in his unbelief; and he is too honest and courageous not to try to do one or the other. If he were a religious man, he would be one of the most truly religious and reverential; he has a very high and noble nature, and better worth immortality than most of us.[27]

Indeed a note of something close to passive nihilism, certainly of exhaustion and submission, sounds again and again in the stories and sketches of these years.

This is not, however, the quality which chiefly distinguishes these writings. That quality is a profound compassion, a poignant, all-pervading concern for each chosen exemplar of the human lot: Bartleby, Israel Potter, Hunilla, Jimmy Rose, The Fiddler, Dom Benito, even for the monster Oberlus, self-styled "the host." Whatever else Melville salvaged or lost in the "dark night of the soul" through which he passed in the months and years following the writing of *Moby Dick,* he retained his sympathy for humanity. All the writings show that this was the one thing he had left to cling to spiritually after the wreck of *Pierre.*

Melville also emerged from his period of silence with a new mastery of his medium. Whatever may have been the quality of the abortive and discarded literary undertakings of this period, the prose of the *Piazza Tales* (the title of the volume in which the stories were collected in 1856) displays a firmness, an economy, a consistency of control in vocabulary, imagery, and rhythm, which Melville had not before been able to sustain.

The same excellence of style distinguishes the enigmatic book with which Melville somewhat contemptuously closed the door on his career as a writer of prose fiction for publication, *The Confidence-Man* of 1856. Most readers of this book are so absorbed in the effort to understand what Melville is saying that they fail to give adequate attention to how he is saying it. Actually the stylistic achievement of *The Confidence-Man: His Masquerade* is extraordinary: a spare, hard, hard-hitting prose which is supremely appropriate to the book's content and purpose.

At first examination that content and purpose seem to be of marked importance from the standpoint of Melville's religious thought. I agree with the thoughtful reading of Elizabeth Foster, that the "man in white" who appears on the crowded decks of a Mississippi River steamboat in the novel's first chapter and, unable to communicate with the passengers in any other way, writes on a slate and holds up to view phrases from the new Testament, is a Christ-figure.[28] The modern world—typified by the varied crowd sailing on the *Fidele*—has only indifference or derision for the man in white and for his message. He takes refuge in "a retired spot on the forecastle," falls asleep, and disappears from the book.

His place at the center of attention is taken by the "confidence-man," a strange, perhaps supernatural creature who appears in many different disguises (*His Masquerade* is the sub-title of the book). His sole purpose at first appears to be to obtain money, in varying amounts according to their means, from his fellow passengers by exploiting their greed, their credulity, their vanity, or their own actual need. It gradually becomes clear that he is less interested in robbing his victims of their money than he is in destroying their confidence in their fellowmen. Miss Foster has shown that Melville is careful to associate the confidence-man with the Devil by many details, and it may be that in Melville's conception this clearly evil creature is the Evil One himself, at his work of destroying in men what most makes them human. If this is so, all the more effective is the sardonic account of his encounter with Mark Winsome, who denies the reality of evil (and seems related to Emerson) and his practical disciple, Egbert. They are too much for the Devil and beat him at his own game. Chagrined, he is reduced to the level of cheating a suspicious barber and seducing an infirm and pious old man, whom he leads into the darkness in which the book ends.

Certainly there are revelations or suggestions of its author's religious bearings in *The Confidence-Man.* If Miss Foster's (and my own) reading of the man in white is correct, the book is for one thing, in totally different tone and terms, a restatement of the thesis of *Pierre:* that the teachings of Christ are but imperfectly applicable to the modern world. Indeed the confidence-man's chief stock in trade is a perversion of the concept of charity, which he peddles in various disguises and under various names. Further, there are such minor thrusts as the association of the Bible with a bogus "Counterfeit Detector."

The Confidence-Man may also give the impression of pessimism, indeed of a hatred of mankind like that asserted by Mark Twain in his references to "the damned human race." There is no doubt that in *The Confidence-Man* Melville sees some of the passengers of the *Fidele* as damned indeed, by their surrender to the confidence-man through their own greed. But there are those who resist his blandishments and on worthier grounds than the enlightened self-interest displayed by Mark Winsome and his disciple. Certainly, too, one of the basic assertions of the book is that of the reality of evil, in human life and in human nature. Yet in repeated readings I have been increasingly convinced that the dominant and ultimate impression left by *The Confidence-Man,* as to its writer's attitude toward his fellowmen, is not that of hatred, or contempt and ridicule, but simply and essentially that of compassion, of intense personal concern in the distress and suffering of the world: a quality which aligns it with the great stories of the immediately preceding years—"Bartleby the Scrivener," "The Encantadas," "Benito Cereno"—rather than with *Pierre* or any earlier work. What makes Melville's pity for his people difficult to detect is in part the stylistic quality of reserve, of Senecan economy and Anglo-Saxon understatement, which characterizes the novel—the extraordinary degree to which aesthetic distance is preserved. There is not a sentence that even hints of sentimentalism in all these pages. Though *The Confidence-Man* is no more a Christian novel than *Moby Dick,* it shares with the best of the *Piazza Tales* a Christlike compassion for mankind not similarly expressed in the earlier work. (This would seem to be the only ground Melville had retained, in the years of his deepest spiritual suffering, as a guide for life.) There is no facile appeal to the reader's emotion—only the stark statement of the factual details, often touched with grim humor of phrase or incident. What is involved between writer and characters is something far deeper than ordinary sympathy or immediate pity, something so profound and so consistent as to have become not only a way but *the* way of viewing life: if not indeed the end of life, the reason for living.

This is also the conclusion reached by Elizabeth Foster. She notes that in this book Melville's "compassion for man the cosmic waif was balanced by his judgment, his intelligence, his humor, his sense of the absurdities of man the victim of his own follies"[29] and maintains:

If Melville now found the tragic hero to be, not the great

man flexing mighty muscles, but the mere human being, and the universal tragedy to be what happens to the least of these, his choice of little men for characters is the outward sign, neither of mental decline from concern with the grand to concern with the petty, nor of misanthropy, but of an immense compassion.[30]

This basic attitude is perhaps most clearly dramatized in the novel in Melville's portrayals of the one-legged man, the Missourian, the cripple, and the old man who is led away into the darkness by the confidence man at the end of the novel.

V

In 1859 Elizabeth Shaw Melville wrote to her mother: "Herman has taken to writing poetry. You need not tell anyone, for you know how such things get around."[31] Perhaps his wife's dismay proceeded from the realization that the shift from prose fiction to poetry meant that Melville had given up any hope of making money by writing. He was still to write one of his most important novels, *Clarel:* the fact that this work is in verse does not at all cancel its fictional achievement in characterization, structure, plot, and thematic content. However, it is the fact that after *The Confidence-Man* Melville never again tried to publish prose fiction and indeed wrote very little of it.

His first book of poems, by-products of the trip to the Mediterranean countries from which *Clarel* also grew, failed to find publication. The Civil War brought a new and engrossing interest into Melville's life. He followed its changing fortunes closely, visited Washington and the field command post where his cousin, Col. Henry Gansevoort (only son of Uncle Peter Gansevoort) was trying to outwit the Confederate raider Mosby. At war's end Melville poured the fruit of his observation and thinking, brooding and emotion, into a volume of poems rapidly composed but remarkable for their substance and in many cases for their form. They are akin to his prose of the 1850's in conciseness and intensity, also startlingly anticipatory of some of the most important developments in poetic form of recent decades. With the poems Melville published a prose "Supplement" which to some readers (including myself) seems closer to the spirit of Abraham Lincoln's "Second Inaugural Address" than any other document of the time. It is a quiet but eloquent appeal to Northern readers for justice in their thoughts and charity in their actions toward the defeated South: "Let us be Christians toward our fellow-whites, as well as philanthropists toward the blacks, our fellow-men. In all things, and toward all, we are enjoined to do as we would be done by."[32] The "Supplement" pleads for an attitude which can only be called, as Melville called it, Christian.

The *Battle-Pieces* are full of references not only to the Bible but to Christian religious concepts in general. In comparing the *Battle-Pieces* with *The Confidence-Man* and the flaccid early poems, one can only feel that in some strange way his vicarious participation in the agony of the Civil War revitalized Melville, broke down barriers and repressions, released new energies. The events that followed support that inference, for very soon he was steadily at work at one of the two most ambitious and difficult projects of his entire career.

The seven months from October, 1856, to May, 1857, Melville had spent in a journey to England—which included the final meeting with Hawthorne previously noted—and thence in an extended cruise to the Mediterranean countries, including Palestine. Throughout this pilgrimage Melville kept a concise but detailed journal, which has survived. From its entries he drew some of the materials for a lecture on "Statues in Rome," one of three prepared lectures with which in 1858 and 1859 Melville tried unsuccessfully to obtain a share of the prosperity many literary men were finding in the lecture field.[33] Also from this journal and the experiences recorded in its brief entries came the substance of most of the poems for which Elizabeth Melville vainly sought publication in 1859–60, while Melville was again absent on a long sea voyage—this time frankly in quest of renewed health, as a cabin passenger to San Francisco and back on a vessel commanded by his younger brother, Thomas.

The most important fruits of the Mediterranean journey, however, came twenty years after the event, in the long novel in verse called *Clarel,* published in two small volumes in 1876 at the author's expense—through an outright gift from Uncle Peter Gansevoort. Intention of later literary utilization is implied in all parts of the journal, in the rich notation of concrete details and the often cryptic suggested parallels and elaborations. This is especially true of the entries dealing with Melville's experience in Palestine. It is quite possible that use of a tour of the Holy Land as a vehicle for exploring the religious horizons of his own and his world's experience had suggested itself to Melville during the journey or even before it. However, it was probably not until after the emotional and intellectual reawakening which is revealed in *Battle-Pieces* and its "Supplement" that Melville actually began work on this project.

When he did, however, it was with a will. In some ways Melville's actual achievement as a writer, the demonstration of his productive and creative capacities, is more astounding in the case of *Clarel* than in any other work of his career. In 1866 he accepted an appointment as an inspector of customs at the Port of New York. For twenty years thereafter he was at work at the Custom House or on the wharves for eight hours a day, forty hours of every week, except for his two-week vacations invariably spent with his family in visits to relatives or at New England resorts. Most of the time he walked the several miles to and from his work. The voluminous family correspondence excerpted in Eleanor Melville Metcalf's *Herman Melville: Cycle and Epicycle*[34] shows how urgent and unremitting were the family demands upon him during these years, in spite of protestations to the contrary. Yet somehow, despite all obstacles and distractions, Melville kept at it, day after day, week after week, until the great story-poem attained its massive completed form of four books, hundreds of sections, 27,000 lines.

Walter E. Bezanson's careful study[35] has shown that in the early stages of the writing of *Clarel* Melville read very widely in travel literature on the Holy Land and borrowed extensively from his reading—descriptive details, characters, even complete incidents. The basic poetic form he adopted, that of irregularly rhyming tetrameter, he had experimented with in some of the war poems and other earlier work. Probably the use of this form by Matthew Arnold in "Stanzas from the Grande Chartreuse," so clearly similar in tone, dramatic situation, and ultimate meaning to Melville's far longer poem, was influential. Arnold was closely read by Melville in these years. However, by far his most important resources were the brief entries in some thirty pages of the pocket journal he carried and used on the journey of 1856–57.[36] His actual stay in Palestine lasted only nineteen days, from January 6 to January 26, 1857, but Dr. Bezanson has shown that from the journal entries of this period Melville drew more than one hundred actual characters and incidents of the narrative of *Clarel*. It is quite evident that in the years which separated the actual and the recreated experience the essential components had both deepened and broadened in Melville's consciousness, to make possible the remarkable immediacy of the reader's vicarious experience, its notable authenticity and intensity.

It is not surprising to anyone at all acquainted with the literary atmosphere of the 1870's that *Clarel* received little attention and almost no understanding at the time of its appearance. What is deplorable, however, is the fact that in the whole period of more than forty years of Melville revival *Clarel* has remained (save for the much less important *Israel Potter*) the most neglected of his works. It is evident that no small portion of the numerous self-styled critics of Melville have never read this major work. And apparently even some of the very thoughtful and constructive readers who have made substantial contributions to Melville criticism have read *Clarel* only partially or carelessly, if at all, with the result that their published comments on it present startling discrepancies with the facts. These circumstances are extremely unfortunate because *Clarel* constitutes the fullest, indeed the definitive delineation of the religious inquiry generally recognized as central in the whole body of Melville's work. At the same time it presents the broadest, the most perceptive and creative statement of the religious dilemma of the nineteenth century which the literature of that century affords.

In its basic pattern and method *Clarel* closely resembles the experimental *Mardi* of almost thirty years before: Melville assembles a group of men of widely differing backgrounds and widely divergent points of view and lets their adventures, observations, and conversations provide the substance of the book. In its achievement, however, *Clarel* is vastly superior to its prototype of Melville's immature years. This pilgrimage is to no imaginary lands, but is very firmly set among the stones and deserts of Judaea and the squalid streets of Jerusalem, as Melville himself had experienced these places in 1857. Even more important, and the major factor in *Clarel's* value as fiction, is the fact that the people of the story are as real as the terrain. Without exception they are realized within the texture of the narrative firmly and sharply and at the same time with depth, as living consistent-inconsistent human beings. Finally, the book has a definite and positive focus which *Mardi* lacks. The central character, Clarel, is a young American divinity student who, assailed by doubts as he neared the completion of his theological studies, has come to the Holy Land in the hope that direct experience of the places associated with the Scriptures and especially with the life of Christ will resolve his tormenting uncertainties, one way or the other.

Like the real pilgrim Herman Melville, Clarel is repelled by the commercialization and sectarian exploitation of the Holy Places and depressed by the blankness and deadness of Jerusalem. He has two significant encounters with a young man whose situation is very similar to his own, though they never speak to one another. This youth, Celio, is a hunchback and the son of an aristocratic Roman family which has destined him for the Church. However, he is even more skeptical and rejecting than

Clarel. Melville's free narrative method enables him here and throughout the work to introduce material independently of his central character's point of view; and he puts into the mouth of Celio—before his despairing death, of which Clarel hears indirectly—an indictment of Christ, on the ground that His example is inappropriate for the modern world. This incident, of course, carries strong echoes of *Pierre*.

By chance, Clarel meets an elderly American who calls himself Nehemiah, a harmless and selfless monomaniac who has come to Palestine to convert the Jews to Christianity (by distribution of tracts) and persuade them to rebuild the Temple. Through him Clarel becomes acquainted with another family of American origin: Nathan, a former Midwestern farmer converted to Judaism who is determined to revive agriculture in the Holy Land; Hagar, Nathan's Jewish wife; and their daughter, Ruth, with whom Clarel falls in love. When Ruth's father is killed by Arabs and Judaic law prevents Clarel's seeing her for a fortnight, he decides—though reluctantly and with forebodings—to join the other travelers he has met in an expedition to Bethany and the Jordan, the Dead Sea and the monastery of Mar Saba, and to Bethlehem.

The itinerary is not imaginary but, as Dr. Bezanson has shown, a regular route followed by thousands of American and European travelers in Melville's time and the actual course he himself followed. Melville's masterly treatment of the physical background of this journey, its desolation, and his projection of the emotional tone of Clarel's experience and that of his companions are perhaps the highest aesthetic attainments of the novel.

Three men, in addition to Clarel, are constant figures of the journey. The first is Rolfe, a vigorous middle-aged American, independent in thought and speech, who represents the refusal of many nineteenth-century Americans to become deeply involved in or disturbed by the religious problems of the age, though they are aware of them. The second member of the party is Vine, withdrawn and usually silent, aesthetically sensitive, sometimes given to wry humor, in whom most thoughtful readers have found a significant portrayal of Hawthorne. He is wholly reticent as to his religious position, ignoring or repulsing Clarel's timid overtures toward friendly discussion. And the third major figure is Derwent, possibly on simple grounds of fictional craftsmanship Melville's most remarkable creation in this novel. A young Anglican clergyman, affable, easygoing, Derwent is all but secure against distress in his confidence that all things work together for good, yet he is not insensitive, selfish, or even self-centered. He represents the popular and prosperous contemporary clergyman's refusal to become involved in the religious conflicts of his time—his dependence on conduct and interests established as acceptable. With each of these three Clarel tries to talk intimately of his personal doubts and needs, but without success or satisfaction.

Other important characters are of the company for only parts of the journey. One of these is the visionary and saintly Nehemiah, who dies by the Dead Sea. Christlike aspects of his character may be suggested by the fact that his mount on the journey is an ass. Another is Mortmain, a disillusioned and embittered revolutionary, born the illegitimate son of a Swedish nobleman, whose all but suicidal rejection of God and man carries echoes of Pierre's rantings. His tortured journey ends at Mar Saba, but his place in the company is taken—as spokesman of extreme social pessimism and religious negation, by Ungar, an American from the South who has opposed slavery but has fought for the Confederacy and is now a soldier of fortune. He is a passionate hater of democracy, and Melville puts into his speeches something of the dismay he himself must have felt as he viewed the United States in the 1870's, the most corrupt period in our political history.

Still other figures join the company more briefly or are encountered by the way, to add still other voices and viewpoints to the broad and searching examination of the world's situation in the late nineteenth century which constitutes the major content of the central portion (Books II and III) of the novel. A young Dominican priest gives the pilgrims an eloquent and forceful statement of the claims for Catholicism in the modern world. At the other extreme, a geologist named Margoth voices the extremest pretensions of science and an unmitigated materialism.

Nor are these parts of the novel merely talk. The sensitive, seeking Clarel is constantly present, listening, evaluating. Though it is clear that Melville is exploring and displaying the conflicting points of view and divergent sets of values partly for their and his own sake, through his successful creation of Clarel as a person he gives the work aesthetic focus and dramatic progression.

Clarel's motive for and purpose in the journey is never lost sight of. As a divinity student, preparing to enter the ministry in some unspecified Protestant denomination, he has encountered the religious problems of the nineteenth century raised by the new findings in science, the "higher criticism" of the Bible, and the fragmentation of mutually intolerant sects, and has come to Palestine in the hope that he may find resolution for his doubts. In prolonged and recurring conversations with his fellow travelers he tries to discover their positions of belief or disbelief in the hope of solving his own problems. For the most part he is disappointed. In Rolfe he finds a positive and practical acceptance of life and a refusal to go beyond its day-to-day demands and opportunities. Rolfe is a man of deeds, not of words or expressed beliefs, and there is no help for Clarel in him. His relation to Vine is one of frustration. Deeply, perhaps excessively, attracted to Vine as a person, Clarel repeatedly tries to open his heart to him, to achieve an intimacy which would enable him to share his doubts and problems; but he is always repulsed. In Derwent, himself a minister, Clarel hopes to find fruitful counsel. But he soon discovers that Derwent, though likeable, is a shallow optimist who successfully evades serious confrontation with the problems of the age. Content with his success in the merely social functions of the ministry, he is not a thinker and is incapable of responding to Clarel's deeper needs.

Herman Melville

At Bethlehem Clarel, still plagued by his doubts and burdened by forebodings, is briefly attracted by the wholehearted hedonism preached by a young Levantine with whom he shares a room and a long conversation. As the party approaches Jerusalem the forebodings are realized. They surprise a burial party outside the walls: Ruth and her mother have died of a contagious fever.

Melville's handling of the final section of *Clarel* seems to me an important contribution to his aesthetic achievement in the work. It is Holy Week in Jerusalem; and we see the throngs of pilgrims, the tawdry processions, the ceremonies and the participants, for the most part externally from the viewpoint of the impersonal narrator rather than from Clarel's. Clarel himself is in and out of the reader's vision, seen for the most part momentarily or incompletely. The reader is left to discover for himself the depth of Clarel's emotion—of his own imaginative volition to share with Clarel his new experience of the meaning of the agony in the garden, the betrayal, the crucifixion. Clarel is last seen on Whitsuntide, one of the crowd on the Via Crucis. By this withdrawal from immediate contact with the dramatic center of his novel Melville risks much, it is true. But he gains aesthetic distance, and the universalization of Clarel's case which I believe he desired.

He also prepares, in a purely technical way, for the shift in person and perspective found in the "Epilogue": a direct address and admonition to Clarel. It is quite evident that Melville has been carefully building toward this poem, which is different in prosodic form from the rest of the book. And it is equally clear that this is the most significant direct statement on central religious problems of Melville's whole career. It requires quotation in full:

> If Luther's day expand to Darwin's year,
> Shall that exclude the hope—foreclose the fear?
>
> Unmoved by all the claims our times avow,
> The ancient Sphinx still keeps the porch of shade
> And comes Despair, whom not her calm may cow,

And coldly on that adamantine brow
Scrawls undeterred his bitter pasquinade.
But Faith (who from the scrawl indignant turns),
With blood warm oozing from her wounded trust,
Inscribes even on her shards of broken urns
The sign o' the cross—*the spirit above the dust!*

Yea, ape and angel, strife and old debate—
The harps of heaven and dreary gongs of hell;
Science the feud can only aggravate—
No umpire she betwixt the chimes and knell:
The running battle of the star and clod
Shall run forever—if there be no God.

Degrees we know, unknown in days before;
The light is greater, hence the shadow more;
And tantalised and apprehensive Man
Appealing—Wherefore ripen us to pain?
Seems there the spokesman of dumb Nature's train.

But through such strange illusions have they passed
Who in life's pilgrimage have baffled striven—
Even death may prove unreal at the last,
And stoics be astounded into heaven.

Then keep thy heart, though yet but ill-resigned—
Clarel, thy heart, the issues there but mind;
That like the crocus budding from the snow—
That like a swimmer rising from the deep—
That like a burning secret which doth go
Even from the bosom that would hoard and keep;
Emerge thou mayst from the last whelming sea,
And prove that death but routs life into victory.[37]

This capstone of *Clarel's* tremendously complex but wholly controlled artistic fabric has much in common with the at once retrospective and prophetic summary of Melville's religious experience which appears in *Moby Dick,* "The Gilder":

Oh, grassy glades! Oh, ever vernal landscapes in the soul; in ye,—though long parched by the dead drought of the earthy life,—in ye, men yet may roll, like young horses in new morning clover; and for some few fleeting moments, feel the cool dew of the life immortal on them. Would to God these blessed calms would last. But the mingled, mingling threads of life are woven by warp and woof: calms crossed by storms, a storm for every calm. There is no steady unretracing progress in this life; we do not advance through fixed gradations, and at the last one pause:—through infancy's unconscious spell, boyhood's thoughtless faith, adolescence' doubt (the common doom), then skepticism, then disbelief, resting at last in manhood's pondering repose of If. But once gone through, we trace the round again; and are infants, boys, and men, and Ifs eternally. Where lies the final harbor, whence we unmoor no more? In what rapt ether sails the world, of which the weariest will never weary? Where is the foundling's father hidden? Our souls are like those orphans whose unwedded mothers die in bearing them: the secret of our paternity lies in their grave, and we must there to learn it.[38]

If the "Epilogue" seems to elaborate, at least by cautious suggestion, one of these "Ifs"—the possibility of personal immortality—in doing so it is consistent, not only with writing which Melville was yet to do, but also with the central religious inquiry and impulse of Melville's younger contemporaries, Howells and James.

With the completion of the great labor of *Clarel,* Melville did not stop writing, but he never again tried a work of major length. He spent much time on poetry and in 1889 published a small group of selected poems, including some from the rejected volume of 1861, in an edition of twenty-five copies. In the year of his death, 1891, he issued another group of poems in the same way. He left a third volume in manuscript but carefully arranged and edited, and inscribed to his wife. He left also, as every reader of Melville knows, the manuscript of *Billy Budd, Sailor,* on which he had worked intermittently from as early as 1886 almost up to the time of his death. This is the story of the "handsome sailor," with the single defect of a speech impediment, universally admired and loved but for the morbid hatred of a petty officer who accuses him falsely and is unintentionally killed by a blow from Billy's fist, and of Billy's subsequent trial and execution. It has become the most widely read and certainly the most variously interpreted of Melville's works.

Billy Budd, found among Melville's papers at the time of his death, remained unpublished for over thirty years. Finally it appeared in the thirteenth volume of the edition of Melville published in 1924 by Constable and Company in London and edited by Raymond Weaver. The British critics who, with Weaver, initiated the "Melville revival" in the 1920's and 1930's, recognized the importance of this last of Melville's prose fictions; their interpretation of its relation to the whole body of Melville's thought is indicated by the title of an article by E. L. Grant Watson: *"Billy Budd:* Melville's Testament of Acceptance."[39] Watson read the short novel as a dramatization of the conflict between good and evil in an imperfect world and the necessity of accepting that imperfection in man and in his society.

Early discussion of the novel by American critics in most cases followed this interpretation. In his sensitive reading in *Herman Melville: The Tragedy of Mind,* William Sedgwick adopted partially Watson's term "acceptance," recognized the consonance between the story and Melville's later poems, and found in it reminders of the mood and meaning of Shakespeare's last plays: *"Billy Budd* stands in the same light to *Moby Dick* and *Pierre* that Shakespeare's last plays—*Pericles, The Winter's Tale, Cymbeline,* and *The Tempest*—stand to the great tragedies."[40] Sedgwick concludes his discussion of *Billy Budd* and his whole study of Melville's thought with this paragraph:

> Such is the force of Melville's final insight that the innocence and loveliness and joy of life is represented on board a man-of-war, Melville's own symbol for the world in its most opposite aspects to life as he had identified it with Typee valley. True, this innocence suffers a shameful death at the

hands of this man-of-war world. Yet, in Billy's death there is more promise of salvation for the world than there is of damnation in his death. And Melville has partaken of its salvation. His intellectual passion spent, and illuminated by his insight of a mind which by accepting its limitations has transcended them and has found within itself, at its own mysterious centre, a calm not to be found elsewhere, Melville has been restored to the radiant visage of life, whose shining secret is, it has its salvation in its own keeping.[41]

But in the 1950's earlier interpretations of *Billy Budd* were widely and violently challenged in a flood of critical articles heralded by Joseph Schiffman's "Melville's Final Stage, Irony: A Re-examination of *Billy Budd* Criticism"[42] and most violently and extravagantly in Lawrence Thompson's assertion, in *Melville's Quarrel With God,* that "Melville has sarcastically and bitterly contrived the entire story of *Billy Budd* to illuminate his own reactionary interpretation of a Calvinistic text."[43] Most of these writers find in *Billy Budd* the same indictment of Christianity and of life that Melville had written in *Pierre,* thus implying that he had not changed in forty years. If these critics read the *Battle-Pieces* with its "Supplement," or especially *Clarel,* Melville's major creative achievement of the four decades, they give scanty evidence of it.

A clarified perspective of *Billy Budd* became possible through the appearance, in 1962, of a corrected text of the story accompanied by a thorough and authoritative study of the whole range of critical commentary. This was the collaborative work of Harrison Hayford and Merton M. Sealts, Jr: *Billy Budd, Sailor (An Inside Narrative).*[44] The volume presents a corrected "reading text," from which errors and corruptions in all preceding editions are removed, and also a "genetic text" showing graphically the growth of the manuscript and the changes made during the six years Melville was working on it. The editors also examine objectively the various critical approaches to the story. They provide adequate reason for rejecting the theory advanced by some that Melville's original intention was to present a disguised version of the "Somers Mutiny" affair—a historical incident in the United States Navy in 1842, when three young sailors were hanged at sea, without adequate trial, on suspicion of conspiring to provoke mutiny. Melville was very much aware of this incident, because his cousin, Guert Gansevoort, was an officer on board the *Somers* when it occurred, and the *Somers* case is specifically referred to in the text of *Billy Budd*. Hayford and Sealts show that there are major differences in the cases and conclude that "The commonly accepted view that the *Somers* mutiny case was in effect the 'source' of *Billy Budd* must be modified."[45] I feel little doubt, however, that the authority and immediacy of the narrative as Melville wrote it proceed in part from his emotional involvement in the *Somers* incident.

The importance of an accurate reading of *Billy Budd* as an expression of Melville's ultimate religious position is emphasized by the evidence within the story of his intention to suggest in the execution of Billy parallels to the crucifixion of Christ. Billy Budd's last words, spontaneously echoed by the assembled crew, are "God Bless Captain Vere!" The language used to describe the actual hanging is strongly suggestive:

> . . . the vapory fleece hanging low in the East was shot through with a soft glory as of the fleece of the Lamb of God seen in mystical vision, and simultaneously therewith, watched by the wedged mass of upturned faces, Billy ascended; and ascending, took the full rose of the dawn.[46]

We are told, too, in the brief final paragraphs of the story, that "The spar from which the foretopman was suspended was for some years kept trace of by the bluejackets. . . . To them a chip of it was as a piece of the Cross."[47] Less concrete, but still resembling the New Testament story are some elements in the accounts of the trial and of the experience of the night preceding the execution.

Another source which may shed light on Melville's intention in *Billy Budd* (though the question ultimately turns on the implications of tone and detail in the story itself) has been suggested by Sedgwick[48] and again by F. Barron Freeman[49] but has been ignored by most critics of the story. This is the documentation as to Melville's temper of mind and attitude toward life afforded by the poems of his final years, written during the same period as *Billy Budd*. For the most part, these are the poems chosen and arranged by Melville for the volume inscribed to his wife and left unpublished at his death. True, most of them are slight; some are frankly sentimental. Of the few that go deeper and state or imply attitudes toward life, death, even God, it might conceivably be argued that Melville was writing them for his wife's pleasure and hence they cannot be taken quite seriously. But whatever else the student of Melville's religous thought and experience may conclude, he will hardly escape the decision that Melville was an honest man. The notion that he may have been lying about religious insights and intimations, merely to please his wife, is simply not tenable. It is my belief that in a few of these last poems, notably "Pontoosuce," Melville defines rather clearly the religious viewpoint he has finally reached.

This last poem of Melville's about water deals not with the sea but with a hill-circled lake. In irregularly rhyming iambic tetrameter varied by pentameter, Melville records and interprets the experience of a walk in the woods overlooking the beautiful lake near Pittsfield, Massachusetts. Here in "autumnal noon-tide" the poet views the pines and the brilliant hardwood forest in autumn color, the far-off mountains, the farms with ripened corn and fruited orchards. The meaning of autumn comes to his mind as a "thought intrusive":

> The present hour but foreruns the blast
> Shall sweep these live leaves to the dead leaves past.

The poet turns for reassurance to the slope where thriving pine-tree "pillars" grow between the "low tawny mounds" that are relics of earlier trees. The poem proceeds with swift concrete summation of the evidence of mutability, with certain details that suggest his own experience or link the poems with his earlier work, to arrive at its quiet, wholly controlled, and unequivocal affirmation:

"Dies, all dies!
The grass it dies, but in vernal rain
Up it springs and it lives again;
Over and over, again and again
It lives, it dies and it lives again.
Who sighs that all dies?
Summer and winter, and pleasure and pain
And everything everywhere in God's reign,
They end, and anon they begin again:
Wane and wax, wax and wane:
Over and over and over amain
End, ever end, and begin again—
End, ever end, and forever and ever begin again!"

. . . .

"Since light and shade are equal set
And all revolves, nor more ye know;
Ah, why should tears the pale cheeks fret
For aught that waneth here below.
Let go, let go!"[50]

This is not Christian affirmation, certainly. It holds not even
the muted hope of personal immortality that sounds in the
"Epilogue" of *Clarel*. But it is not rebellion. It offers nothing
that can be twisted into the semblance of a petty and spiteful
lifelong quarrel with God. In word and image and in the very
heartbeat of the lines are wholehearted, courageous, and even
triumphant acceptance: acceptance of death with life, of the
will of God so far as man can know it or understand. Other
poems of these last years assert unequivocally that life holds
much good, that the living of it, even the enduring of it, has
been more a blessing than a curse, that personal, requited love
is strong enough to transcend the inevitable defeats, infirmities,
and even death. Here, in the final years of his long search for
religious faith, Herman Melville found peace—neither through
victorious resolution of his dilemma nor in mere resignation,
but in the clear-sighted recognition of gains as well as losses and
the acceptance of the total given fact of life itself.

4

Mark Twain

THE PUBLICATION OF *Letters from the Earth* IN 1962 AND OF "Reflections on Religion" in 1963 emphasized what was already abundantly clear: that among the major American novelists of the nineteenth century, Mark Twain was the most outspoken in his reactions to the religious tensions of the times. It is not certain that his distresses were keener than those of his contemporaries and predecessors, but his expression of them was notably more direct and more voluble. It is not an overstatement to say that in the last decades of his life Twain became obsessed by religious problems and his denials and denunciations became compulsive. Efforts to find biographical explanation for this fact have not been altogether well-directed nor fully successful.

In the book which initiated modern critical study of Twain, *The Ordeal of Mark Twain* (1920), Van Wyck Brooks ascribed what he considered to be Twain's failure as a literary artist to three factors: the cultural poverty of the frontier; the impact of Calvinism, especially as imposed by Twain's mother, Jane Lampton Clemens; and the inhibiting influence of the censorship of his work by his wife, Olivia, and his friend, William Dean Howells. The notion of the cultural poverty of the frontier as a factor in Twain's development was effectively exploded

THE DARKENED SKY

by Bernard De Voto in his *Mark Twain's America* (1932); recent study of manuscipts and proofs has shown that the supposed "censorship" exercised by Olivia and Howells was much less substantial than Brooks had thought and indeed was usually beneficial. The one item in Brooks's dark picture which has remained largely unchallenged is the idea of the calamitous impact on young Sam Clemens' mind of "hellfire damnation" Calvinism as preached in Hannibal, taught in Sunday school, and especially as imposed by his mother. Since this concept is obviously essential in any consideration of Twain's religious experience as a whole, it calls for careful examination.

II

The impression that Sam Clemens was subjected to a rigid Calvinistic upbringing appears to come primarily from three sources: the treatment of religious matters in his autobiographical fiction, notably *The Adventures of Tom Sawyer;* the idea of his mother as an overly strict, pious, and domineering parent —which was probably derived from a combination of the characterization of Aunt Polly with Twain's recollections of the promises his mother exacted from him at the times of his father's death and of his leaving home; and his frequent references throughout his life to his "Presbyterian conscience." Upon close examination, the evidence thus afforded seems less than adequate.

It is true that Sam did attend Sunday school and a Presbyterian church during some of his years at Hannibal, and the sermon reported in the fifth chapter of *Tom Sawyer,* which "dealt in limitless fire and brimstone and thinned the predestined elect down to a company so small as to be hardly worth the saving,"[1] is of a tenor probably often paralleled at the church Sam attended. But Twain's account of the experience carries a built-in negation of the idea that the boy was left with any profound impression. Tom counts the pages of the sermon—"after church he always knew how many pages there had been, but he seldom knew anything else about the discourse;" he is briefly attentive only when "the minister made a grand and moving picture of the assembling together of the world's hosts at the millenium when the lion and the lamb should lie down together and a little child should lead them . . . and he said to himself that he wished he could be that child, if it was a tame lion."[2] What is memorable in Mark Twain's recounting of the Hannibal church service is not the Calvinistic sermon but the gorgeous episode of the pinch-bug. Of a piece with this incident is the incongruously placed recollection of the cat, the pulpit, and the flypaper in *What Is Man?* So far as the published writings show, Twain's only clear recollections of church services in his boyhood were farcically humorous.

The reference to a revival, in Chapter 12 of *Tom Sawyer,* is purely burlesque in tone, and the point-of-view character, Tom Sawyer, is completely external to the supposed emotional experience. Similarly, the treatment of the camp meeting in the twentieth chapter of *Huckleberry Finn* is altogether objective. It is vivid and may embody remembered details and impressions, for there had been camp meetings near Hannibal in Sam's boyhood and he may have attended one.[3] But there is no hint of a serious emotional impression.

The accounts in *Life on the Mississippi* of the drowning of Lem Hackett (supposedly a sinner) and of Dutchy (a very good boy) demand attention. Dutchy's death is made painfully vivid, with specific details which strongly suggest that Twain may have been recalling an actual experience. The other account is completely colorless, and it is hard to believe that it has any basis in reality. Yet both are followed by accounts of storms and of extravagant terror, remorse, and good resolutions. These become ludicrous in their effect, especially the resolutions. Tone and content alike make it clear that, if he is in fact writing of events which occurred in his boyhood, Twain is exaggerating the attendant emotions.

The atmosphere of dread which, as critics have noted, is built up effectively in the earlier chapters of *Huckleberry Finn*

nothing to do with Calvinism or with Christianity. As in
Tom Sawyer, this atmosphere is achieved by use of details of
Negro folklore and of local or regional superstition. In short,
there is no real indication, in the books which rest directly on
Twain's Hannibal experience, of religious repressions or pro-
found religious impressions of any kind during his boyhood.

Further, the actual character of Jane Lampton Clemens
proves, upon objective examination, to be signally unlike the
supposed paragon of piety and doctrinal conformity who imposed a Calvinist faith on her son. Brooks asserted that "the
stronger her will was, the more comprehensive were her repressions, the more certainly she became the inflexible guardian of
tradition."[4] Thus, in Brooks's view, the creative impulse in
young Sam was stifled: "He was in his mother's leading-strings,
and in his mother's eyes any sort of personal assertion in choices,
preferences, impulses was, literally, sinful. Thus the whole
weight of the Calvinistic tradition was concentrated against
him at his most vulnerable point."[5]

It was this "embodiment of cast-iron Calvinism" who named
her oldest son "Orion" because he happened to be born under
that constellation; who delayed joining the Presbyterian church
at Hannibal for four years, after moving to that town from
Florida, Missouri; and who did not attend church at all in St.
Louis, after she went there to live with her daughter, though
she sometimes took her granddaughter to the Jewish synagogue.
This granddaughter wrote of her:

> She loved every kind of excitement. She seemed to be always
> going to a parade, a circus, or a funeral—it was all one to
> Grandma. . . . She kept her beauty to the last, as well as her
> love of color and dancing. I have known her to dance when
> she was seventy-five. . . . Grandma's room was always a per-
> fect riot of red; carpets, chairs, ornaments, were all red. She
> would have worn red, too, if she had not been restrained. She
> was modern in her ideas and insisted on wearing her skirts
> shorter than was conventional.[6]

This granddaughter, who lived with Jane Clemens for twenty-
five years,

and heard her mention about everything that was in her mind, does not remember that she ever referred to the retribution of a stern Calvinistic God, or similar subjects. . . . Of course if there was anything queer about a religion or theory Jane Clemens took a fancy to it at once, and followed it up, though not to the point of becoming a convert. Anything out of the common infatuated her, and the queerer the religion the greater her interest in it. She was fascinated by the St. Louis doctor who had not taken a bath for thirty years because he was afraid he would lose his magnetic force. She took the same interest in him that she would in an elephant, or any other queer beast.[7]

Aunt Polly, the repressed and repressive matron of *Tom Sawyer,* seems to owe little to the lively lady who was the real Jane Clemens except her faculty for being the victim of a boy's jokes and her readiness to forgive them. As long as she lived, Mark Twain enjoyed playing jokes on his mother. From the West—in commentary on her habit of using any blank piece of paper for correspondence—he sent her a letter written entirely on small scraps, which she sorted out indignantly. Another letter from the West, impressively marked "Private," proved to be written in Chinese characters. Later in their lives a slip of the pen let Jane write to her son "Kill Susy for me" instead of "Kiss Susy for me;" and her son replied with a detailed account of how he had sawed off the child's head while a friend held her. In short, the available evidence—only partially sampled above—makes wholly unconvincing the traditional picture of Jane Clemens as a dourly devout mother imposing a rigid and terrifying Calvinism on an impressionable son.[8]

There is, however, a still more substantial reason for rejecting the view that Twain's religious experience began with heavy doses of undiluted Calvinism. Jane Clemens was not the only adult with whom he had a significant relationship. His father, John Marshall Clemens, died March 24, 1847, in Sam's twelfth year. That he was clearly remembered is demonstrated by his appearance as a recognizable character in both published and unpublished writings of Mark Twain. It is evident from the tenor of these references that while there was no close tie of affection between father and son, Sam's attitude toward his father was one of unqualified respect. And this unloved but deeply respected parent was a free-thinker, a representative of a restricted but important minority in the religious pattern of frontier towns. The precise nature of John Marshall Clemens' "free" thinking seems to defy recovery. Probably it included rejection of literal interpretation of the Bible and questioning of the divinity of Christ—as a frontier echo of Unitarianism. All that we can be sure of is that John Marshall Clemens did not go to church regularly,[9] and that young Sam Clemens could not have been unaware of divergent and conflicting views on religious matters within his own family. Even though his filial affection was reserved for his mother, the respect shown by the community and by Jane Clemens herself for the intelligence and integrity of his father must have given Sam good reason to ponder that father's judgment in the field of religion.

Nor was Sam's inoculation against wholehearted acceptance of Calvinism limited to the force of his father's example. The Clemens children spent their summers—Sam, at least probably until he became a printer's apprentice at the age of twelve or thirteen—at the farm of John and Patsy Quarles. Patsy was Jane Clemens' sister. These summers were remembered by the adult Mark Twain with extreme pleasure. As Henry Nash Smith observes, "The evocation of the Quarles place in the *Autobiography* is a reverie, almost an incantation."[10] His memories are of natural beauty, of abundant food and play, of happiness. Central in these memories was the warm and kindly character of John Quarles, an indulgent father (in contrast to Sam's own father), prosperous (as John Marshall Clemens was not), benevolent to his slaves, respected in the community—in spite of the fact that he was an acknowledged Universalist, a believer in universal salvation. This was an opinion even more unorthodox and objectionable, especially to Calvinists, than ordinary "free-thinking." Minnie M. Brashear, in *Mark Twain: Son of Missouri*, surmises that Jane Clemens may have tried

to warn her children against the insidious influence of John
Quarles' heresy; and this is the more likely because Jane Clemens
persisted for many years in the completely false notion that
Quarles was unkind to her sister, Patsy. But as Miss Brashear
notes, that the "generous man was such an object of censure
could make him all the larger a hero to the young inquirer into
the ways of life."[11]

Closely examined, then, the evidence fails to support the
legend that Calvinism had a traumatic impact on Mark Twain
in childhood. The real character of his mother belies the claim
that she subjected him to terrors of hell fire, and the example
of his father and his uncle was fully adequate to counteract
such Calvinistic pressures as did accrue. The legend was, admittedly, nurtured by Twain's frequent references to his "Presbyterian" upbringing, and his blatant determinism in later
years bears a superficial resemblance to the Calvinistic doctrine
of predestination. But these biographical facts are susceptible
of other and sounder explanation. The ascertainable specific
evidence indicates that as he emerged from boyhood into youth,
contributed to his own and his family's support as a printer's
apprentice, and set out at the age of eighteen to make his own
way Sam Clemens was not at all a convinced Calvinist, but a
confused and uncertain boy insofar as he gave serious thought
to religious matters at all. His mother's teaching had had definite effect, of course. He had read the Bible extensively and
intensively, with results to be noted later. At the same time, the
example of dissent set by his father and his uncle must have
undermined every impulse toward conforming belief. That the
effect of conflicting influences on the Clemens children was
uncertainty and lack of secure faith seems to be born out by
the experience of Pamela and Orion, the only others of the six
children who survived into maturity. Both appeared, in their
earlier years, to be devout Presbyterians. Pamela, as the sister
eight years older than himself, doubtless had an important part
in Sam's religious training. But of Pamela in her later years
her grandson wrote: "As I remember my grandmother . . . it

seems to me that she was always searching for absolute truth.
. . . In religion Pamela never did seem to reach a satisfactory
goal."[12] As for Orion, he changed religious positions almost as
frequently as he changed jobs—which was very often indeed—
and in 1879 achieved the distinction of being expelled and
excommunicated for heresy by a church in Keokuk, Iowa.[13] His
little brother, Sam, was to follow a less erratic course to a less
equivocal final position.

III

For a period of fifteen years, from his departure from Hannibal at the age of eighteen, to the ratification by her parents
of his engagement to Olivia Langdon when he was thirty-three,
Mark Twain was on his own—in matters of money, of morals,
and of religion. It is noteworthy—and a strong confirmation of
the view developed in the preceding section—that the pledge
Jane Clemens asked of and received from her son when he left
home contained no religious clause. "I do solemnly swear that
I will not throw a card or drink a drop of liquor while I am
gone"[14] was the Bible-sworn oath that he gave—and kept for a
substantial period. Either Jane Clemens was less strict and rigorous than she has been pictured, or she realized Sam was
already beyond a point at which he could be expected to pledge
himself to Bible reading, attendance at Sunday school, and the
like. Probably both conclusions are valid.

In regard to Mark Twain's development in religious attitudes
during his *wanderjahre* as a printer, from the time he left
Hannibal until he became a Mississippi River pilot, much
attention has been given to the account in the *Autobiography*
of his friendship in Cincinnati with a man named MacFarlane,
a self-educated mechanic and fellow lodger, who held many
of Twain's later views. In a recently published important article, however, Paul Baender[15] has shown that MacFarlane is primarily if not entirely a fictional creation, on whom the aging
Twain projected backward his own later attitudes. Though

130

it is probable that Twain's reading during this early period brought him into contact with much of the religious controversy of the time, the specific evidence is extremely limited. One concrete item of some importance appears in a letter written to an Annie Taylor on May 25, 1856, while Sam was working as a printer for his brother's paper at Muscatine, Iowa. In both tone and material, it strikingly anticipates later writings. At this time Miss Taylor was a student at Iowa Wesleyan College at Mt. Pleasant, Iowa. The letter is long and carefully written, evidently deliberately designed to make a favorable impression and elicit a reply. It contains a rather lengthy burlesque account of "a religious mass meeting of several million" insects of various kinds which had assailed Sam as he worked at his press, and is fully developed in religious terminology with such phrases as "grand anthem" and "devoutly responded." That Miss Taylor might have enjoyed such mild irreverence is suggested by the fact that her official record at Iowa Wesleyan contains the exceptional notation, "very irregular at prayers."[16]

Another very early comment on religious matters is distinctly suggestive of views which were to be powerfully expressed by Twain nearly fifty years later, in such characteristic writing as "To the Person Sitting in Darkness." It occurs in a letter written from St. Louis and published in his brother's newspaper, the Muscatine *Tri-Weekly Journal,* on February 28, 1855, under the caption "Correspondence of the *Journal*":

A widow woman with five children, destitute of money, half starved and almost naked, reached this city yesterday from some where in Arkansas, and were on their way to join some relatives in Illinois. They had suffered dreadfully from cold and fatigue during their journey, and were truly objects of charity. The sight brought to mind the handsome sum our preacher collected in church last Sunday to obtain food and raiment for the poor, ignorant heathen in some far off part of the world; I thought, too, of the passage in the Bible instructing the disciples to carry their good works into all the world—*beginning first at Jerusalem.*[17]

The notebooks and family letters from five years Twain

spent in Nevada and California throw little light on his religious attitudes. To these years belong the first of a long series of friendships with ministers, and there are incidents in which he gives assistance to religious enterprises. But there is nothing to suggest that Twain was ill-adjusted in a society in which religious affiliation was rare and religious activity minimal. It is safe to infer that whatever provisional views he had arrived at were strengthened during this period and that these views would have been regarded as heretical by the orthodox.

In the letters from the Sandwich Islands to the Sacramento *Union,* written during Twain's visit in 1866, we first encounter themes which were to reappear with increased emphasis in later years: criticism of missionaries and condemnation of an established or state-supported church. Twain tries hard to be fair to the missionaries and objective in his comments on them and their work, and he goes to great lengths to persuade the reader of his impartiality. By way of self-defense, he notes that the missionary inevitably judges a stranger by his own lights:

> . . . and with a tranquil simplicity of self-conceit, which is marvelous to a modest man, he honestly believes that the Almighty, of a necessity, thinks exactly as he does. I violate the injunction to judge not, also. I judge the missionary, but, with a modesty which is entitled to some credit, I freely confess that my judgment may err. Now, therefore, when I say that the Sandwich Island missionaries are pious; hard-working; hard-praying; self-sacrificing; hospitable; devoted to the well-being of this people and the interests of Protestantism; bigoted; puritanical; slow; ignorant of all white human nature and natural ways of men, except the remnant of these things that are left in their own class or profession; old fogy— fifty years behind the age; uncharitable toward the weaknesses of the flesh; considering all shortcomings, faults and failings in the light of crimes, and having no mercy and no forgiveness for such—when I say this about the missionaries, I do it with the explicit understanding that it is only *my* estimate of them—not that of a Higher Intelligence—not that of even other sinners like myself.[18]

Mark Twain

Twain is harshly critical of the English bishop of Honolulu and finds the English Church as "established" in Hawaii at the time of his visit to be corrupt in its organization and mistaken in its policies. In contrast, he has only warm commendation for "the French Roman Catholic Mission here." He praises the educational work of the priests, and asserts:

> The American missionaries have no quarrel with these men; they honor and respect and esteem them and bid them God-speed. There is an anomaly for you—Puritan and Roman Catholic striding along, hand in hand, under the banner of the Cross![19]

These comments in the letters from the Sandwich Islands reveal as a whole an objective attitude; while they are indicative of no significant religious commitment on Twain's part, on the other hand they show no actual hostility toward religion.

Similar attitudes mark *The Innocents Abroad,* which offers much richer documentation of its writer's religious views. It is, indeed, a major presentation of the position he had reached at the age of thirty-two, when the letters to the *Alta California* and the *New York Tribune* which formed the basis of the book were written. Three aspects of Twain's treatment of religion-related subjects in this book justify special attention.

One of these is the continuing drama of his relationship with the several clergymen included in the passenger list of the *Quaker City* expedition to the Mediterranean. The expedition had been organized in Henry Ward Beecher's church, and clergymen were in control of it. Mark was not altogether happy about this aspect of the matter but had to accept it. On June 1, 1867, while waiting to sail, he wrote a letter to his mother which expresses his attitude—and also supplements what has been said earlier about Jane Clemens, in its revelation of the broad-mindedness her son could expect from her:

> I am resigned to Rev. Mr. Hutchinson's or anybody else's supervision. I don't mind it. I am fixed. I have got a splendid, immoral, tobacco-smoking, wine-drinking, godless room-

mate who is as good and true and right-minded a man as ever lived. . . . But send on the professional preachers—there are none I like better to converse with. If they're not narrow-minded and bigoted they make good companions.[20]

For the most part Mark got on well enough with his fellow passengers, ministers and others, but he did become exasperated by what he considered the selfishness and self-righteousness of some of the more pretentiously pious, whom he called the "Pilgrims." He was especially incensed by the callous cruelty of these men to the horses and pack animals, when they insisted on covering an excessive distance in one day in order to avoid having to travel on Sunday. The inconsistencies of the pretentious and self-satisfied pious were to afford targets for some of Twain's most brilliant writing in later years.

More important in *Innocents Abroad,* however, is the revelation of Twain's attitudes toward Catholicism. In Hannibal, while Sam Clemens was still there, there was discussion in the newspapers as to whether or not the Catholics should be permitted to establish a church in the town. Except for the reference to the French missionaries noted above, no evidence of contact with Catholics or observation of Catholicism appears in Twain's writings or personal letters before *The Innocents Abroad.* Once the *Quaker City* had crossed the Atlantic, however, Twain was confronted by Catholics and Catholic institutions almost continuously until the return voyage began. Predictably, his reactions were generally adverse and often sharply hostile. In Italy he noted unfavorably the same things Cooper and Hawthorne had objected to: tawdry pretentiousness in some churches, altars, and ceremonies; excessive duplication and questionable authenticity of relics; the great numbers and well-fed appearance of the clergy; the prevalence of beggars and the extreme poverty and apparent ignorance and apathy of the common people.

Twain made a conscious effort to be fair, however. He coupled praise of an individual—Saint Borromeo—with adverse criticism of the way in which, at Milan, his memory was exploited.[21] In one instance he made a positive effort to give honor where it was due—though his bland assurance of the superiority of the Protestant faith (which he claims as his own here) gives his comment a curious twist:

> I feel that after talking so freely about the priests and the churches, justice demands that if I know anything good about either I ought to say it. I *have* heard of many things that redound to the credit of the priesthood, but the most notable matter that occurs to me now is the devotion one of the mendicant orders showed during the prevalence of the cholera last year. I speak of the Dominican friars. . . . They must unquestionably love their religion, to suffer so much for it. . . . surely the charity, the purity, the unselfishness that are in the hearts of men like these would save their souls though they were bankrupt in the true religion, which is ours.[22]

Unlike Cooper and Hawthorne, Twain makes excursions into the history of the Catholic Church in order to make a case against it. He had apparently, before this time, read a popular history of the Inquisition from a Protestant viewpoint. Late in the journey Twain objects to the exploitation of sacred places in the Holy Land, but at the same time expresses gratitude to the Catholics for preserving them. Finally, as the travelers are almost ready to turn westward again, Twain frankly admits conscious prejudice: "I have been educated in enmity toward everything that is Catholic, and sometimes, in consequence of this, I find it much easier to discover Catholic faults than Catholic merits."[23] This is followed by a generous expression of appreciation for the kind treatment of all travelers, Protestant and Catholic alike, by the Convent Fathers of Palestine.

One of the most interesting of Twain's comments on Catholicism involves his personal reverence for the name and person of Christ. He was shocked to discover in Rome so few churches, so few pictures and inscriptions specifically devoted to veneration of Christ, in comparison to the number dedicated to the Virgin Mary and to various saints. To this indictment he appends a comment that is characteristic of this book: "I may be wrong in this . . . but it *is* my judgment. . . ."[24]

The narrative in *Innocents Abroad* of Mark Twain's experience in the Holy Land indicates rather clearly that at this time he felt a sincere reverence for Christ and accepted the biblical account of his life as historically true. Henry Nash Smith has shown that in preparing the manuscript for book publication, working with the letters he had written en route, Twain had help and advice from Mrs. Fairbanks, a woman journalist who had become his friend and mentor on the trip—and perhaps, in final revision of the proofs, from Olivia Langdon as well.

> *The Innocents Abroad* as finally published in 1869 was irreverent enough to evoke hostile criticism; Mark Twain had not renounced his role as humorist. But his eagerness to rise to the social and cultural level represented by Livy and Mrs. Fairbanks led him to make substantial changes in the *Quaker City* letters as he transformed them into a book. He deleted many phrases of the sort Mrs. Fairbanks regarded as slang, and some entire passages that seemed likely to offend refined readers.[25]

It might be supposed that the desire to please these critics led Twain to insert the element of reverence for Christ in the course of his revision. But this was not the case, for his notebook jottings on the scene, as he visited the places of the Gospel narratives, convey the same essential attitude as that expressed in the book:

> Nazareth. The hill in the rear of the town whence an extensive view can be had—Tabor—Hermon—Carmel—Esdraelon—he saw all these—one's thoughts run on the boyhood of Christ so connected with these scenes. Here his mother marked the sayings of the Christ and pondered them in her heart.[26]

At Jacob's Well, Twain made this notebook entry:

> This is an interesting spot. Jesus rested here on his journey from Jerusalem to Galilee while his disciples went to the city to buy meat. 2000 years have not changed the scenery

and the customs of the inhabitants remain the same—women with water-pots on their heads. This well, these mountains, yonder city were looked on by the Saviour.[27]

In the text of the book Twain included a very interesting and not irreverent speculation about the attitude of family and friends when He came "back to Nazareth a celebrity." Twain marvels at the neglect of these people:

Who wonders what passed in their minds when they saw this brother (who was *only* a brother to them, however much he might be to others a mysterious stranger who was a god and had stood face to face with God above the clouds) doing strange miracles with crowds of astonished people for witnesses?[28]

At some of the sacred places Twain frankly confesses his inability to feel anything at all. He mocks some claims of the miraculous, is exasperated by the "Pilgrims'" insistence on discovering literal fulfillments of prophecies, and gives his humor free rein on some of the Old Testament stories. He is disappointed in the grapes which are offered as the same as those brought back by Joshua from his exploring trip:

. . . in the children's picture books they are always represented as bearing one monstrous bunch swung to a pole between them, a respectable load for a pack-train. The Sunday-school books exaggerated it a little. The grapes are most excellent to this day, but the bunches are not as large as those shown in the pictures. I was surprised and hurt when I saw them, because those colossal bunches of grapes were one of my most cherished juvenile traditions.[29]

The reputed grave of Noah comes in for some of Twain's best fun in the whole book:

. . . the grave of the honored old navigator is two hundred and ten feet long. . . . He must have cast a shadow like a lightning rod. The proof that this is the genuine spot where Noah was buried can only be doubted by uncommonly incredulous people. The evidence is pretty straight. Shem, the son of Noah was present at the burial, and showed the place to his descendants . . . lineal descendants of these introduced themselves to us today.[30]

Humor is of course a prevailing component of *The Innocents Abroad,* and no small part of the humor is directed toward subjects which were regarded by some of Twain's companions with unquestioning reverence. Mark's own reverence is reserved primarily for places chiefly associated with the life of Christ and for references to Christ. As of 1867–68, this reverence remained as a positive element in his generally indifferent or negative religious attitude.

IV

The ten years following his formal engagement to Olivia Langdon on February 4, 1869—roughly his fourth decade—were crucial for Mark Twain. In these years he learned, with difficulty, that he was a writer first, a journalist and lecturer only secondarily, and—also with difficulty—he made good his claim to be considered a serious writer, not merely a humorist. He achieved great fame during this period and, when compared to his earlier years, great wealth. His religious attitudes also underwent decisive development so that by the end of the decade the lines of force had become established, the prevailing patterns had become evident which would mark his religious experience almost to the end of his life.

In the first phase of this development, from before the actual engagement to a time perhaps a year after the marriage, he earnestly endeavored to find in himself the makings of a conventional Christian. His heterodoxy (or worse) was one of the reasons his acceptance as a suitor was delayed by Olivia and her family, and he was required for some months to write to her only "as a sister." Clearly his desire to remove this barrier was a powerful motive in his effort for improvement in spiritual matters which is recorded in almost every one of his letters during the courtship. But these letters also make it clear that it was not primarily a matter of an externally imposed barrier to Mark; rather, he felt in himself a genuine need to achieve some measure of spiritual assurance, of belief, for his own happiness in their relationship as well as for Olivia's. He could not feel worthy of her unless he could approach her ideal of manhood—which was that of the Christian gentleman. It seems to me false and unfair to suppose, as some critics have suggested, that the fervent resolutions and hopes for improvement voiced in Mark's letters were little more than a calculated stratagem. I feel, indeed, that his motivation was probably even deeper than Mark himself realized. After all the years of poverty, of uncertainty—the printing offices and the cheap boardinghouses, the gaudy drama of the river and the diggings, the hecticness and hazards of journalism as he had known it—Mark had at last tasted in the Langdon and Fairbanks homes the flavors of security and respectability. They tasted good. He wanted Livy, and he wanted Livy's world, too. Professed Christian faith was a part of it, or seemed to be; and on such grounds as the Reverend Thomas Beecher (the Langdons' liberal pastor) represented, that didn't seem too great a requirement. Mark wanted to meet it sincerely—or thought he wanted to, which amounted to the same thing.

Hence the letters to Livy during the engagement and the months immediately preceding it are filled with expressions of religious aspiration and hope, coupled with some of discouragement. Mark exults over Livy's promise to pray for him, thanks her for sending him each week Henry Ward Beecher's sermons in pamphlet form (with her markings), tells her of attending church and praying regularly when on his lecturing trips. One of these letters, recounting for Livy his attendance at a church service in a small town, is of interest in relation to the suggestion made earlier that there is no evidence of profound emotional experience in connection with church services in Twain's boyhood. "It was as if twenty-five years had fallen away from me like a garment and I was a lad of eleven again in my Missouri village church of that ancient time." There follows a detailed description of the church interior, and then a satirical account of the "distinguished visiting minister from the great town a hundred miles away," and a broadly burlesqued treatment of the choir and congregation.[31] The account, even in this intimate letter to Livy and within the context of Mark's current religious aspiration, contains no seriousness.

Mark did not conceal from Livy the fact that he encountered difficulties in his task of spiritual self-regeneration. In a long letter of January 6, 1869,* he chooses a prophetic word to define his state:

> I am "dark" yet—I see I am still depending on my own strength to lift myself up, & upon my own sense of what is right to guide me in the Way—but not always, Livy, not always. I see the Savior dimly at times, & at intervals, *very near.*
> . . . Sometimes it is a *pleasure* to me to pray, night & morning, in cars & everywhere, twenty times a day—& then again the whole spirit of religion is motionless (not dead) within me from the rising clear to the setting of the sun. . . .[32]

In general, Mark's references to his religious aspirations decrease in number and in length month by month during the year-long engagement, though they do not disappear. On January 8, 1870, less than a month before the wedding, Mark wrote from Troy, New York, a letter which Livy should have regarded as an omen, and perhaps did:

> I have been reading some new arguments to prove that the world is very old, & that the six days of creation were six immensely long periods. For instance, according to Genesis, the *stars* were made when the world was, yet this writer mentions the significant fact that there are stars within reach of our telescopes whose light requires 50,000 years to traverse the wastes of space and come to our earth. . . .
> How insignificant we are, with our pigmy little world!— an atom glinting with uncounted myriads of other atom worlds in a broad shaft of light streaming from God's coun-

---

tenance—& yet prating complacently of our speck as the Great World, & regarding the other specks as pretty trifles made to steer our schooners by & inspire the reveries of "puppy" lovers. Did Christ live 33 years in each of the millions & millions of worlds that hold their majestic courses above our heads? Or was *our* small globe the favored one of all? . . .

I do not see how astronomers can help feeling exquisitely insignificant, for every new page of the Book of the Heavens they open reveals to them more & more that the world we are so proud of is to the universe of careening globes as is one mosquito to the winged & hoofed flocks & herds that darken the air & populate the plains & forests of all the earth. If you killed the mosquito would he be missed? Verily, What is Man, that he should be considered of God?[33]

This letter clearly indicates directions which Twain's thinking and writing were soon to take, and retain. Both the idea of Christ's ministry in other worlds and the concept of the vastness of space are expressed in the story "Captain Stormfield's Visit to Heaven," first drafted about this time.

The changes in attitude and conduct which Twain had achieved for Livy's sake—and his own— lasted for several months, perhaps for a year or more. In the first month of his engagement Mark had written, on February 14, 1869, to his newly found friend, the Reverend Joseph Twichell of Hartford, telling of his plans: ". . . my future wife wants me to be surrounded by a good moral and religious atmosphere (for I shall unite with the church as soon as I am located,) & so she likes the idea of living in Hartford."[34] The church membership did not materialize. In his biography of Twain, Albert Bigelow Paine says that when Mark's old friend of Nevada days, Joe Goodman, visited the newlyweds in the summer after their marriage, he was "dumfounded to see Mark Twain ask a blessing and join in family worship. Just how long these forms continued cannot be known today." Probably they did not last long. Paine ascribes the ending of these family religious observances to a specific dramatic incident:

"Livy," he said one day, "you may keep this up if you want to, but I must ask you to excuse me from it. It is mak-

141

ing me a hypocrite. I don't believe in this Bible. It contradicts my reason. I can't sit here and listen to it, letting you believe that I regard it, as you do, in the light of gospel, the word of God."[35]

Paine's biography (based, of course, largely on information given him near the end of Twain's life) includes another dramatic incident said to have marked the later termination of Twain's discussion of religious matters with Twichell, but this is clearly apocryphal.[36] Hence it is not necessary to assume that Mark put an end to the family's observance of religious practices in the way described.

It is evident, however, that religious practice soon ceased to play the part in the lives of Twain and his wife that he had expected before their marriage. Howells remembered that in the beginning of their residence in Hartford the Clemenses attended church regularly but ceased to later on. Letters from Livy to Mark while he was on a lecturing trip, within two years of their marriage, not only show distress over her irregular church attendance, but suggest something deeper. On December 2, 1871, she wrote:

> It is so long since I have been to church that I was mellowed by the very atmosphere I think, Mr. Twichells prayer touched me and made me cry, he prayed particularly for those who had fallen away and were longing to come back to God—Youth I am ashamed to go back, because I have fallen away so many times and gone back feeling that if I should ever grow cold again, it would be useless trying. . . .[37]

A little later Livy wrote again in the same vein:

> This morning . . . Mr. Twichell gave us a *very good* sermon. . . . When I went in and saw that it was the communion service, my heart sank because I do feel so unfit to go to the table of communion, yet cannot bear to go away from it. Mr. Twichell gave such an *earnest* invitation to all who were feeling cold and far away from God and discouraged to stay and get comfort that I could not come away. I staid, and of course my prayers were for you and myself.[38]

Mark Twain

Not only did Mark relinquish his attempt to cultivate in himself religious convictions harmonious with those of his wife, but at the same time Livy's own religious position was collapsing. In later years Twain blamed himself for robbing his wife of her religious faith. Indulgence in emotional orgies of self-recrimination was a specialty of his from boyhood on. In this case his remorse was not without justification.

It is quite possible that Twain's inability to accept the orthodox view of the Bible was an important element in his abandonment of the attempt to meet Livy's ideal in religious matters, within a year or two after their marriage. He knew the Bible thoroughly before he left Hannibal and was certainly aware even then—by his father's attitude—that its literal meanings were open to question. His visit to the Holy Land led him to extensive and careful rereading. His notebooks were crammed with specific biblical references of book, chapter, and verse, and as we have seen in *Innocents Abroad* he experimented in mildly satirizing some points of Old Testament legend. Also, both just before and just after his marriage he was very keenly interested in science, especially in astronomy and geology. He and Joe Goodman were observed poking through the old quarry at Quarry Farm (the Clemens' summer home for many years), looking for fossils.[39]

The fresh rereading of the Bible occasioned by the trip to the Holy Land, and in part by the effort to meet Livy's expectations, and the newly acute interest in science interacted to produce such thoughts as those expressed in the letter to Olivia of January 8, 1870, quoted above. Paine assigns to the period of Twain's brief partial ownership and editorship of the Buffalo *Express,* 1869–70, the writing of an article "on the human idea of God, ancient and modern," which Paine says Twain's wife "prevailed upon him not to print." These sentences from the portion of the article given by Paine are especially important in relation to Twain's emerging religious views:

The difference between that universe and the modern one revealed by science is as the difference between a dust-flecked

143

ray in a barn and the sublime arch of the Milky Way in the skies. Its God was strictly proportioned to its dimensions. His sole solicitude was about a handful of truculent nomads. He worried and fretted over them in a peculiarly and distractingly human way. One day he coaxed and petted them beyond their due, the next he harried and lashed them beyond their deserts. . . . When the fury was on him he was blind to all reason—he not only slaughtered the offender, but even his harmless little children and dumb cattle. . . .

To trust the God of the Bible is to trust an irascible, vindictive, fierce and ever fickle and changeful master; to trust the true God is to trust a Being who has uttered no promises, but whose beneficent, exact, and changeless ordering of the machinery of his colossal universe is proof that he is at least steadfast to his purposes; whose unwritten laws, so far as they affect man, being equal and impartial, show that he is just and fair; these things, taken together, suggest that if he shall ordain us to live hereafter, he will be steadfast, just, and fair toward us. We shall not need to require anything more.[40]

It should be noted at this point that Twain's later determinism is implicit in his conception of the "true God" as expressed here—the God whom he sees as demanded by modern science, who is marked by the "changeless ordering of the machinery of his colossal universe"—though that implication is by no means fully grasped as yet. Twain's determinism was not derived from Calvinism but from his reading of science.

From the combination of refreshed interest in the Bible and new exploration of science there emerges, then, at the beginning of the 1870's, one of three major aspects of Twain's expression of religious attitudes which were to continue to appear almost to the end of his life. This first aspect takes primarily the form of exploiting more or less humorously the legendary material of the Old Testament, as well as other orthodox ideas. In this same period Twain was working on a book about Noah, which is mentioned in his correspondence. Paine ascribes what would seem to have been a portion of this work, entitled "Shem's Diary," to 1870. Bernard De Voto put together a group of unpublished writings dealing with Old Testament characters under the title of "Papers of the Adam Family," belatedly published in *Letters from the Earth* in 1962. He did not find the "Shem's Diary" of 1870, but identified two "Extracts from Methuselah's Diary" as from the middle 1870's, probably the summer of 1876.[41] By then Twain had begun to use Old Testament substance for heavy-handed satire directed toward his own times. He kept returning to the Old Testament stories almost throughout his writing lifetime; the best and most well-known of these efforts is the "Eve's Diary" of 1905. Twain dealt humorously not only with Old Testament material but with such religious traditions as that of the conventional heaven.

A second significant element in Twain's religious thought during this period is his increased attention to discrepancies between profession and practice on the part of supposed Christians. Three times within three years he published vigorous attacks on well-known clergymen. The first of these incidents preceded his marriage and was occasioned by the action of the ministerial association of Elmira, New York, in expelling from its membership the Langdons' pastor, the Reverend Thomas K. Beecher, without stated cause. The only discoverable reason for the action was that Beecher's preaching was attracting congregations so large that only the Opera House would hold them, while those of other ministers were shrinking proportionately. Twain had come to know and like Beecher, and was outraged. He wrote a scorchingly ironic account of the affair and submitted it to the Langdon family. With their approval it was published in the Elmira *Advertiser*, signed "S'cat."[42]

The other attacks on Christian ministers for unchristian conduct were among Twain's contributions to *The Galaxy*, in the department he conducted for that magazine under the title "Memoranda" in 1870 and 1871. The first, "About Smells," appeared in the issue for May, 1870. Twain begins by quoting accurately a passage from an article by Rev. T. Dewitt Talmage, a regular contributor, in *The Independent*, on the topic "How?"

I have a good Christian friend who, if he sat in the front

pew in church, and a working man should enter the church at the other end, would smell him instantly. My friend is not to blame for the sensitiveness of his nose. . . . The fact is, if you had all the churches free, by reason of the mixing up of the common people with the uncommon, you would keep one-half of Christendom sick at their stomach. If you are going to kill the church thus with bad smells, I will have nothing to do with this work of evangelization.[43]

Twain continues:

We have reason to believe that there will be laboring men in heaven; and also a number of negroes, and Esquimaux, and Terra del Fuegans, and Arabs, and a few Indians, and possibly even some Spanish and Portuguese. All things are possible with God. We shall have all these sorts of people in heaven; but, alas! in getting them we shall lose the society of Dr. Talmage.

The article proceeds, with admirably controlled sarcasm, to a positive conclusion:

Now, can it be possible that in a handful of centuries the Christian character has fallen away from an imposing heroism that scorned even the stake, the cross, and the axe, to a poor little effeminacy that withers and wilts under an unsavory smell? We are not prepared to believe so, the reverend Doctor and his friend to the contrary not withstanding.[44]

And there is the eloquent and justly famous diatribe, "The Indignity Put Upon the Remains of George Holland by the Rev. Mr. Sabine." Sabine had refused to permit the funeral of a highly respected and widely beloved actor, George Holland, to be held in his fashionable New York church. Twain denied that ministers and churches held a monopoly on Christianity and its propagation:

It is almost fair and just to aver (although it is profanity) that nine-tenths of all the kindness and forbearance and Christian charity and generosity in the hearts of the American people today, got there by being filtered down from their fountain-head, the gospel of Christ, through dramas and tragedies and comedies on the stage, and through the despised novel and the Christmas story . . . and NOT from the drowsy pulpit.

All that is great and good in our particular civilization came straight from the hand of Jesus Christ, and many creatures, and of divers sorts, were doubtless appointed to disseminate it; and let us believe that *this seed and the result* are the main thing, and not the cut of the sower's garment. . . .

Twain completed his rebuke with the suggestion that we should:

whisper to the Sabine pattern of clergyman, under the breath, a simple, instructive truth and say, "Ministers are not the only servants of God upon earth, nor His most efficient ones either, by a very, very long distance." Sensible ministers know this, and it may do the other kind good to find it out.[45]

The theme of the gap between Christian profession and practice had of course appeared in *Innocents Abroad,* in the attacks on the "Pilgrims" for their cruelty to animals and for other offenses, and in the criticism of Catholic clergymen in Italy and in Palestine. It remains as a recurring motif throughout Twain's writings: in the irony of the churchgoing feudists in *Life on the Mississippi* and *Huckleberry Finn,* in the indictment of churchmen and an established church in *A Connecticut Yankee at King Arthur's Court,* in the scathing denunciation of missionaries in "To the Person Sitting in Darkness" and related works. It is evident that the genuine indignation which Twain could readily summon in relation to the derelictions of professed Christians afforded a major emotional support for his increasing negation of all religion over the years.

The third factor foreboding that ultimate negation was Twain's contempt for man. In the 1870's came the first utterances of what was to build into a resounding damnation of the human race, which became a sufficiently reiterated theme song of Twain's last years and writings. There are hints of this attitude in some of the descriptions of city crowds and rural villagers in *The Innocents Abroad,* but it is expressed much more seriously, though still indirectly, in *The Gilded Age.* As Kenneth Andrews remarks, "In a very real sense . . . *The Gilded Age* is a reactionary book. It exhibits the reservations about political democracy that its authors formulated in the seventies. Warner and Mark Twain imply that with universal suffrage corruption in high places is inevitable."[46] Only in a superficial reading of *The Gilded Age* will one see it as an attack merely on corrupt politicians and venal journalists. The novel goes behind the congressman to his constituents, behind the reporter to his readers. It is a direct response to the age to which it gave a name, to be sure; but it sees the source of contemporary evils in human greed and grossness.

There are similar pessimistic views of human nature in *The Prince and the Pauper,* though these are veiled and softened for the most part by the historical framework and the juvenile point of view. The clearest expression of this attitude is in Twain's minor writings of the 1870's—in "The Curious Republic of Gondour" (published in the *Atlantic Monthly,* unsigned, in 1875), in "The Revolution in Pitcairn" (*Atlantic,* 1879), and in the "Fables" written at Quarry Farm in 1874 and published in revised form in *Sketches New and Old* in 1875.

In "The Curious Republic of Gondour" the satire is political. In Gondour it has been recognized that it is a fatal mistake to give the ignorant and unprincipled man equal political power—that of one vote—with the wisest and most humane and unselfish. Accordingly a multi-vote system has been established. Every man has one vote, but some have many more. "The Great Revolution in Pitcairn" is also primarily political. It tells how an unscrupulous American, Butterworth Stavely, overthrows temporarily the peaceful government of Pitcairn Island, with its eighty or so people, and makes himself dictator. The selfishness and venality of the ordinary citizen are dramalized, and religious satire enters also, for Stavely first arouses the people by suggesting that they need even longer prayers in their church services and more hours of Sunday school.

In accepting, on September 8, 1874, the manuscript which was to become Twain's first contribution to the *Atlantic Monthly,*

"A True Story," Howells rejected on religious grounds another piece Twain had submitted at the same time, "Some Learned Fables, For Good Old Boys and Girls." He wrote Mark:

> . . . The Atlantic, as regards matters of religion, is just in that Good Lord, Good Devil condition when a little fable like yours wouldn't leave it a single Presbyterian, Baptist, Unitarian, Episcopalian, Methodist or Millerite *paying* subscriber—all the deadheads would stick to it, and abuse it in the denominational newspapers. Send your fable to some truly pious concern like Scribner or Harper, and they'll extract it into all the hymnbooks. But it would ruin *us.*[47]

The editors of the *Mark Twain—Howells Letters* give what seem adequate reasons for Howells' rejection in their description of the work:

> The story concerns a scientific expedition sent out by "the creatures of the forest." Howells as editor must have been wary of *Atlantic* readers' potential objections to the comment, "Thus inscrutable be the ways of God, whose will be done!" when the "stinking" Tumble-Bug and the "illustrious" Duke of Longlegs lie down together, drunk, after the animals chance upon a jug of whiskey; to the havoc wrought within a single week by a detachment of missionaries, among a "timid, gentle" race of "heathenish" spiders, "not three families being by that time at peace with each other or having a settled belief in any system of religion whatsoever" . . . and to the conclusion of Professor Woodlouse that Man "imagined he had a soul, and pleased himself with the fancy that it was immortal."[48]

The "Fables" contain rather vicious satire aimed directly at religious notions and slogans, together with—somewhat surprisingly—satirical implications as to the sensational findings of scientific expeditions. The chief target of the work, however, is human nature itself: these are insects, paralleling the conduct and matching the character of an equally contemptible race, mankind.

At first glance the implications of the distrust of man stated or implied in these writings of the 1870's may seem political or social rather than religious. But the concept of man is of course essential in Christianity: man as possessing the capacity for spiritual growth and significant relation to God. The contemptible and obnoxious human being glimpsed repeatedly in these writings, viewed in relation to the universal and changeless God of Twain's new scientific vision, leads to his determinism. The view of man which is emerging in Twain's writings of this period, it must be insisted, is not Calvinistic. The individual may be a miserable creature in Calvinism, predestinated to perdition, but as a human soul he is central in the drama of creation. In a view of life built on light years and Old Red Sandstone, rejecting all revelation, the individual human being is of an inexpressible insignificance. Twain was never able to give over abusing man for what he thought him to be.

By the end of the 1870's, then, of the faith Twain fought for before his marriage and of whatever religious baggage he may have brought with him on the long journey from Hannibal to Elmira, not much was left: only two items, in fact. One of these was his belief in that remote, changeless, and exact modern God of science, who could, however, be depended on to be "steadfast, just, and fair." The other item was reverence for Jesus Christ. Emphasis on Christ as the source of all that is good in our lives will have been noted in the denunciation of the Reverend Sabine, and similar expressions of attitude mark the whole decade from *The Innocents Abroad* on through. On March 23, 1878, Twain wrote to his brother Orion, concerning a manuscript Orion had sent to him for criticism:

> And mind you, in my opinion you will find that you can't write up hell so it will stand printing. Neither Howells nor I believe in hell or the divinity of the Savior, but no matter, the Savior is none the less a sacred Personage, and a man should have no desire or disposition to refer to him lightly, profanely, or otherwise than with the profoundest reverence.[49]

The position so taken, the attitude so expressed, may be thought to be inconsistent; but there can be no doubt that it was genuine. Reverence for Christ, as the sole exception to Twain's ruthless iconoclasm, persisted almost until the end of his life.

V

Early in the 1880's, according to Paine, Twain wrote out—perhaps merely for his own satisfaction—a statement of his religious views as of that time. In this document he asserted his belief in God Almighty but declared that "the Old and New Testaments were imagined and written by man." He acknowledged that "the goodness, the justice, and the mercy of God are manifested in His works; I perceive that they are manifested toward me in this life. . . ." He violently rejected the idea of eternal punishment and declared himself "wholly indifferent" as to the question of a future life.[50] Actually a considerable anxiety about the problem of personal immortality is expressed —largely by denying the anxiety; over half the total statement is devoted to the question of rewards and punishments, focused in an attack on the conventional notion of hell.

Heaven fared no better in these years. The *Notebook* indicates that in 1883, "working again on his Captain Stormfield story," Twain made the following note: "Stormfield must hear of the man who worked hard all his life to acquire heaven and when he got there the first person he met was a man he had been hoping all the time was in hell—so disappointed and outraged that he inquired the way to hell and took up his satchel and left."[51] It was perhaps when he was working on *A Connecticut Yankee at King Arthur's Court,* later in the decade, that Twain made a further entry for the Stormfield story:

Captain Stormfield finds that hell was originally instituted in deference to an early Christian sentiment. In modern times the halls of heaven are warmed by radiators connected with hell, and the idea is warmly applauded by Jonathan Edwards, Calvin, Baxter & Co., because it adds a new pang to the sinner's suffering to know that the very fire which tortures him is the means of making the righteous comfortable.[52]

THE DARKENED SKY

Midway of the decade Twain received from Charles Warren Stoddard, who had been his secretary for a time during one of his visits to England, a copy of Stoddard's autobiography, in which he narrated his conversion to Catholicism. Twain wrote to Stoddard on June 1, 1885, in acknowledgment and comment:

My dear Charley—

I have read it. Yes, I think you were right to print it: for there are all sorts of people, & they require all sorts of comforting; consequently there are those who require this sort— I mean this sort of comfort that is found in what is called religion. Peace of mind is a most valuable thing. The Bible has robbed the majority of the world of it during many centuries; it is but fair that in return it should give some to an individual here & there. But you must not make the mistake of supposing that absolute peace of mind is obtainable only through some form of religious belief; no, on the contrary, I have found that as perfect peace is to be found in absolute unbelief. I look back with the same shuddering horror upon the days when I believed, as you do upon the days when you were afraid you did not believe. Both of us are certain now; and in certainty there is rest. Let us be content. May your belief & my unbelief never more be shaken in this life.

You have told your story eloquently, beautifully,—how well a gifted man *can* argue from false premises, false history, false everything!

But dear old boy, I love you just the same!

Sincerely Your old Friend,
S. L. Clemens[53]

The "perfect peace" asserted here did not last long, if indeed it existed at all beyond the dimensions of the letter; but the name "serenity of unbelief," as Seymour L. Gross calls the mood in his article about this letter,[54] seems more appropriate for the first five years of the 1880's than for any other period in Twain's adult life. This was a time of health for his wife and children and profound happiness in family life, the time of the full flowering of his significant friendships with How-

152

ells, Twichell, and others, a time of great financial prosperity and of already worldwide fame. Perhaps most significantly for Twain's inner self, it was the period in which the twice-abandoned story of *Huckleberry Finn* was at last completed, published, and recognized at least by Howells and a few others as the very great book that it is.

The religious values in *Huckleberry Finn* are controlled, balanced, and positive. Huck breaks the crushing grasp of a conditioned conscience, molded by every social sanction and religious precept he has known, in an act of conscious sacrifice of self for love of a human being: a close approach, far closer than any other in Twain's career, to a dramatic typing of the Atonement. The drift toward unpitying contempt for humanity is apparent in the portrayal of the riverside communities, but it is modified by the kindness of the Grangerfords and by the sympathetic presentation of Mary Jane Wilks and is fully balanced by the positive human goodness of Nigger Jim and of Huck himself.

It was in the early 1880's that Twain cultivated the friendship of Robert J. Ingersoll, the prominent free-thinker and brilliant lecturer whom Twain respected on both grounds. Also at this time he became a subscriber to *The Truth Seeker*, a prominent magazine of "Free Thought" founded in New York in 1873—a subscription which he kept up through the last year of his life. The writings of Ingersoll and many articles in *The Truth Seeker* specifically parallel expressions of Mark Twain's thinking at this time. These details do not demonstrate an indebtedness on either side, or conscious or unconscious derivation; but the facts of Twain's friendship with and respect for Ingersoll, and of his loyal interest in *The Truth Seeker*, cannot be questioned.

Twain had read Lecky's *History of European Morals* as early as 1874. I believe that he read also Winwood Reade's *The Martyrdom of Man*, perhaps in its second edition of 1876, and *The Bible for Learners* by a Dutch theologian, Dr. H. Oort, shortly after its publication in three volumes by Roberts Brothers in

1878. Parallels between these works and Twain's increasingly bitter denunciation of the Bible and the Bible's God are striking. *The Bible for Learners* is a richly detailed and documented treatment of the findings of the "higher criticism," especially in regard to the Old Testament, and it is often sarcastic.

Five years elapsed between the appearance of *Huckleberry Finn* and the publication of Twain's next book, *A Connecticut Yankee at King Arthur's Court,* in 1889. In the interval, as Kenneth Andrews remarks, Twain "was thinking of himself as a captain of industry and only intermittently working on the manuscript of *A Connecticut Yankee.*"[55] This was the period in which the Paige typesetting machine was making prospective millions for Twain every month, and the Webster Publishing Company was making actual thousands at the same rate: a period, in short, when there was little financial incentive for writing and when, on the other hand, preoccupation with money-making was the dominant aspect of Twain's life. Nowhere else in this study do we find a major writer so completely immersed in the dominating material movement of his times as was Twain in these five years. Not only was he giving lavishly of his time and thought to the typesetter and pouring funds from his generous income into it; we see him speculating in a dozen other financial ventures and cultivating a friendship with Andrew Carnegie!

Along with the "intermittent" work on the *Yankee,* Twain was thinking and occasionally writing along the lines projected in the previous decade. Elaborate burlesque of conventional religious concepts and practices is combined with brilliant dramatization of the gulf between pretension and practice in a brief work of 1887 (De Voto's estimate) called "Letter from the Recording Angel." The "letter" purports to be a detailed statement of the account of a wealthy coal merchant with the "Office of the Recording Angel, Department of Petitions," and includes classification of and action taken upon all his prayers, both public and private, for a given week. Public Sunday school prayers don't count, it appears. The climax of this brilliant satire recounts the astonishment and jubilation in heaven over the gift to an impoverished cousin, a widow, of *"fifteen whole dollars"* out of a monthly profit of over $20,000 (she needed fifty).

> There was not a dry eye in the realms of bliss; and amidst the handshakings, and embracings, and praisings, the decree was thundered forth . . . that this deed should . . . be recorded by itself upon a page of its own, for that the strain of it upon you had been heavier and bitterer than the strain it costs ten thousand martyrs to yield up their lives at the fiery stake; and all said, "What is the giving up of life, to a noble soul, or to ten thousand noble souls, compared to the giving up of fifteen dollars out of the greedy grip of the meanest white man that ever lived on the face of the earth?"
>
> And it was a true word. And Abraham, weeping, shook out the contents of his bosom and pasted the eloquent label there, "RESERVED"; and Peter, weeping, said, "He shall be received with a torchlight procession when he comes"; and then all heaven boomed, and was glad you were going there. And so was hell.
>
> Signed
> The Recording Angel   Seal
>
> By Command.[56]

As early as 1883 Twain's notebook shows an entry concerning the insignificance of man in relation to the universal God, an idea Twain was to tinker with for the rest of his life: "I think we are only the microscopic trichina concealed in the blood of some vast creature's veins, and it is that vast creature whom God concerns himself about and not us."[57] By 1885 or 1886 this concept had been elaborated:

> Special Providence! That phrase nauseates me—with its implied importance of mankind and triviality of God. In my opinion these myriads of globes are merely the blood corpuscles flowing through the arteries of God and we but the animalculae that infest them, disease them, pollute them; and God does not know we are there and would not care if He did.[58]

The idea remained in Twain's mind, and received its most ambitious application in *Three Thousand Years Among the Microbes,* which occupies nearly one hundred and twenty-five pages in *Which Was the Dream?* (1966), the volume of unfinished fictions edited by John S. Tuckey. Tuckey's study shows that the manuscript was written in just over a month of steady work, in 1905.

The universal God characterized by goodness and justice and mercy, of the beginning of the decade, is somehow fading, in these years of violent involvement in a world of technology and of commerical competition. Twice in this period Twain recorded ideas for essays for his Hartford discussion club (composed in part of ministers) which show other phases of his continued thought about the problem of man, especially in relation to Christ:

> Club essay: The little man concealed in the big man. The combination of the human and the god. Victor Hugo; Carlyle; Napoleon; Mirbel; Jesus; Emerson and Washington . . . Grant; Mahomet; in them (including the Savior) was allied the infinitely grand and the infinitely little.[59]

> Club subject: The *insincerity* of man. . . . When a merely honest man appears he is a comet—his fame is eternal—needs no genius, no talent, mere honesty—Luther, Christ, etc.[60]

The search for some firm position was still going on, clearly enough, in spite of all preoccupations.

Meanwhile, with repeated interruptions, Twain wrote the confused and confusing story *A Connecticut Yankee at King Arthur's Court.* Twain's intention in this book has been variously interpreted, and with reason, for it is notably inconsistent and self-contradictory. Yet it is, I believe, a work of great importance in the study of the development of Twain's thought. It seems clear that his excitement over the typesetting machine was one of the conditioning forces in the book's conception, and it may be felt that the work is a celebration of technology as the means of human progress. Conceivably this was at least part of Twain's conscious intention. But if this is so, the intention was most curiously realized. The only applications of technology to the conditions of sixth-century Britain actually dramatized in the novel are for purposes of deception (the blowing-up of Merlin's tower, the "miracle" at the Valley of Holiness), of destruction (the slaughter of knights by a dynamite bomb, and the holocaust at the end), and of commercial exploitation (the knights-errant selling toothpaste, and the conversion of the Table Round into a stock exchange). It is Lancelot's unscrupulous greed in a stock market transaction, in fact, which precipitates the novel's catastrophe.

Further, the Yankee is a very strange hero, if the purpose is to glorify technological progress and he is its avatar, for Hank Morgan is for the most part an extremely disagreeable creature, as deserving of contempt as any creation of Twain's genius save a very few. He has Twain's own weakness for theatrical effects (for example, the Hartford house, the white suits) and is never satisfied without them. He preens himself over petty triumphs—the discomfiture of the guests at his four-dollar dinner, for instance. He is frankly greedy for money and lustful for power. He takes a sadistic pleasure in mutilation, dismemberment, and slaughter. Indeed, only one character in the novel is comparable to Huck and Jim and worthy to be their successor as a human person in the procession of Twain's characters. This is, ironically, King Arthur. Or is it ironical? What *was* Twain's target? If one were to chart his purpose literally from the dramatic action of the book and from its chief characters, it would not be hard to view its treatment of technological progress and the machine man as negative rather than positive —to see it as strangely parallel to another "dream" novel of the same year, William Morris' *News from Nowhere*. If Twain actually did mean to celebrate technology and assert the superiority of the late nineteenth century over the age of Arthur, we can only view the book as a dismaying indication of the degree to which he was indeed in these years the creature of his times, submerged and self-deceived.

THE DARKENED SKY

Another guess at Twain's intention in *A Connecticut Yankee at King Arthur's Court* is Kenneth Andrews' suggestion that we may find in it "a defense of American democracy that is markedly more Jacksonian and affirmatively equalitarian than *The Gilded Age*. The difference between these books reflects less specifically a political development in Mark Twain than a growth in his emotional sympathy for the downtrodden."[61]

Intense sympathy for the downtrodden is indeed expressed in this novel, in a dozen incidents that give the book almost its sole value apart from variety-show entertainment. The family afflicted by smallpox, the prisoners in Morgan Le Fay's dungeon, the young mother condemned to death for stealing to feed her starving child—no reader will forget these scenes and others like them. But equalitarian affirmation is a value less unequivocally present. The Yankee finds thousands of promising candidates for the developing and perfecting experience of working in his factories, learning to read, and otherwise assisting in bringing in the technological millenium. But when the showdown comes there are only fifty-two—all teen-agers—who are judged worthy to preside at the fatuous slaughter of ten thousand knights.

The blame for this, of course, is laid on the tyranny of custom, the conditioning power of education and environment. The Yankee is sure that if he could have had more time he could have reformed and reshaped England. But is Twain sure? Or are the implications of the tale consistent with the low estimation of man which he had previously expressed and would restate over and over until he died?

It may be noted, of course, in explanation of the book's abrupt and artificial ending, that having erected the fantasy of a sixth-century industrial revolution in England, it was necessary to find some way of getting out from under it. This helps to account for the Yankee's ultimate failure, but scarcely for the wholesale slaughter.

Whatever the conscious intention of *The Connecticut Yankee* and whatever we may feel to be the degree of its success, the book's chief interest to the thoughtful reader of Mark Twain may be found in elements not accountable as part of that intention. The volume is crowded with images of violence —of mayhem, dismemberment, stabbing, beating, strangling, mass slaughter: these within a rather flimsy frame of mock-Arthurian lingo and faded-seeming castles, hovels and city streets, and all this within an almost forgotten margin of the peace and beauty of an unspoiled English countryside. So largely does the major action of the novel deal in violence, rising to the senseless horror of the Yankee's gloating over the technologically achieved massacre, that I cannot but agree with Henry Nash Smith, in his highly perceptive study of this novel, that "one is tempted to seek a psychological explanation for it."[62]

As for its overt religious content, the chief element in *A Connecticut Yankee* is its identification of an established church—specifically the Roman Catholic Church of the Dark Ages—as the chief obstacle to progress, the stronghold of tyranny. The institutions of royalty and aristocracy are the objects of direct attack, but the Church is seen as the source and patron of these institutions, their chief support as well as their chief beneficiary. Although this attack on historical Catholicism is the most outspoken Twain had yet made, he was careful, as always, to be fair to individual clergymen. Early in the book the Yankee explains his own notion of a desirable religious system and confesses frankly (in one of those incidents in which he is human and likable) that the goodness of some of the priests is an obstacle to him:

> Something of this disagreeable sort was turning up every now and then. I mean, episodes that showed that not all priests were frauds and self-seekers, but that many, even the great majority, of these that were down on the ground among the common people, were sincere and right-hearted, and devoted to the alleviation of human troubles and sufferings.[63]

Later, the abbot and other churchmen at the Valley of Holiness are treated distinctly as comedy characters,[64] but not unkindly. The highest point of eloquence and emotion in the entire novel is reached in the young priest's fervent protest against the laws which condemn a young mother to death for stealing to feed her starving child and in his promise to care for the orphan. Although it is the Interdict which presumably breaks the Yankee's power, fear of the church that alienates all of his promising men except the youthful fifty-two, these developments are not effectively dramatized and their significance rests—as does very largely the whole thesis of the stultifying power of tradition, custom, education and environment—on the Yankee's mere assertion. This fact, combined with the general scattering of effect, results in something less than full effectiveness in the attack on the Church—as established and in its political and social effects—which Twain clearly intended in this book and at times achieved. The *Connecticut Yankee* is of major importance in the record of Twain's religious experience because in it for the first time he made institutional Christianity as a whole a target for attack, and that motive is obvious despite the uncertainty regarding other aims. The implication is that underlying the commercial and technological preoccupations of these years was a more and more acute consciousness of religious problems.

That implication is borne out by a personal document of the end of this decade which is especially worthy of our attention, a long letter written by Mark Twain to his wife on July 17, 1889. It was occasioned by the death, two weeks before, of Theodore Crane, the husband of Livy's sister, who had been their host for many summers at Quarry Farm, and Mark's beloved friend with whom he had discussed religious matters many times. The letter begins with a reference to a letter from Howells, which Livy evidently had seen. Howells too was mourning a recent death, that of his first child and older daughter, Winifred. Howells had said:

> I read something in a strange book, *The Physical Theory of Another Life*, that consoles a little; namely, we see and feel the power of Deity in such fullness that we ought to infer the infinite Justice and Goodness which we do not see or feel.[65]

Mark Twain

Mark wrote:

> Livy darling, this that Howells speaks of appeals to one's reason; it sounds like sense. We do see & feel the *power* of what we call God; we do see it & feel it in such measureless fulness, that we "ought to infer"—*not* Justice and Goodness from *that*; but we may from another thing, namely: the fact that there is a large element of Justice & Goodness in His creature man. . . .

Indeed, Mark argues, we must conclude that "there is far more goodness than ungoodness in man, for if it were not so man would have exterminated himself before this." He concludes with the assurance that "I am plenty safe enough in *his* hands" —those of the Deity who has thus shaped man. He declares: "I don't *know* anything about the hereafter, but I am not afraid of it."[66]

It could be argued that Mark was writing in this letter only for Livy's comfort and in the hope of deceiving her as to his true feeling. It seems more probable, however, that he is trying here to convince himself, to regain a conviction, or at least to state provisionally a course of reasoning which attracts him. The predication in this letter of the prevailing goodness of men, as a basis for deductions concerning the nature of God, strongly supports the interpretation of *The Connecticut Yankee* as positively humanitarian. The attitude toward the question of a future life which the letter expresses is similar to the position taken in the "manifesto" of the early 1880's and to the view expressed in the essay on "the ancient and the modern God" of ten years earlier. The decade about to end had been the happiest of Twain's life, and it had brought him closer to religious security—in his belief in the remote and majestic yet good and just Deity reasoned toward in this letter— than he had been before or would be again.

VI

Hank Morgan, the "Connecticut Yankee," had been a shop foreman at the Colt's Arms Factory at Hartford. It was at this factory that Twain first saw the model of the Paige typesetting machine, as early as 1880. By the time Twain's book about Hank Morgan was published, the machine had consumed for several years the labor of a small army of men—paid with Twain's money—in efforts to perfect it. Twain's income during the preceding decade had been ample indeed; but more and more of it had been going into the typesetter, which, he expected, was to make him a multimillionaire: the letters in which he counts the prospective profits sound as though they had been written by Col. Sellers! The publishing company Twain had organized, primarily for the subscription sale of his own books, had been enormously profitable for a few years. But C. S. Webster, Twain's relative by marriage who had built up the business, withdrew, broken in health by the burden of the business itself coupled with Twain's inordinate demands for personal services. His successor was loyal but less able. In order to keep the costly work on the typesetter going, Twain drew from the publishing business the capital funds needed to carry on that business. In short, by 1890 the well-paved road to great wealth had become a quaking bog.

In 1890 Mark Twain still had twenty years to live—years in which he would be accorded worldwide fame such as no other American writer has ever known. But they were to be years punctuated by disasters. In the autumn of 1890 came the death of Jane Clemens, followed in just one month by that of Livy's mother. The typesetting machine had been "completed" several times during the 1880's, but each time the inventor had elected to tear it down and start over in order to achieve some added improvement—after extracting the necessary money from Twain. By 1890 Twain could no longer furnish the added money. His resources were exhausted: royalties, assets of the publishing firm, personal borrowings, even property of his wife. He undertook the formation of a stock company to take over the development of the machine. Early in 1891 it was evident that this effort had failed. Twain turned to his writing, relatively neglected in recent years, for desperately needed income. A little later a new friend, H. H. Rogers of the Standard Oil Company, became his business manager and took over his tangled affairs. The publishing company could not be saved, and in April, 1894, it went into bankruptcy, leaving Twain in debt for some $70,000. For a time it appeared that the typesetter might still succeed. But it failed decisively in a final test at which Rogers was present, and at the end of 1894 Twain had to accept the fact that the long-cherished dream of great wealth from that source was false.

Within a few months he had arranged for a round-the-world lecturing tour, and he hoped to pay his debts from the proceeds. Livy and their second daughter, Clara, accompanied him. For reasons which later were to seem inadequate the eldest girl, Susy, and the youngest, Jean, were left at home. The trip was a great triumph, personal and financial. When the engagements ended, Twain had planned to remain in England for a period of writing. Then word came Susy was ill. Before her mother and sister could reach America she died, a victim of meningitis.

The remaining years of Livy's life she and Mark spent chiefly abroad and in relative seclusion. Livy developed an organic heart disease which made her health most precarious. Repeatedly during these final years she was under the care of nurses for months at a time, while Mark was permitted to see her for only minutes a day if at all. After her death in Italy in 1904, Mark and his remaining daughters returned to America. Clara, the elder of the two, who had borne part of the burden of caring for her mother, suffered a nervous collapse and spent most of a year secluded from her family in a rest home. Later, as a student of music, she was rarely with her father for more than short periods, and in 1909 she married and went to Europe. Jean, the youngest child, who became a victim of epilepsy in her later years, died in 1909. Of her Mark wrote after her death that he had never known Jean until the last days of her life. It was against this background of personal experience that Twain did his writing in his last twenty years and that his religious attitudes took their final shape.

The first fruit of his renewed writing activity under the

acute financial pressure at the end of the 1880's was *The American Claimant,* a tale of rather attractive potentialities badly botched by Twain's misguided attempt to salvage in it portions of an abortive play presenting Col. Sellers as a spiritualist. Next in order of publication is *Pudd'nhead Wilson,* which was serialized in the first half of 1894. It is another product of hasty literary carpentry, embodying parts of an unfinished work in which Twain's always treacherous taste was close to its lowest ebb, *Those Extraordinary Twins.* But in the parts unblighted by the portentous twins there is fiction of high quality. The limited religious interest of the work lies partly in the fact that one of the chief characters, the kindly Judge Driscoll, is one of the two free-thinkers of Dawson's Landing, a Mississippi River town closely resembling Hannibal. Very possibly his character owes something to John Marshall Clemens. The other member of the "Free-thinkers' Club" is Pudd'nhead himself. The wryly skeptical apothegms ascribed to "Pudd'nhead Wilson's Calendar," which are used as chapter headings in this novel, no doubt represent some of Twain's thinking at this time; they are in no way related dramatically to Wilson himself, who is only thinly characterized in any personal sense. He remains relatively outside the main texture of the story, entering it primarily as one who furnishes the solution to a murder mystery, through scientific means, and sees justice done. The best characterization in this novel is that of Roxy, the Negro mother. Her childlike religious attitudes are treated at some length, lightly but with full sympathy.

We are now confronted by one of the strangest events, externally one of the most puzzling, in the whole field of this study: the writing by Mark Twain, at the depth of his financial trouble and in a time of defeat and despair, of his *Joan of Arc.* The writing of this book—destined to be punctuated by frantic cablegrams and interrupted by futile business trips to the United States—was begun in Italy in 1893 and continued in France in 1894 and early 1895. On April 29, 1895, Twain wrote H. H. Rogers: "At six minutes past seven, yesterday evening,

Joan of Arc was burned at the stake. . . ."[67] The novel was serialized in *Harper's Magazine* in 1895 and published in book form in 1896, while Twain was still on his round-the-world tour.

Twentieth-century critics for the most part have viewed *Joan* with condescension or disdain, in contrast to nineteenth-century readers including Howells and Twain himself. This is a good example of the failure of modern critics to fully recognize religious values. Some have disregarded Twain's *Joan* because they were unimpressed by Joan's life in itself and could not understand why he should write about it. At the moment, however, we are not concerned with the question of the book's literary merit or lack of it but with Twain's reasons for taking up this theme and with its meaning in relation to his religious situation. It is not necessary to accept the story that a wind-blown leaf from a biography of Joan fixed Mark's attention on her in his boyhood, but it is true that more than twenty years before he wrote Joan's story he had compiled a list of reference books related to it—and he himself claimed he had started the book several times. Further, we can see that under circumstances of tension and when interruptions were likely this project would be attractive on merely technical grounds, because it called for no long-range planning, no balancing of alternatives or working-out of plots. The outward form of the story and the whole essential sequence of events were "given" by the facts of history.

But the degree of authority and immediacy achieved in his rendering of the historical narrative makes it clear that the writing of Joan's story was something more than an opportune use of attractive fictional material. No doubt the book was in part, consciously or unconsciously, a tribute to the writer's virgin daughters—particularly to Susy who was at this time just of the age of the Maid of Domremy and in whose nature her father felt depths he could not penetrate. Something of Twain's idealizing love for his wife, and of his reverence for all womanhood, went into this book as well. But as Howells saw, and as the reader of today will see if he looks with clear vision,

the story of Joan of Arc held for Mark Twain a meaning even
deeper still. George N. Shuster recognized that ultimate significance when he remarked, "What a startling confession of spiritual unrest is *Joan of Arc!*"[68]

There was that in Mark Twain's nature which recoiled from
the darkness and cried out for affirmation of man's higher
nature. For the lifelong lover of history there was one out-
standing, fully authenticated story, and only one, that exempli-
fied beyond dispute or denial the operation of supernatural
forces in the lives of men. Howells expressed the issue well in
his review:

> What can we say, in this age of science, that will explain
> away the miracle of that age of faith? For these things really
> happened. There was actually this peasant maid who believed
> she heard voices from Heaven bidding her take command of
> the French armies and drive the English out of her country;
> who took command of them without other authority than
> such as the belief of her prince and his people gave her; who
> prophesied of the victories she would win, and won them;
> who broke the power of the invaders; and who then, as if
> God thought she had given proofs enough of her divine com-
> mission, fell into their power and was burned for a heretic
> and an idolater. It reads like a wild and foolish invention,
> but is every word most serious truth. It is preposterous, it is
> impossible, but it is all undeniable.[69]

Could one—I think Twain asked himself, perhaps unconsciously—by realizing through one's art the very flesh and breath
of a life of supreme faith, come to know what faith is? At
least, in a time of failure and defeat the wonderful tragic
story could hold new meaning and his heart could be warmed
by living for a time in the presence of that shining faith. He
could forget his burdens in complete dedication of his highest
powers to a sustained act of devotion and veneration which was
as close as Twain ever came to worship. "Possibly the book may
not sell, but that is nothing—it was written for love."[70]

It is essential to note that Twain's treatment of religious
elements in *Joan of Arc* is wholly impartial, absolutely non-

commital. He abhors Cauchon the traitor, to be sure, censures other priests who were the willing tools of Joan's enemies, is kindly disposed toward those who befriended the Maid. But as to the source or nature of the Voices, he suffers no slightest hint of his attitude to appear. He gives the reader only the authenticated facts of history.

Whatever meaning the character of Joan may have held for Twain, whatever the effect of his vicarious immersion in her experience during a crisis of his own life, he faced his situation in 1895 with courage and resourcefulness. He assumed voluntarily the burden of debt which the law would have permitted him to evade. He set out cheerfully on the immensely arduous lecturing tour around the world and keenly enjoyed its bizarre variety of experiences, even the hardships, exulted in the personal kindness and the public adulation with which he was everywhere received—in short, had the time of his life. He completed the whole journey triumphantly—to face unwarned at its end the catastrophe of Susy's death: the beloved, idolized eldest daughter, the one who was, I feel, a major inspiration for his writing of *Joan of Arc,* had developed an unsuspected disease during her parents' year-long trip and died while their ship was crossing the Atlantic.

That event initiated the final phase of Mark Twain's religious experience. In the writings of his last fifteen years there is much repetitious emphasis on religious matters, all negative, and chiefly in work not intended for publication. It is a dismal and painful record, and I shall not pursue it in full detail.

Twain's first resource, once the family had found refuge in London, was work on the book which became *Following the Equator,* based on voluminous notebooks kept during the trip. His steady effort brought the long book to completion by May 18, 1897. References to religion in *Following the Equator* are generally minor and facetious; an example is the comment on an impostor encountered in India: "the bearer's recommendations were all from American tourists; and St. Peter would have admitted him to the fields of the blest on them—I mean if he is as unfamiliar with our people and their ways as I suppose he is."[71] However, there are more serious entries in his notebook. In New Zealand, in November, 1895, he reflected:

> It is the strangest thing that the world is not full of books that scoff at the pitiful world, and the useless universe and violent, contemptible human race—books that laugh at the whole paltry system and deride it. Curious, for millions of men die every year with these feelings in their hearts. Why don't *I* write such a book? Because I have a family. . . .[72]

In India, after describing the appearance and conduct of certain Fakirs or holy men, he noted: ". . . all for the glory of God. Human beings seem to be a poor invention. If they are the noblest work of God where is the ignoblest?"[73]

It was Bernard De Voto's impression, stated in his *Mark Twain at Work,* that the two years and a half after the completion of *Following the Equator* constituted for Twain a comparatively barren period, one of consciously recognized impotence and failure.[74] Further investigation of the Mark Twain papers, in addition to facts which were already available but ignored by De Voto, shows that the actual case is just the opposite—that the period from the summer of 1897 to the end of the century was a time of extremely intense and fruitful activity for Twain, though much of the work was left unfinished. Much of what he had still to say about religion found expression in these years.

To begin with we may note, as the least significant of the points to be made, one curious aspect of the essays on Christian Science, the first of which was published in October of 1898. The basis of what is perhaps Twain's sternest condemnation of Mrs. Eddy is that he believes she is placing herself on an equal footing with the Trinity, especially as equal or superior to Christ. He remarks: ". . . unconscious profanations are about as common in the mouths of the lay membership of the new church as are frank and open ones in the mouths of their consecrated chiefs."[75] It is clear that Twain had not yet entirely lost the feeling of reverence for Christ which he had voiced in the letter to Orion more than twenty years before.

Mark Twain

Much more important for our purpose is the fact that within this period, probably at Vienna in 1898, Twain finally gave fairly definite form to his theory of determinism, what he called his "Gospel." It was not printed until 1906, in a small unsigned edition entitled *What Is Man?* which was distributed anonymously. As we have seen, the concept of human life as externally determined because a part of a universal machine had been implicit in the ideas Twain had drawn from his reading of popular science as early as 1869. The view had developed in his mind over the years and had become consciously complete perhaps as early as 1890. Twain's Gospel makes dreary reading. De Voto's harsh words are not unjustified: "When he tried to form a system of his intuitions he wrote only 'What Is Man?', a statement of the mechanistic view in the metaphors of John Watson's Behaviorism, and as perfectly accommodated to the minds of sophomores."[76]

De Voto is also justified, I feel, in his speculation as to the inner motivation of this unhappy book:

> *What Is Man?* is not only a treatise on man's instability, weakness, cowardice, cruelty, and degradation. . . . *What Is Man?* is also a plea for pardon. In describing man's helplessness, it pleads that man cannot be blamed. In asserting man's cowardice, it asserts also that man is not responsible. . . . No one, I think, can read this wearisomely reported argument without feeling the terrible force of an inner cry: Do not blame me, for it was not my fault.[77]

Mark Twain's conscience was a product of temperament, not of training. Its sanctions were psychological, not religious. It was a sufficiently unfortunate possession. The list of things for which he had blamed himself with a torturing intensity—and usually without the slightest rational reason—from the death of his brother Henry on, was already a long one; and he would go on adding to it to the end of his life. I agree that *What Is Man?* is a brief for man's blamelessness in his errors, his cowardices, his sins. Yet I do not think that Twain found in it, or wanted to find, any actual relief from his own remorse (and accompanying self-pity) in the long series of incidents in which he blamed himself, for these emotions were a part of his picture of himself and were in a sense dear to him.

It must be insisted that there is no Calvinism in any accurate sense in Twain's determinism, as has been sometimes suggested. In 1902 Twichell loaned Mark his copy of Jonathan Edwards' *On the Freedom of the Will,* for reasons I can only guess at. Perhaps Twichell was merely curious as to what would happen. At any rate, he got a reaction. The book and its ideas were evidently entirely new to Twain. Up to a point he not only followed the argument of the great Calvinist, but approved. But his own account of his reaction from that point on is worth quoting:

> . . . continuously until near midnight I wallowed and reeled with Jonathan in his insane debauch; rose immediately refreshed and fine at 10 this morning, but with a strange and haunting sense of having been on a three days' tear with a drunken lunatic. It is years since I have known those sensations. All through the book is the glare of a resplendent intellect gone mad—a marvelous spectacle. No, not *all* through the book—the drunk does not come on till the last third, where what I take to be Calvinism and its God begins to show up and shine red and hideous in the glow from the fires of hell, their only right and proper adornment. By God I was ashamed to be in such company.[78]

In this same fruitful period Twain gave his view of man as cowardly, greedy, and generally contemptible its most effective embodiment in all his fiction in "The Man That Corrupted Hadleyburg," which was published in *Harper's Magazine* for December, 1899. Although church members are among those who falsely claim the "corrupting" reward in this story, its purpose is not to denigrate organized religion as such, but to dramatize the Twainian view of the "damned human race." In Twain's most important published work at the beginning of the new century, however, the attack on hypocrisy is a major motive and factor.

This work consists of the series of brilliant pieces of journalism inspired by current events: "To the Person Sitting in Darkness" and "To My Missionary Critics" in 1901, "Defense of General Funston" (1902), "The Tsar's Soliloquy" (1904), and "Leopold's Soliloquy" (1905). The humanitarian impulse is dominant in all these essays, of course. Each is an impassioned commentary on human suffering and on the greed or callousness or cruelty responsible for it. It is noteworthy, however, that the sufferers are Chinese or Filipinos or Congolese in most of the essays and that in all the inflictors of suffering are professed Christians. In other words, the familiar theme of the contrast between profession and practice, which had been important in Twain's expression of his attitudes since the 1870's, is still very much in evidence. Indeed this theme has never been dealt with more powerfully than in these papers, by Twain or anyone else.

We must go back to the final years of the nineteenth century for the beginnings of one of the most interesting and important developments in Twain's later literary production, the writing of *The Mysterious Stranger* and related works. John S. Tuckey's perceptive and thorough study[79] has corrected earlier datings of *The Mysterious Stranger* and has traced the full and highly interesting story of the three widely different drafts Twain made. The version we know was begun late in 1897 or early in 1898 and was completed in 1900—except, significantly, for the final chapter, which was not written until 1904 (as a part of another draft) at a time very near to Livy's death.

De Voto believed that *The Mysterious Stranger* was written in the last years of Twain's life, after the death of Livy, and that it was his final completed work. On this assumption he viewed this work as representing the final stage in Twain's thinking on religious and related matters. This would make the final speeches of Satan, in the eleventh chapter, in their absolute negation, their nihilism, Mark Twain's last word as well:

"*Nothing* exists; all is a dream. . . ."

". . . there is no God, no universe, no human race, no earthly life, no heaven, no hell. It is all a dream—a grotesque and foolish dream."

171

De Voto found this resolution of all life's problems by denying life's reality a satisfying one for Twain. Tuckey's discoveries show, however, that the view of the ending of *The Mysterious Stranger* as Twain's last word on life's problems is wholly erroneous. We have a considerable body of writing done by Twain after *The Mysterious Stranger* was completed. That writing is by no means characterized by wintry calm. Though there is a certain attractiveness in the picture of Twain at the end of his life reaching a point of rest, a Prosperolike calm, even though that calm had been gained at the expense of the ultimate denial, of nihilism, it is perhaps really more satisfying and certainly more characteristic and consistent with his whole career to find him still battling for truth along familiar lines. There is no hint of reconciliation in the writings of the final years, no hope of solution. There is stubborn and angry courage, and no loss of eloquence.

The "Reflections on Religion" are dated by their editor, Charles Neider, as belonging to the summer of 1906 and included in the autobiographical dictation of that time. These essays mark one important change in Twain's religious thought, a new attitude not expressed before. The reverence for the character of Jesus, which as we have seen persisted long after Twain had lost faith in His divinity, has been extinguished at last. The Old Testament God is once more indicted for His "vindictive, unjust, ungenerous, pitiless and vengeful nature."[80] But now Christ is identified with Him as another half of the same Deity, and even more cruel, inconsistent, and unworthy of worship. This view is based on Twain's impression, now arrived at, that the concept of eternal punishment originated with Christianity, or—as he puts it—that Christ invented hell. The first of the "Reflections," dated June 19, 1906, is devoted to the development of this viewpoint, which obliterates henceforth the earlier and long-lasting respect for Christ.[81]

Another new item in the "Reflections" of 1906, at least in the degree to which it is emphasized, is Twain's attack on what he calls the doctrine of the Immaculate Conception. What he is really talking about, in the second "Reflection" in which he charges the Christian Bible with borrowing the idea from earlier holy books, is the Virgin Birth of Christ. He constantly confused the two dogmas.

A further novelty in this phase of Twain's attitude toward religious matters is his violent condemnation of the Bible on the ground of obscenity. "There has never been a Protestant boy or a Protestant girl whose mind the Bible has not soiled,"[82] he declares, in a passage so vehement as to carry painful autobiographical overtones.

Finally, in the fourth of this series of dictations, for June 23, 1906, we have a last and most significant step in the fashioning of Twain's ultimate religious position. The essay begins with phrasing which suggests the view of "the real God . . . the authentic creator of the *real* universe . . . that God of unthinkable grandeur and majesty,"[83] which Twain had first expressed in the letter of January, 1870, when he had just read some of the new science, and which had persisted, with frequent restatement, down to the end of the century or perhaps later. As this essay proceeds, we find that this "real God" is no longer beneficent, no longer to be trusted. He is indifferent—worse, he is infinitely and universally cruel: "We stand astonished at the all-comprehensive malice which could patiently descend to the contriving of elaborate tortures for the meanest and pitifulest of the countless kinds of creatures that were to inhabit the earth."[84] In this view, the real and universal God is no better than that of the Old Testament. In essential character they have coalesced and become one demoniac and malevolent tyrant. Against that cosmic malevolence Twain's wrath was inexhaustible.

Earlier and relatively less incendiary elements in Twain's general religious position persisted, too. The triviality of man in relation to the course of evolution as revealed by the geological record, long a favorite subject, was never more happily treated than in a brief essay to which Twain gave the title, "Was the World Made for Man?" It took 99,968,000 years to prepare the world for man, according to the authorities Twain cites, "impatient as the Creator doubtless was to see him and admire him."[85] The first nineteen million years went into the fashioning of the oyster.

> An oyster has hardly any more reasoning power than a scientist has; and so it is reasonably certain that this one jumped to the conclusion that the nineteen million years was a preparation for *him*; but that would be just like an oyster, which is the most conceited animal there is, except man.

Eventually came man, who:

> has been here 32,000 years. That it took a hundred million years to prepare the world for him is proof that that is what it was done for. I suppose it is. I dunno. If the Eiffel Tower were now representing the world's age, the skin of paint on the pinnacle-knob at its summit would represent man's share of that age; and anybody would perceive that that skin was what the tower was built for. I reckon they would, I dunno.[86]

De Voto ascribes this essay to the period 1905–1909 and notes justifiably that it is in Twain's "best vein."

"The Turning-Point of My Life," published in *Harper's Bazar* in 1910, was the last article written by Twain definitely for publication. According to Paine and the Howells correspondence, it was produced in the last year of Twain's life. It constitutes a condensed and pointed restatement of the deterministic arguments of *What Is Man?* with the same absence of definite religious application except as this is implied in the mechanistic view of life. Its point is, of course, that there is no "turning-point" in a life—that each event follows another in an unbroken causal sequence—a view which Twain tries to support from his personal experience.

What seems to be the final substantial body of Twain's writing is the series of essays called "Letters from the Earth," which Paine identifies under that title as written in the autumn of 1909. They were published in the book by the same title in 1962. The essays begin with an account of the creation, as observed by the archangels and explained by the Creator, and this is followed by a letter written by Satan from the Earth.

Mark Twain

The pretense that the letters are reports of Satan's observations is soon abandoned, or at least lost sight of, and we have in eleven letters (some 25,000 words) a final restatement of already familiar matters, with a modicum of new material. It is especially interesting to discover, for example, that precisely the point made in the letter to Olivia of January, 1870, is elaborated in the third letter: to the effect that Genesis is inaccurate in its chronology of creation because of the length of time it takes for light from the fixed stars to reach the earth. Another favorite target vigorously exploited here is the story of Noah and the Deluge. Heaven is once more scaldingly satirized—and a new factor is added, that of the absurdity of the exclusion of sexuality from the Christian heaven. This leads to a digression in which the physical capacities of the sexes in man are contrasted and the Creator is charged with a stupid error for the inequality. Finally, Twain's recent discovery that Christ was the supremely evil manifestation of the Deity was violently restated in the tenth "letter":

> . . . it was as Jesus Christ that he devised hell and proclaimed it.
>
> Which is to say, that as the meek and gentle Savior he was a thousand billion times crueler than ever he was in the Old Testament—oh, incomparably more atrocious than ever he was when he was at his very worst in those old days![87]

Insofar as these "Letters from the Earth" afford a cross section of what was in the mind of the man of seventy-five, they are sufficiently depressing. There is a shrillness about them and a coarseness of fibre, an unrelenting emphasis on the ugly detail, which are new and revealing. Their most poignant revelation, it seems to me, is that of Twain's ultimate inability to face his life and judge himself—his passionate search even at this date for a scapegoat (God), for an excuse (temperament). Perhaps his hysterical unwillingness to accept responsibility is simply the other side of that abnormal capacity for remorse and self-accusation which he tried to account for by calling it a Presbyterian conscience.

175

THE DARKENED SKY

Fortunately we have as the very last scrap of Twain's writing something which, while it voices his characteristic mockery of the traditional Christian heaven, does so in more appealing accents. This is the "advice" which he wrote for Albert Bigelow Paine, his friend and secretary, during his last visit to Bermuda only weeks before his death. It is entitled "concerning deportment on reaching the Gate which St. Peter is supposed to guard," and the Helen referred to here is Mrs. Paine.

> Upon arrival do not speak to St. Peter until spoken to. It is not your place to begin.
>
> Do not begin any remark with "Say."
>
> When applying for a ticket avoid trying to make conversation. If you *must* talk let the weather alone. St. Peter cares not a damn for the weather. And don't ask him what time the 4:30 train goes; there aren't any trains in heaven, except through trains, and the less information you get about those the better for you. . . .
>
> Don't try to kodak him. Hell is full of people who have made that mistake.
>
> Leave your dog outside. Heaven goes by favor. If it went by merit you would stay outside and the dog would go in.
>
> You will be wanting to slip down at night and smuggle water to those poor little chaps [the infant damned], but don't you try it. You would be caught, and nobody in heaven would respect you after that.
>
> Explain to Helen why I don't come. If you can.[88]

5

William Dean Howells

A PECULIAR CIRCUMSTANCE OF OUR STUDY IS THE FACT THAT TWO
of the six writers considered in this book, William Dean
Howells and Henry James, were significantly influenced by doctrines of one of the smallest and least widely known religious
denominations: the Church of the New Jerusalem, founded on
the writings of Emanuel Swedenborg. Howells ceased, early
in his life, to profess actual adherence to Swedenborgianism;
James never did profess such adherence; but both were profoundly and lastingly influenced by its teachings.

Emanuel Swedenborg, 1688–1772, was first a scientist of
worldwide distinction, then a man of large practical affairs and
influence in his native country of Sweden, and finally a writer
on religious subjects. In 1743 a series of intense personal experiences culminated in Swedenborg's conviction that he had been
granted revelation of religious truth; and from that time until
his death in 1772 he continued to elaborate his beliefs and
experiences in a stream of books, variously published in Holland and other countries since Lutheran authority prohibited
their appearance in Sweden. Swedenborg himself founded no
formal religious organization; but shortly after his death
readers and believers in England came together to establish a
denomination called the Church of the New Jerusalem, devoted

to the promulgation of Swedenborg's teachings and the circulation of his writings.

The new sect gained adherents in Europe and America; the first Swedenborgian society in the New World was founded at Baltimore in 1789. A century later New Church societies in the United States numbered 154, with only some 7,000 members. Thus the New Church (as it was commonly called by its adherents in contradistinction to all prior Christian organizations, Catholic or Protestant, which were grouped together as "the Old Church") never attained large numbers of societies or members, though it penetrated almost all parts of the nation. One of its most fruitful fields was the newly settled Middle West, especially in Ohio, Indiana, and Kentucky; and among the converts was William Cooper Howells, the father of the novelist.

Three elements in the teachings of Swedenborg and the doctrines of the New Church were of major influence in the life and writings of William Dean Howells. The first of these is the freedom of the will. At the opposite pole from Calvinism, Swedenborg taught that the individual is free to choose good or evil and that by his choices he makes his own heaven or hell. He is neither predestined to damnation nor elected to salvation. Throughout his life here on earth he has free choice, and he becomes for eternity what he chooses to become. Those who go to hell go there because they prefer it, as they have preferred evil on earth.

A second tenet, of vital importance to the reader of Howells, is that of the constant penetration, in what we call our natural lives, of spiritual beings from the spiritual world. The individual human soul is constantly in the company of spirits, both good and evil, and constantly chooses between their suggestions and examples. Large parts of Swedenborg's writings are devoted to elaborately detailed accounts of his visits to the spiritual world and his conversations with those who have died. Swedenborg taught that the "influx" from the spiritual into the material world could be decisive for positive conduct, or the natural man could be "let into his evils" by the withholding or with-drawal of spiritual aid. Dreams, premonitions and presentiments, telepathic communication, all that has been called "extra-sensory perception," found explanation and authority—as either heavenly or infernal in origin and effect—in Sweden-borgianism.

A third Swedenborgian doctrine, of major importance in understanding Howells as man and writer, is that of the sacred-ness and permanence of marriage. Rejecting the views of celi-bacy as a means to virtue and of sexual relations as intrinsically evil, Swedenborg taught that marriage is a means of spiritual growth and that men and women attain their fullest and high-est good only through the married state. Further, he held that the marital relationship, once established, is eternal, lasting for good or evil according to its nature throughout the future life. Marital infidelity and abuse or degradation of marriage and of sexual relations in general he considered major evils. Howells' attitudes toward marriage and sexual matters in his fiction and criticism had their basis in Swedenborgian doctrine.

In his affectionate introduction to his father's book of remi-niscences, Howells described his father's happiness in his Swedenborgian faith:

> It was the delight of his life . . . a tranquil joy, a peace that passed understanding. It was easy for him, whose being was in some sort a dream of love and good will, to conceive all tangible and visible creation as an adumbration of spirit-ual reality; to accept revelation as the mask of interior mean-ing; to regard the soul as its own keeper, and the sovereign chooser of heaven or hell. . . . To his essential meekness and unselfishness it was natural that he should think of himself as nothing in himself, but only something from moment to moment through influx from the Lord. He had a profound belief in this philosophy, which served to answer every ques-tion and satisfy every need of his spirit. He did not try to make it equally sufficient for others. He scarcely urged it even upon his children. . . .[1]

Though the Howells children were not constrained, were

"scarcely urged," to grow up as Swedenborgians, most of them did; and for William Dean, Swedenborgianism permanently affected his perception of life and colored its expression.

II

The first twenty-four years of Howells' life—lived almost wholly in Ohio, from his birth at Martin's Ferry on March 1, 1837, to his departure for Italy as American consul at Venice in November, 1861—are much more fully documented by his own hand than is the corresponding period in the life of any other of our six writers. *A Boy's Town* (1890), *My Year in a Log Cabin* (1893), and *Years of My Youth* (1916) are frankly autobiographical. *The Flight of Pony Baker* (1902) and *New Leaf Mills* (1913) are fictional treatments of segments of the experience of these early years. It is necessary to bring all these sources into focus, and to supplement them with insights afforded by other writings, in order to measure fully the effect on Howells' fiction of his early religious experience and impressions.

First of all, Howells' home was one of love. This is clear not only throughout the autobiographical writings but also in the record of lifelong intimacy and affection: in Howells' frequent visits to his family in Ohio; in his constant correspondence with his father, his brother, Joseph, and his sisters; and in his generous financial aid in their later years. It was also a home of work. The newspapers conducted by William Cooper Howells at Hamilton, the "Boy's Town," at Dayton and Ashtabula, and ultimately at Jefferson, were in truth family enterprises; and probably the best-known single fact about the life of William Dean Howells is that he became an accomplished typesetter before he was ten years old, while he still had to stand on a box or chair in order to reach the case. He had little formal education; he estimated that his total attendance at schools did not exceed one year. But his father had an exceptionally large and well-chosen private library, and the reading aloud of good books was a regular part of the family life. As William's literary interests developed, his father shared and encouraged them, not only by providing books but also by reading and discussing these with the precocious boy.

Finally, the Howells home was religious. At Hamilton, where William Dean spent his boyhood, and again at Jefferson, the village of his adolescent years, there were no local societies of the New Church; and though the children were permitted to attend the services of other churches, including the Roman Catholic, the Howells family had no part in regular public religious observances. In their place, on Sunday evenings the father read to the family passages from the writings of Swedenborg, doubtless with comment and interpretation, while an engraved portrait of Swedenborg, in a mahogany frame, looked on from a prominent place in the room. It is clear that a rather firm and explicit grounding in Swedenborgian doctrine was part of the preparation for life which William Cooper Howells sought for his children.

In the vivid imagination of his second son, not surprisingly, Swedenborg's graphic accounts of the world of spirits, of the heavens and hells and their inhabitants and of conversations with these beings, became interwoven and fused with some of the more sensational aspects of the religious attitudes which prevailed in the little towns and which the boy encountered in his playtime with other children. Ghosts and apparitions, premonitions and presentiments, all the folklore of the supernatural which was characteristic of the time and place and seemingly sanctioned by parental acceptance of Swedenborg's revelations, became obsessive realities in the sensitive boy's inner life. For years he believed that he was destined to die at the age of sixteen. A superficial injury from the bite of a dog gave him the persistent and torturing notion that he had contracted hydrophobia. The future novelist was born too late to experience the full flower of religious hysteria as his father had known it in camp meetings on the earlier frontier and as he himself was to analyze it in his last major work of fiction, *The Leatherwood*

God (1916); but excessive emotionalism, antagonism between denominational groups, and gross discrepancy between profession and conduct on the part of prominent church members were factors of his environment and contributed to the element of neuroticism which Edwin H. Cady has recognized in Howells' childhood and youth.[2]

No Ohio village of the time lacked its village atheist or at least "free-thinker;" and as Howells' experience widened, when he joined his father at Columbus (the elder Howells had been given a political appointment as secretary to the state legislature), and as he began to earn his own living as a newspaper writer well before he was twenty, he encountered further varieties in religious attitude and in belief or disbelief. There is difference of opinion among critics as to when Howells lost confidence in Swedenborgian doctrine and in religious belief as a whole. Arnold B. Fox concludes: ". . . there is little doubt that the poem 'Lost Beliefs,' which appeared in 1860, refers at least in part to his loss of faith."[3] The text of the poem (Howells' third to appear in *The Atlantic Monthly*) seems scarcely to admit of any other interpretation:

> One after one they left us;
> The sweet birds out of our breasts
> Went flying away in the morning:
> Will they come again to their nests?
>
> Will they come again at nightfall,
> With God's breath in their song?
> Noon is fierce with the heats of summer,
> And summer days are long!
>
> Oh my Life! with thy upward liftings,
> Thy downward striking roots,
> Ripening out of thy tenderest blossoms
> But hard and bitter fruits,—
>
> In thy boughs there is no shelter
> For my birds to seek again!

William Dean Howells

> Ah! the desolate nest is broken
> And torn with storms and rain.[4]

Fox continues:

> I am inclined to believe that Hannah Graham Belcher places the emphasis misleadingly when she says that Howells became increasingly skeptical in his religious beliefs during the late eighties and early nineties. It is apparent that his skepticism dates from a much earlier time.[5]

The reference is to Miss Belcher's careful study of "Howells's Opinions on the Religious Conflicts of His Age as Exhibited in Magazine Articles."[6]

I feel that the lack of agreement arises from the fact that there were two major phases in the process of Howells' loss of the religious faith of his early youth. The first was his discovery that he could no longer believe in Swedenborgianism as a total system or in any other formulated doctrine or institutional creed, and this, I think, occurred in his early twenties and is expressed in "Lost Beliefs." The second phase was the loss of confidence in personal immortality. In one of the last writings published before his death, an essay titled "Eighty Years and After,"[7] Howells said:

> Until I was thirty-five years old I had no question but if I died I should live again; yet the swift loss of that faith, through the almost universal lapse of it in the prevailing agnosticism of the eighteen seventies and 'eighties, was a relief from that fear of death. I had hitherto felt that, being a sinner, as I did not doubt I was, I should suffer for my sins after death; yet, now that the fear of hell was effectively gone, a certain stress was lifted from me which had weighed upon my soul. When I was a well-grown boy I used to pray before I slept at night that I might not die before morning and that I might not go to hell, but neither of my petitions had been inspired by the wise and kind doctrine of Swedenborg which I had been taught from my earliest years.[8]

Howells indicates here how largely the religious views and values of the communities in which he grew up had invaded, in his boyhood, the teachings of his home. The "Lost Beliefs" of 1860 appear to have been the conventional and generally accepted religious attitudes of the times, rather than the distinguishing tenets of Swedenborgianism with its primary assumption of personal immortality.

III

The fifteen volumes Howells wrote during his first twenty years of book publication—from *Poems of Two Friends* in 1860 through *The Lady of the Aroostook* in 1879—offer little reflection of his religious ideas and experience. These were years of extremely rapid growth and development, personal and professional, which may be summarized under three aspects. The first was the impact of European experience. In recognition of his writing a "campaign biography" of Abraham Lincoln, Howells was given an appointment as American consul at Venice. He sailed for Europe in November, 1861, and remained for four years. Since consular duties were light in wartime, Howells devoted most of his attention to study of the Italian language and literature and to travel in Italy. From his experience in Italy he wrote the two books which first made his reputation as a writer, *Venetian Life* (1866) and *Italian Journeys* (1867).[9]

A second phase of Howells' development in this period was his rapid rise in the field of journalism. After a brief but significant association with E. L. Godkin and the New York literati as a staff writer for *The Nation* (1865), he became assistant editor of *The Atlantic Monthly* in 1866, and was editor of that magazine from 1871 to 1881. During these years he was experimenting in the writing of fiction and plays, and gradually clarifying his preferences in both materials and methods, from *Suburban Sketches* (1871) through *The Lady of the Aroostook* (1879).

Most significant in Howells' personal life of the events of these years were his marriage and the births of his children. In his last year at Columbus he had met Elinor Gertrude Mead, who was visiting relatives there from her home at Brattleboro, Vermont. (The Meads were Unitarians and were prominent people in Vermont.) At the end of 1862 Elinor came to Europe to marry him. Their first child, Winifred, was born in 1863; John Mead in 1868, and Mildred in 1872. Howells' marriage was as supremely important for him as was Twain's, which in certain respects it strangely paralleled.

Together with his wife Howells faced the religious conflicts of the nineteenth century at what may have been their climax of intensity. One must explore the magazines of the 1860's and 1870's to realize with any degree of adequacy the impact of Darwinism (especially after Huxley's lectures in America), and of the new findings in astronomy, on American thought.[10] As assistant editor and later chief editor of *The Atlantic Monthly*, Howells was at the center of the storm.

Though Howells reviewed many books during his first years on *The Atlantic Monthly*, most of those specifically religious in content were assigned to other reviewers.[11] For example, O. B. Frothingham reviewed a translation of Lessing's *Nathan the Wise* (February, 1868), which he said we may call "the confession of faith of the modern theist;" Thomas Wentworth Higginson handled objectively Max Muller's *Essays on the Science of Religion* (June, 1869); Henry James, Jr., did a brilliant job of demolition on Henry Ward Beecher's *Lecture-Room Talks* (July, 1870).

When in his years as assistant editor of the *Atlantic* Howells did review books which might raise religious questions, he was careful to avoid arousing controversy. His review of *The Secret of Swedenborg*, by Henry James, Sr. (December, 1869), is strictly, even painfully noncommittal both as to Swedenborgianism itself and as to James's version of it. He does venture the comment that Swedenborg's doctrine is "peculiarly distasteful to the intellectualized spirit of this age, in which men seem to exist only in their self-consciousness."[12] Reviewing Daniel G. Brinton's *The Myths of the New World* in the issue for October 1868, Howells concludes: ". . . that doubt, scarcely more merciful than atheism, whether man might not somewhere be destitute of belief in God and his own immortality, is removed, so far as concerns the Americans."[13] Howells' treatment of Lecky's *History of European Morals* (November, 1869) is at once highly appreciative and determinedly noncontroversial. Of Oliver Wendell Holmes's *Mechanism in Thought and Morals,* Howells says frankly (May, 1871), "we are rather glad that it is no business of ours to pronounce upon the correctness of his ideas."[14]

However, in the reviews of these early years, Howells did afford a few glimpses of his own religious thought. In his very long and enthusiastic review of three stories by Björnstjerne Björnson in April, 1870, Howells wrote: ". . . Björnson's religious feeling is not pietistic; on the contrary, it teaches . . . that a cheerful life of active goodness is the best interpretation of liberal and hopeful faith."[15]

At this time, Howells was approaching the second religious turning point suggested above. In July, 1869, Mrs. Howells' father died. In an interrupted letter to Henry James, Howells wrote of this experience:

> For a man who never intended to recognize death as among the possibilities, except in an abstract and general sort of way, I have, within a year, seen enough of it to convince me of an error in my theory of life. It can never again seem the alien far-off thing it once did; and yet acquaintance with it has robbed it of something of its terrors. Shall I say it has been at once realized and unsubstantialized? I had always thought to find death in the dead; but they are "but as pictures"; I feel the operation of a principle which seemed improbable formerly, but I am not frightened at its effect as I had always thought to be. I don't mean, of course, that I don't fear to die—God knows I do—but in other times, the mere imagination of death was enough to fill me with unspeakable anguish.[16]

Sometime shortly thereafter, Howells and his wife undertook a program of systematic religious reading, evidently including, if not consisting wholly of, works of Swedenborg. Two letters of Howells to his father early in 1872 report the results of this undertaking. On January 28 he wrote:

> . . . for the past week we've suspended our theological readings. The fact is the subject has grown a little too exciting, and I should willingly never resume it if I did not think it a duty to do so. In Swedenborg I'm disappointed because I find that he makes a certain belief the condition of entering the kingdom of heaven. I always tho't it was a good life he insisted upon, and I inferred from such religious training as you gave me that it made no difference what I believed about the trinity, or the divinity of Christ, if only I did right from a love of doing right. Now it appears to me from the Testament that Christ was a man directly, instead of indirectly, begotten by a divine father; and for this persuasion, which I owe to the reason given me of God, Swedenborg tells me I shall pass my eternal life in an insane asylum. This is hard, and I can't help revolting from it. I am not such a fool as to think I can do the highest good from myself, or that I am anything in myself; but I don't see why I cannot be humble and true and charitable, without believing that Christ was God. I am greatly disappointed, and somewhat distressed in this matter. At times I'm half minded never to read another word of theology; but to cling blindly to the moral teachings of the gospels. I should like extremely to talk with you.[17]

Less than a month later, on February 25, he expressed again his lack of satisfaction in Swedenborg and his wish that he could discuss these problems, specifically that of immortality, with his father:

> I suppose that I understand Swedenborg very dimly, but if I do understand him, it seems to me that man's state hereafter, whether in bale or bliss, is one of less dignity than on earth—that there is less play for his powers, and that the very union of his will and intellect deprives him of individual consciousness, and cripples him.—There are a thousand points I'd like to talk with you upon.[18]

In his remaining reviews for the *Atlantic*, Howells gave much fuller and franker indication of his personal religious attitudes than he had in the preceding years. Sometimes the expression is merely playful, as in the comment—in a review of Leigh Hunt's *Wishing-Cap Papers* (May, 1873)—on the author's "tenderness for all mankind—even Calvinists."[19] Sometimes it is satirical, with an overtone of bitterness. In reviewing Christopher Pearce Cranch's *Satan,* in March, 1874, Howells wrote:

> The tendency of modern liberalism to ignore the chief of the fallen angels has been one of the most painful spectacles which conservative theologians have had to contemplate; and but for the consoling reflection that these liberals were destined to be very much astonished at their last day, their behavior would have been well-nigh insupportable. . . . It is . . . a question of the very existence of the power which had so long frightened mankind into being good, and must thus have been largely instrumental in bringing us to our present millenial condition.[20]

Of John Foster's *Life of Charles Dickens,* volume III, Howells wrote in the *Atlantic* for May, 1874:

> It is a solemn lesson that the exercise of genius is in itself only a momentary escape from the *ennui* that torments all of us who have not provided ourselves with some sure retreat from the world within the world. Religion used to be highly recommended for this purpose; we suppose that nowadays Evolution is to console and support us—not with the hope of heavenly peace somewhere, but with the elevating consciousness of primordial jelly.[21]

In a careful review of George Eliot's *The Legend of Jubal and Other Poems,* in July, 1874, Howells asserted:

> It is the disadvantage—the artistic disadvantage, at least—of the materialistic creed, that it can appeal to nothing but the intellect; it tends to deathly allegory, and it preaches the Worm and the Grave much more tiresomely than Eternal Life can be set forth. . . .[22]

Not infrequently the reviews of the early 1870's touch the problem of personal immortality, with a certain pained wistfulness. In his review of John Morley's *Rousseau* (July, 1873), Howells wrote:

There was sufficient occasion, in writing of Rousseau and his
times, to celebrate mortality and the worm at the expense of
those fond hopes of eternal life which most of us cherish. . . .[23]

Of Harriet W. Preston's *Love in the Nineteenth Century,*
Howells wrote in the *Atlantic* for September, 1873:

The whole episode [of the death of a young wife] is given
a sort of resentful sorrow, as if in indignation that men
should be scienced out of what can alone sustain and console
them under supreme trial; and it is the wholesome use of
Miss Preston's book, in all its precepts, to cast doubt upon
doubt.[24]

Howells' review of Oliver Wendell Holmes's *Songs of Many
Seasons* (January, 1875) speaks of "those fond dreams of a
future life which some of us still furtively indulge, despite the
hard skeptic air of our science-smitten age,"[25] and of Mrs. S.
M. B. Piatt's *That New World and Other Poems* he wrote in
January, 1877: "Certain of the poems strike one with awe for
the fierce sincerity with which the cut-flowers of consolation
are thrust aside, and the ineffable loss through death is confronted."[26] Not least impressive is the comment, following a list-
ing of Spanish proverbs in a review of *Popular Sayings of Old
Iberia* (September, 1877): "proverbial passages, the last of
which is deeper and better than many theologies: 'I can forgive
anything for love,' said a Spanish boatman, 'and so, I suppose,
can the almighty'."[27]

In his own books published between *Venetian Life* (1866)
and *The Lady of the Aroostook* (1879), Howells gave relatively
little indication of his religious thought. The only important
element is that of criticism of institutional religion. In the
books growing out of his experience in Italy, the target naturally is Roman Catholicism; and we may justifiably suppose
that, in part, Howells saw in the Roman church what he expected to see. This would be conditioned not so much by what
he may have gleaned of Swedenborg's condemnation of established churches as by the endemic prejudice of his American
and Midwestern environment. In *Venetian Life* he declared:

"The ceremony of baptism . . . is performed, like all religious services in Italy, without a touch of religious feeling or solemnity."[28] He supports this general assertion by an account of a funeral, which is strongly condemnatory in tone and implication.[29] Similar comments occur in *Italian Journeys* (1867).

After his successful experiments with American materials, largely autobiographical, in *Suburban Sketches* (1871), *Their Wedding Journey* (1871), and *A Chance Acquaintance* (1873), Howells returned to Venice for the significant settings and the central character of his first truly ambitious novel, *A Foregone Conclusion* (1875). In it he dramatized fully one phase of his hostility toward institutional religion. As James Woodress comments:

> Howells did not hesitate to use the novel as a forum for criticizing the Catholic church. He had observed at first hand the corruption of the clergy in Italy, and he blamed for at least part of its rottenness the priestly vow of celibacy. . . . His outspoken attack on this phase of Catholicism is of a piece with the scattered criticisms of the Church in his travel books. . . .[30]

When Howells returned to American scenes for his next novel, the ill-fated *Private Theatricals* (serialized in *The Atlantic Monthly* from November, 1875, through May, 1876, but not published in book form until 1921, under the title *Mrs. Farrell*), he extended his overt criticism of religious institutions to include those in his native land. In his account of West Pekin's "First Church," Howells wrote:

> Even the theology preached them was changed. It was the same faith, no doubt, but it seemed to be made no longer the personal terror it had been, nor the personal comfort. . . . faith, like all life in West Pekin, had shrunken till one might say it rattled in its shell.[31]

The book also contains, as Mildred Howells noted in her introduction to the posthumously published volume, an observation "which is of his latest, as well as his earliest philosophy."

It is Mrs. Farrell's admission that "Nothing that's wrong can be one's own affair. . . . it belongs to the whole world."[32]

In *The Lady of the Aroostook* (1879) Howells reaffirms the judgment which he had voiced in *Private Theatricals:* that there has been a general lessening of genuine religious feeling and faith. His touch is light as he treats the religious attitudes of most of the voyagers in the novel. But there is serious satire in his account of the views and conduct of Mrs. Erwin, the aunt who assumes charge of Lydia Blood after Lydia has crossed the Atlantic as the sole feminine passenger on the *Aroostook.* Howells has Mrs. Erwin take Lydia to a service of the Church of England, having previously advised her as to religious matters:

> "But things have changed very much of late years, especially with all this scientific talk. In England it's quite different from what it used to be. Some of the best people in society are skeptics now, and that makes it quite another thing."[33]

IV

As he entered a new decade, Howells was ready to publish the first of his novels in which a religious subject was of paramount importance. *The Undiscovered Country* was serialized in *The Atlantic Monthly* from January through June, 1880, and appeared as a book immediately thereafter. It was written as Howells approached the end of his triumphant career as editor of the *Atlantic,* when he was soon to declare that he was "terribly, miserably tired of editing." It was followed by the climactic year in which he resigned the editorship of the *Atlantic,* wrote the first of his greatest novels—*A Modern Instance*—and sustained the only prolonged and serious illness of his adult life: ". . . some sort of fever . . . . the result of long worry and sleeplessness from overwork," he wrote to his father on November 15, 1881.[34]

The Undiscovered Country is given extended treatment by Kermit Vanderbilt in his excellent recent book, *The Achieve-*

ment of William Dean Howells: A Reinterpretation.[35] It is also carefully studied by Olav W. Fryckstedt in *In Quest of America* (pp. 185–191). Fryckstedt shows the notable resemblances between the novel and Turgenev's *Rudin*, and recognizes in the work—as well as in the novels immediately preceding it—Turgenev's influence (which Howells repeatedly acknowledged) on the development of Howells' purposes and methods. Fryckstedt regards Dr. Boynton, the central person of *The Undiscovered Country*, as "in fact one of the great figures in Howells' world of fictional characters, on a level with such portraits as Bartley Hubbard and Silas Lapham."[36] Boynton is a small-town physician who has become an ardent champion of spiritualism and has come to Boston to proclaim and advance the cause. In his seances he uses his daughter, Egeria, as a medium, in a relationship similar to that of the father and daughter at the beginning of Henry James' *The Bostonians* (1886). In line of duty a young journalist named Ford attends a seance and sees Egeria suffer a nervous collapse in the course of it. He becomes interested in the girl and tries to interfere, feeling that her father is exploiting her unjustly. The reader shares both Ford's initial suspicion that Boynton is a conscious impostor and his later realization that the doctor is wholly sincere in his attempt to explore the world beyond death and to demonstrate the fact of personal immortality.

The weakness of the novel is largely structural. Through an arbitrary sequence of events, the scene is transferred to a Shaker village—a setting which Howells knew well from a summer spent there with his family and used also both as the subject of an essay in *Three Villages* (1884) and as the background for his last completed novel, *The Vacation of the Kelwyns* (1920). Egeria undergoes a long and severe illness, and is lovingly cared for by the Shaker sisters. Boynton plans a grand demonstration of spiritualism for the Shaker community as soon as Egeria is sufficiently recovered. In announcing his plan to the Shakers, Boynton uses language reminiscent of Howells' observations in earlier novels and in reviews:

William Dean Howells

"But you who dwell here, in the security, the sunshine, of this faith [in personal immortality] have little conception of the doubt and darkness in which the whole Christian world is now involved. In and out of the church, it is honeycombed with skepticism. Priests in the pulpit and before the altar proclaim a creed which they hope it will be good for their hearers to believe, and the people envy the faith that can so confidently preach that creed; but neither priests nor people believe."[37]

When Ford, aware of the girl's extreme reluctance and positive fear of appearing as her father's medium again, tries to persuade Boynton to give up the plan, the doctor becomes furious, strikes Ford, and suffers an apoplectic stroke. The crux of the novel's serious intention appears in the final chapters, in which Ford cares for the dying man and faces his insistent questions. When Ford is summoned by Boynton—who is, Ford thinks, about to die—Ford's reflections suggest in part the early recollections of Howells, as he was to record them in the third person in the last year of his life:

. . . all through his childhood and his earlier youth the thought of death had been agony to him, probably because it was related to fears of the life after death, which survived in his blood after they ceased to be part of his belief. . . . Life was not a good, he knew that; but he felt now that it was something, and beyond it there was not even evil.[38]

But Boynton does not die at once, and in his extended conversations with Ford, he expresses respect for science:

"The refusal of science to believe what it cannot subject to its chemic tests has its sublime side. It is at least absolute devotion to the truth, and it involves martyrdom, like the devotion to any other religion."[39]

He appeals, with a humility new in him, for a way out of his dilemma as he faces death:

". . . Give me some hope! A word comes from you at times that does not seem of your own authority: speak! Say it!"

"You have the hope that the world has had for 1800 years,"
answered Ford, deeply moved.

"Was that first in your thoughts?" Boynton swiftly rejoined.
"Was it all you could think of? . . . But you have rejected
that hope."

"It left me. It seemed to have left me. I don't realize it
now as a faith, but I realize that it was always present somewhere in me. It may be different with those who come after
us, to whom it will never have been imparted; but we who
were born in it,—how can we help it, how can we escape it?"

"Is that really true?" mused Boynton aloud. "And there is
absolutely nothing else but that? Nothing in science?"

"No."

"Nothing of hope in the new metaphysics?"

"No, nothing."

"Nothing in the philosophy that applies the theories of
science to the moral world?"

"Nothing but death."

"Then that *is* the only hope,—that old story of a credulous
and fabulous time, resting upon hearsay and the witness of
the ignorant. . . ."[40]

Boynton concludes at last that all his research in spiritualism
has been in the wrong direction. Spiritualism is equal to materialism, he concludes:

". . . the only thing that I have got by all this research is the
one great thing which it never included,—which all research
of the kind ignores."

Ford perceived that he wished him to ask what this was,
and he said, "What is that?"

"God," replied Boynton. "It may be through an instinctive
piety that we forbear to inquire concerning him of those
earth-bound spirits. What could they know of him? Many
pure and simple souls in this world must be infinitely nearer
him. But out of all that chaos I have reached him. No, I am
not where I started: I have come in sight of him. I was anx-
ious to know whether we should live hereafter; but whether
we live or not, now I know that he lives, and he will take
care. We need not be troubled. As for the dead, perhaps we
shall go to them, but surely they shall not return to us. That
seems true, doesn't it?"[41]

The Shakespearian reference of the title of this novel is

enriched by a speech of Egeria's to Ford, in the course of her convalescence:

> "Yes," she continued looking dreamily at Brother Joseph's flower-beds, "here is prince's feather, and coxcomb, that I hated to touch when I was little, because it seemed like flesh and blood. And here is bachelor's button, and mourning bride, and marigolds, and touch-me-not."[42]

Boynton, dying, asks:

> "Who is it . . . that speaks of the undiscovered country?"
> "Hamlet," replied Ford.
> "It might have been Job,—it might have been Ecclesiastes,—or David. . . . and Hamlet says no traveler returns, when he believes that he has just seen his father's spirit. . . . We must doubt it; we are better with no proof . . . . The undiscovered country—what a weight of doom is in the words—and hope!"[43]

The final sentences of the novel return to its central theme:

> If Boynton has found the undiscovered country, he has sent no message back to them, and they do not question his silence. They wait, and we must all wait.[44]

In *The Undiscovered Country* Howells went farther than he had ever gone before in fictional dramatization of his personal religious experience. The question of personal immortality remained with him in varying degree, expressed in varying terms of hope and doubt; but for the immediate future, and indeed for the next twenty years of his life, his thinking about religious matters was for the most part directed toward the social inadequacies of contemporary religious institutions and conceptions, and the need for the application of Christian principles to the solution of social and economic problems.

V

Leaving unanswered the question of personal immortality—it was never again to be treated at length in Howells' fiction, but was to be raised repeatedly in his writing of all kinds—Howells turned in *A Modern Instance* (1882), so far as religious content is concerned, to examination of the status of contemporary religious practice. Howells lived with this story for six years before he wrote it, and its completion was delayed by the serious illness mentioned above. The germinal idea came to him, he said, after he witnessed a performance of Euripides' *Medea* in Boston in 1875, and he considered calling the novel "A Modern Medea." When an interviewer asked Howells at the height of his fame which of his novels he thought best, he gave *A Modern Instance* as his choice. On other occasions he made other nominations; but the high place of the book in the Howells' canon cannot be questioned.

We see the major characters for the first time and the last against the symbolic background of winter in a small New England town. The opening chapters develop the fiercely possessive and intensely physical love of Marcia Gaylord, only child of an aging and ill-mated couple, for a clever, handsome and self-indulgent young journalist, Bartley Hubbard. Their marriage destroys itself in a prolonged conflict culminating in the most powerful dramatic scenes Howells ever wrote—those of the Indiana divorce trial. We then see Marcia and her child isolated in the old Gaylord mansion at Equity, Maine, while Ben Halleck, a young minister who has ruined his life through an infatuated but unrealized devotion to Marcia, is "on his way to take charge of a backwoods church down in Aroostook County."[45]

In his rich portrayal of the village background in the beginning of *A Modern Instance,* Howells takes time for a deliberate analysis of the religious situation:

> Religion there had largely ceased to be a fact of spiritual experience, and the visible church flourished on condition of providing for the social needs of the community. It was practically held that the salvation of one's soul must not be made too depressing, or the young people would have nothing to do with it. Professors of the sternest creeds temporized with sinners, and did what might be done to win them to heaven by helping them to have a good time here. The church embraced and included the world.[46]

This is promptly balanced by an account of the Boston home of Ben Halleck, an acquaintance of Bartley Hubbard, who has visited there, and Howells speaks lightly and ironically of the religious attitudes in the Halleck home:

> They were rich people, devout in their way, and benevolent, after a fashion of their own . . . their house was richly furnished with cushioned seats, dense carpets, and heavy curtains; and they were visited by other people of their denomination, and of a like abundance.[47]

The fourth chapter returns to Equity and the position of Squire Gaylord in the religious life of the village:

> For liberal Christianity he had nothing but contempt, and refuted it with a scorn which spared none of the worldly tendencies of the church in Equity. The idea that souls were to be saved by church sociables filled him with inappeasable rancor; and he maintained the superiority of the old Puritanic discipline against them with a fervor which nothing but its re-establishment could have abated.[48]

When at the end of the book Ben Halleck enters the ministry, Howells is at pains to show the reader that his action is dictated by personal need rather than by confidence in the church as a social force:

> In entering the ministry he had returned to the faith which had been taught him almost before he could speak. He did not defend or justify this course on the part of a man who had once thrown off allegiance to all creeds; he said simply that for him there was no other course. He freely granted that he had not reasoned back to his old faith; he had fled to it as to a city of refuge.[49]

Edwin Cady sees much Swedenborgianism in *A Modern Instance*. Certainly the Swedenborgian conception of the sanctity of marriage, and the permanence of the relation whether for good or bad, is strongly emphasized; and most readers will sympathize with Cady's condemnation of Howells' "letting a stuffy lawyer named Atherton debate the moral problems of the book in fruitless Swedenborgian meanders,"[50] though Atherton's position is less explicitly Swedenborgian than this comment would imply. Atherton is at least as much a spokesman for the conventional conservative attitude toward divorce in the 1880's. The deeper Swedenborgian elements in the novel are those introduced as the author's comment regarding decisive actions of the characters, especially Bartley Hubbard. Here the emphasis is on Swedenborg's doctrine of free will and the individual's determination of his destiny. A clear example is the statement concerning Bartley's plight when, after deserting his wife and then deciding to return to her, he finds that his money has been stolen: "Now he could not return; nothing remained for him but the ruin he had chosen."[51]

In the 1880's, Howells read for the first time the religious writings of Tolstoi, and he was deeply impressed. As Howells repeatedly acknowledged, he experienced something comparable to a religious conversion under the impact of Tolstoi's ideas and his example in renouncing his high social position so that he might live as a peasant and try to realize the tenets and practice of primitive Christianity. Many religious leaders at that time were shifting their emphasis from doctrine to social action as a religious program. In his praise of Tolstoi's action, Howells was implicitly accepting the tenets of what was coming to be known as the "Social Gospel." George Bennett suggests that in the years preceding his discovery of Tolstoi, Howells was working out these ideas for himself, so that Tolstoi represented "confirmation rather than revelation to Howells":

> These were the years when Howells was consciously working toward a discovery and definition of self. This process affected *The Undiscovered Country*, and one aspect of it, at least, was ended by the relinquishment of the theoretical question of immortality in favor of the more immediate question of how men should live their lives here on earth.[52]

The identification of religious with social responsibility inevitably raised for Howells the problem of social determinism, as opposed to the Swedenborgian teaching of free will and total personal responsibility for conduct. This problem is faced specifically at one point in *A Modern Instance,* when Ben Halleck and his sister, Olive, call on the Athertons to tell them of Ben's receipt of the Indiana newspaper containing the legal notice of Hubbard's divorce suit:

> While Olive told what had happened, he [Ben Halleck] looked listlessly about the room, aware of a perverse sympathy with Bartley, from Bartley's point of view. Bartley might never have gone wrong if he had had all that luxury; and why should he not have had it, as well as Atherton. . . .[53]

But Howells never wholly accepted the idea of social determinism as a corollary to his conviction that the struggle for social justice was the primary religious obligation of his time; he was unable to give up entirely the Swedenborgian doctrine of choice and of personal responsibility. The result was a basic inconsistency, or at least indecisiveness, which betrayed itself occasionally throughout the vast bulk of writing of his remaining years.

The major novels which followed *A Modern Instance* in the 1880's are alike in focusing their religious content on the functions of religious institutions, and specifically of ministers, in the modern world. The characters of *The Rise of Silas Lapham* (1885), *Indian Summer* (1886), *The Minister's Charge* (1887), and *Annie Kilburn* (1889), include in each case a minister or ministers; and each is studied as an example of the ministry in its contemporary social context.

Howells' whole campaign for realism in fiction, waged most notably and vigorously in the "Editor's Study" in *Harper's Magazine* from 1886 to 1892 but constantly a part of his critical and fictional practice throughout his mature life, had a religious base. He recognized the reading of fiction as an important factor in the shaping of human character and conduct. He believed that truth in fiction makes for sanity and rightness in action, while false sentimentalism distorts judgment of right and wrong, and that

> If a novel flatters the passions, and exalts them above the principles, it is poisonous; it may not kill, but it will certainly injure.[54]

199

THE DARKENED SKY

The creation and criticism of literature Howells recognized as his life work: the work which not only expresses and shapes but essentially *is* the life, in a Swedenborgian conception which Howells never abandoned.

In *The Rise of Silas Lapham,* the chief function of the minister, Rev. Sewell, is to point out the viciousness of false sentimentality in fiction and to try to avert its bad effects in the case of the mistake, on the part of most of the parties concerned, as to Tom Corey's intentions in relation to the two daughters of Silas Lapham. The limited social effectiveness of Sewell's church as an institution is implied rather than dramatized.

In *Indian Summer* (1886) a minister again speaks for Howells in condemnation of false sentimentality, this time false sentimentality as found in real life rather than in fiction. Rev. Waters is in Florence studying Florentine history and engrossed by Savonarola. Howells' account of him is notable in its recognition of both what was anemic and what was admirable in the New England religion of the time; of the Rev. Waters' "humble acquaintances" in Florence, Howells writes:

> They could never have understood—nor, for that matter, could anyone have understood through European tradition— the sort of sacerdotal office that Mr. Waters had filled so long in the little deeply book-clubbed New England village where he had outlived most of his flock, till one day he rose in the midst of the surviving dyspeptics and consumptives and, following the example of Mr. Emerson, renounced his calling for ever. By that time even the pale Unitarianism thinning out into paler doubt was no longer tenable with him. He confessed that while he felt the Divine goodness more and more, he believed that it was a mistake to preach any specific creed or doctrine, and he begged them to release him from their service. . . . His people parted with him in terms of regret as delicate as they were awkward, and their love followed him.[55]

The Reverend Sewell of *The Rise of Silas Lapham* appears again in *The Minister's Charge* (1887), this time as the victim of his own mistaken kindness in encouraging the poetic ambitions of an ungifted rural youth, Lemuel Barker. Sewell preaches eloquently, and more definitely than Howells had enunciated it before, the gospel of the duty of the socially and materially advantaged to help their less fortunate fellow-men. His sermons gain point for the reader through the harsh realism of Howells' accounts of the Boston of the poor as he follows Lemuel's experiences through most of the book. But Sewell's attempts to put his doctrine into practice, in the case of Lemuel, are largely ineffective; and the novel as a whole is most notable for its dramatization of his failures, and of the limitations of institutional Christianity in regard to the actual application of Christ's teachings in the modern world.

Annie Kilburn (1889) is a more forceful parable of the same truth. Annie Kilburn, a wealthy woman who after many years in Europe returns to her girlhood home in South Hatboro, Massachusetts, and is inspired by the teaching and example of Rev. Peck to try to "do good" for working people of the newly industrialized town, is one of Howells' most fully realized feminine characters. Peck is no more effective than Sewell, but he is far more fully committed; he preaches Christ's example in such practical matters as wages, housing, and social relations, and loses his pastorate as a result. He dies in a railroad accident as he is about to undertake a project in cooperative housing. Peck is not idealized, however. He is courageous but in some ways stupid, and he fails to recognize his duty to his own child. This inadequately appreciated novel pointed the way toward the greater achievement, at the beginning of the next decade, in *A Hazard of New Fortunes*.

After *The Undiscovered Country*, then—in the 1880's— Howells provided only limited insight into his personal religious views and experience in his fiction, and he ignored in it the problem of personal immortality almost entirely. This reticence is largely paralleled in his reviews of the period, with a single very notable exception. This is in the "Editor's Study" for April, 1886, in which Howells uses reviews of two books by John Fiske, *The Destiny of Man* and *The Idea of God as*

Affected by Modern Knowledge, as prefatory to the announcement of his discovery of Tolstoi. The article is so pertinent to our inquiry that it demands quotation at length:

> The evolution of a believer in a God sensible to human need and in the life hereafter, from a metaphysician so purely scientific as Mr. John Fiske, is certainly one of the most interesting phases of Darwinism. Of course it proves nothing very conclusive, but for the moment one does not realize this; and if one's heart is not altogether at rest in orphanage and nonentity, as we suppose very few hearts are, it comforts, it encourages. So many scientists have denied so many things that it is hard to understand that Science herself denies nothing, to begin with, but seeks only and always to know the truth. . . . he arrives at the conviction that "the everlasting source of phenomena is none other than the infinite Power that makes for righteousness." . . . This will not seem much to those who are accustomed to accept God from authority, and who have always believed what they were bid (which is no bad thing, perhaps, and seems to save time); but it is a good deal as the result of reasoning that begins and ends outside of all authority except that of fact scientifically ascertained; and it is still more as an induction of the Darwinian theory, which teaches Mr. Fiske . . . that a "stage of civilization will be reached in which human sympathy shall be all in all, and the spirit of Christ shall reign supreme through the whole length and breadth of the earth."[56]

In the same department for May, 1888, Howells reviewed H. C. Lea's *History of the Inquisition of the Middle Ages.* A change in Howells' attitude toward Roman Catholicism was already evident in *Tuscan Cities,* the book of travels published in 1885, and this change is also demonstraetd by one comment in the review:

> It is the fate of the Roman Catholic church to bear forever before the world the chief burden of a sin which is no more Catholic than it is Protestant. The means of persecution were first at hand with that Church and its hand was strongest; that is all. . . . Whenever one man hates another for his opinions, there the spirit of the Inquisition is as rife as ever.[57]

William Dean Howells

VI

The year of 1885 was marked by the publication of *The Rise of Silas Lapham* and by negotiation of a new contract with Harper and Brothers which guaranteed a comfortable income, ample time for the writing of fiction, and complete freedom in a new department—"The Editor's Study" in *Harper's Magazine,* previously quoted—to choose what books he would review and to say what he liked about them. All this must have seemed to Howells, as he neared his fiftieth birthday, fruition of his highest hopes. Yet the personal experiences of the next few years were such as to fully justify Edwin H. Cady's calling them, in his perceptive biography, "The Black Time."

First came the crisis in which, above all others, Howells demonstrated the courage of his convictions. In a nationwide epidemic of strikes in 1886—chiefly for the eight-hour day—that at the McCormick Harvester Plant on Chicago's West Side had been particularly marked by violence. When strikers had been beaten and killed by police, Chicago anarchists called a meeting of protest at Haymarket Square. A bomb was thrown, several policemen were killed and others wounded. In the resulting hysteria all professed anarchists in Chicago were rounded up; seven were convicted and sentenced to death, and four were actually hanged, though no evidence was introduced to show that any of them had any direct agency in the bombing. The case was appealed and the conviction sustained. After trying in vain to get the collaboration of such professed liberals as George William Curtis and John Greenleaf Whittier, Howells wrote in November of his fiftieth year, 1887, a vigorous letter of protest and secured its publication in the *New York Tribune* and the *Chicago Tribune.* It was met by a storm of violent abuse. Though history has abundantly confirmed Howells' view of the trial, his public expression of it required extraordinary courage and carried with it extreme distress.

But this was not by any means the severest suffering of this "black time." During the year 1885–86 Winifred, Howells' first child, was to have been presented to Boston society. She had grown into personal beauty, and was sensitive and creative in artistic interests. Howells had bought a house in fashionable Beacon Street and prepared it for festivities. But Winifred's health had been increasingly precarious, and when the time came neither she nor her mother was able to face a winter of parties. Winifred's condition fluctuated between hopeful gain in strength and sudden collapse followed by prolonged debility. Of course the best of physicians were consulted. They told the Howellses that Winifred's troubles were "basically moral." As Cady summarizes their advice, "She must be forced to eat, to exercise, to make herself healthy again."[58] Finally the doctors decided that she must be separated from her parents, placed in a sanitarium. She was at a "rest home," isolated from her family when on March 3, 1889, she died suddenly—two days after Howells' fifty-second birthday.

But even the lonely death was not the worst that Howells and his wife had to bear. The physicians discovered—presumably by autopsy—and ill-advisedly told her parents that Winifred's illness had been organic after all, not mental, and the whole course of treatment had been wrong. The father and mother were left with an intense and lasting sense of guilt for what they had done, however innocently, to their beloved child. Elinor Howells did not recover from the blow. Though she lived on for twenty years, unfailing in her devotion to her husband and younger children, she was never really well again.

It was in the shadow of this prolonged tragedy that Howells wrote his greatest novel. *A Hazard of New Fortunes* (1890) grew out of plans for a series of sketches of New York life which Howells proposed to Harper and Brothers in 1888, while *Annie Kilburn* was still appearing serially. In it Howells evidently intended to embody and apply to the metropolis his new social insights, which he had sharpened by his reading of Tolstoi and which he had applied to a New England small town in the preceding novel. As Howells worked on the material, in intervals punctuated by the recurring crises of Winifred's illness, the sketches grew to be his longest novel and the richest in strongly individualized characters, the most complex in organization, and the most positive in dramatized intention of his whole career. The book was completed during the final year of Winifred's illness; serialization in *Harper's Magazine* began three weeks after her death. Howells himself was well aware of flaws in the book. He wrote to Thomas Wentworth Higginson in 1891:

> . . . you are quite right in your criticism of the opening passages: long stretches of carpentry where I arrived at little or nothing of the real edifice. I may tell you that they were done when we were losing, when we lost, our Winny, and that I was writing in the stress because I *must*. Afterwards I could not change them.[59]

Overtly religious materials in *A Hazard of New Fortunes* are concentrated in the last fifty pages of the novel. They arise largely from the fact that Howells has created in this novel the only veritable Christ-figure in all of his fiction: not by the use of arbitrary and artificial symbols, but in his whole organic conception and authentic realization of Conrad Dryfoos—his lifelong self-giving, his forgivenesses of his father's domination and cruelty, and his innocent death. The significance of this character in Howells' intention is made unmistakably clear in the comments of March, the author's spokesman and "center of illumination" for the novel. When he asks, "And Conrad . . . what was *he* punished for?" his wife gives the answer: "He? . . . he suffered for the sins of others."[60] Of the incident in the streetcar strike, in which Conrad has been killed by a stray bullet while trying to defend his father's foe, Lindau, from the brutality of a policeman, March says:

> ". . . But Conrad—yes, he had some business there; it was his business to suffer there for the sins of others. Isabel, we can't throw aside that old doctrine of the Atonement yet. The life of Christ, it wasn't only in healing the sick and going about to do good; it was suffering for the sins of others. That's as great a mystery as the mystery of death. Why

should there be such a principle in the world? But it's been felt, and more or less dumbly, blindly recognized ever since Calvary. If we love mankind, pity them, we even wish to suffer for them. . . ."[61]

In the character of Margaret Vance, wealthy and well-born, who devotes her life to social service and is last seen in the novel in the garb of a sisterhood, Howells dramatizes—not so firmly as one could wish—the Tolstoian example he so much admired of the renunciation of wealth and ease for love of mankind. In the conversation previously quoted, in a significant speech addressed to his children, March refers to the matter of personal immortality in terms which seem to come directly out of Howells' sorrow over the mistaken treatment of Winifred:

> "Children . . . death is an exile that no remorse and no love can reach. Remember that, and be good to everyone here on earth, for your longing to retrieve any harshness or unkindness to the dead will be the very ecstasy of anguish to you. . . ."[62]

A few chapters earlier in the novel, March has expressed clearly to his wife and his partner, Fulkerson, his belief in immortality —this in connection with the death of Conrad: "When I think what we can be if we must, I can't believe the least of us shall finally perish."[63]

Beginning with the first anniversary of Winifred's death, Howells serialized a novella, *The Shadow of a Dream*, which appeared in book form immediately after serialization was completed. In it Howells used for the first time a type of literary material which he was to continue to work with for many years, in various forms and with varying degrees of success. This was the field of the supernatural, the extrasensory, and the occult. In exploring his memories for the material of *A Boy's Town*, which was being serialized at the same time, Howells perhaps had recognized the large part which such experience had played in his boyhood, as was noted early in this essay. Both these revived memories and some experience (not known to be recorded) related to Winifred's death may have contributed to the power of *The Shadow of a Dream,* Howells' most effective short work of fiction. The story is built upon the effects of an ailing husband's recurring dream that his wife and a young clergyman who is their closest friend are in love and are only waiting for his death to free them for marriage. When after the husband's death they ultimately learn what the dream was, they part. The possible existence of a guilty love below the consciousness of both wife and friend—who have no such feeling knowingly—and its possible impact on the dreaming mind of the diseased husband are problems which Howells suggests but does not resolve. They would be readily susceptible of solution in Swedenborgian terms; and the persistent interest of Howells in such problems is one of several indications of the degree to which Swedenborgianism still entered into his creative life.

In December of 1890 Howells wrote to Howard Pyle, a Swedenborgian, an enthusiastic comment on the manuscript of Pyle's story *In Tenebras,* calling it "true, because it is consonant with the most reasonable conjecture of the life hereafter. . . . it interests me all the more because I have had it in mind myself to write a story of the future life . . . using Swedenborg for my *entourage.*" The letter continues: "I do not always feel sure that I shall live again, but when I wake at night the room seems dense with spirits."[64] The following month Howells wrote to Pyle again. After expressing his thanks for the gift of some drawings, he again speaks freely: "[William] James is one of the few scientific men who do not seem to snub one's poor humble hopes of a hereafter."[65]

In the years immediately following Winifred's death, while Howells was reaching gropingly toward a renewal of faith in personal immortality, external events—the Homestead Strike of 1892 among them—were pushing him toward more positive formulation of his beliefs in regard to social and industrial matters. All students of Howells are indebted to Clara Marburg Kirk for the illumination, in her *W. D. Howells, Traveler from Altruria, 1889–1894* (New Brunswick, New Jersey, 1962), of a period in Howells' career which had been puzzling. For two years after Winifred's death, Howells and his wife lived in Boston. There Howells was associated with a group of able men who called themselves Christian Socialists and were agitating for social and economic reforms on the basis of the practical application of the teachings of Christ to the problems of the day. Howells held major reservations, expressed in a letter to his father on April 27, 1890: "The Christian Socialists are more to my mind than the Nationalists; but I doubt if I shall openly act with either for the present. The C.S. have loaded up with the creed of the church, the very terms of which revolt me. . . ."[66] As events and conditions worsened in the years approaching the depression of 1893, their impact on Howells became more insistent. When he returned to New York he became coeditor of *The Cosmopolitan* with John Brisben Walker, who was trying to build that previously merely popular magazine to a position of eminence. Mrs. Kirk has shown that Howells was impelled to take this step by his hearty approval of Walker's social and economic ideas and his intention of making *The Cosmopolitan* a major forum for their presentation. Their editorial association lasted only six months, though Howells continued to write for the magazine. In 1892 and 1893 *The Cosmopolitan* carried a series of "Letters of an Altrurian Traveler" (published in book form under the title *A Traveler from Altruria* in 1894) in which the "Traveler" pointedly contrasted conditions in America with those in his native "Altruria," where property was held in common and the teachings of Christ were the actual rules of conduct.

Use of a fictional account of an ideal commonwealth for the purpose of social criticism had been recently established anew by the popular reception of Edward Bellamy's *Looking Backward* (1888), and more recently by William Morris's *News from Nowhere* (1891). The crucial difference between these and other utopian fictions of the time, and the work of Howells, was the strong emphasis by Howells on the application of Christian ethics. The impact of the "Letters" was heightened by the inescapable general recognition of the widespread human suffering which accompanied the onset of the depression of 1893. In a second series of the "Letters" in *The Cosmopolitan,* Howells wrote with extreme candor and deep feeling of the condition of the poor in New York City. Some of the essays of this second series were included, in revised and greatly softened form, in the volume *Impressions and Experiences* (1896). Others were used in *Through the Eye of the Needle* (1907), together with an introduction extolling with sharp irony the improved conditions in America, and a new second part. This second part consists of a series of letters in which an American woman who has married the Traveler and returned with him to Altruria describes the life there. As Mrs. Kirk observes, these last of the Altrurian writings have a definitely dreamlike tone, suggesting that though Howells retained in his heart the ideal of Christian socialism, in his mind he had ceased to hope for its realization.

VII

Though Howells took an active part in the campaign for social justice in the early 1890's, he was too wise to think that improved conditions would automatically produce improved people. He was too profound and too honest a thinker (and perhaps too irretrievably a Swedenborgian) to have unqualified confidence in reform as a cure-all. In the two major novels which followed *A Hazard of New Fortunes* in the 1890's, *The Quality of Mercy* (1892) and *The Landlord at Lion's Head* (1897)—both too little appreciated by most modern readers— he attacked this problem of social determinism versus free will and explored it at length. One of the most interesting aspects of *The Quality of Mercy* is the way in which social and personal guilt are presented in relation to each other. The story is built around a trusted businessman's theft of a large sum of money and his flight to Canada to escape punishment. The view that society is to blame for defalcations is fully presented in an article by a journalist, Maxwell, and in conversations of other characters. Yet the idea of personal responsibility, the concept of guilt, and the necessity for expiation dominate the book unmistakably. One is compelled to conclude that Howells was not a social determinist to the extent of relieving such a man as Northwick, the embezzler, from real responsibility and guilt, though he recognized fully the degree to which mistaken values in society do place handicaps and temptations in the way of the individual.

The story of Northwick's flight and ultimate return holds particular interest for our purpose. Not only is it a narrative of guilt and expiation—the expiation finally accepted as an inner decision rather than imposed by outward circumstance—but Howells has employed so many references to God and Providence, and has used the character of Père Etienne, a young Canadian priest, in such ways as to give this central portion of the story a positive religious quality exceptional in Howells. Twice Northwick attempts in his own mind to make a bargain with Providence. Soon after his arrival in Canada he visits a Catholic church and with difficulty resists an impulse to hang the money belt containing the stolen money on an altar. He experiences a conviction that he must "die to the world," and flees into the interior of Canada. When he meets the saintly young priest, he is immediately afraid: one is reminded of the words of Mauriac, "when the devil has his eye on someone, he fears nothing more than that he should meet a saint."[67] The young priest's attitude and motivation are explicitly religious, and his concern for Northwick's soul is profound. Northwick experiences at one point a powerful impulse toward confession and is disappointed in himself when he does not achieve it. Finally he starts back for the United States to accept his punishment. Though he dies suddenly in the course of the journey, the ethical conflict of the book with its deep religious implications has been resolved. As a frequently hostile contemporary critic of Howells, William Morton Payne, observed: "A man like the defaulter Northwick . . . is presumably possessed of something in the nature of the soul, and this is what, with admirable success, Mr. Howells has set himself to discover."[68]

William Dean Howells

In *The Landlord at Lion's Head* (1897) Howells again attacked the problem of personal accountability for conduct but treated it with notably less recognition of distinctly religious values than he had shown in *The Quality of Mercy*. In the later novel the inquiry is focused on the character of Jeff Durgin, who is quite possibly Howells' most completely achieved character. He is shown as a boy who enjoys frightening younger children, as a "jay" at Harvard who takes a savage pleasure in humiliating those who claim social superiority, and ultimately as a ruthless, successful and prospectively wealthy man of business. In a series of debates with the point-of-view character of the novel, a painter named Westover, Jeff repeatedly denies individual responsibility, insists that the good or bad effects of what a person does depend wholly on chance. He does not argue for social determinism, does not deny freedom of choice, but does deny personal responsibility for the effect of conduct on others. Since Howells' sympathy is clearly with Westover in these debates, the novel may be seen as confirming, in less definitely religious terms, the emphasis of *The Quality of Mercy* on the individual's moral and ethical responsibility.

The recurring public concern over the possibility of communication with the spirits of the dead, which marked almost the whole span of Howells' lifetime, became especially prominent in the 1890's and early 1900's with the founding of the Society for Psychical Research and the avowal of interest by Sir Oliver Lodge and other prominent scientists. This contemporary interest is reflected in *The Landlord at Lion's Head*, in which a full chapter is devoted to an account of an experiment with automatic writing, using a planchette. Westover is a witness of the experiment, the results of which are—predictably—ambiguous.

A short and slight novel which immediately preceded *The Landlord at Lion's Head, The Day of Their Wedding* (1896), is interesting in its revelation of the degree to which some of the doctrines of Swedenborg were still potent in Howells' thinking at that time. A young Shaker couple, who have decided to leave the celibate community and be married, go to a minister who is unnamed and unidentified as to denomination. In counseling them to give full and profound consideration to the step they are about to take, this minister gives the young Shakers Swedenborg's teaching on marriage in positive and undiluted form.

Howells' most definite and positive expression of religious experience and attitude in the decade following the death of Winifred is in an essay disarmingly entitled "True, I Talk of Dreams," in the issue of *Harper's Magazine* for May, 1895. It shows that for all his sincere dedication to the cause of Christian Socialism and the realization of Christian ideals in contemporary society, the constant and ultimate religious problem for Howells was that of personal immortality. Howells wrote:

> I think very few of us who have lost their beloved have failed to receive some sign or message from them in dreams, and often it is of deep and abiding consolation. It may be that this is our anguish compelling the echo of love out of the darkness where nothing is, but it may be that there is something there, which answers to our throe with pity and with longing like our own. Again, no one knows, but in a matter impossible of definite solution, I will not refuse the comfort which belief can give. Unbelief can be no gain in it, and belief no loss.[69]

VIII

After the death of Susie Clemens while her parents were still in England on their way home from a trip around the world, Howells wrote to Twain on September 13, 1896. After recalling Twain's sensitive kindness to him after the death of Winifred, he said:

> As for the gentle creature who is gone, the universe is all a crazy blunder if she is not somewhere in conscious blessedness that knows and feels your love. The other night I woke to think, "Why do we bother trying to conceive a state of being beyond this which shall be different from this, when there will really be nothing but something like an earthly separation to bridge over?" You are parted from her a little

longer, and that's all, and the joint life will go on when you meet on the old terms, but with the horror and pain gone forever. This is the easiest and the most reasonable thing to believe, and it is not to be refused because it is so old and simple.[70]

Though it is clear that Howells was keenly aware of the elements of delusion and self-delusion in the excitement about spiritism in the late 1890's and early 1900's, it is also clear that the question of personal immortality was central for him in this period, with gravity and immediacy accruing from the impact of Winifred's death, the continuing debility of his wife, and his own sense of advancing years. The finest creative expression of this concern took the form of poetry, as had the immediate response to Winifred's death: that of a brief poetic drama published in May, 1900, in *Harper's Monthly*, under the title "Father and Mother, A Mystery." The father and mother, alone in their house after the funeral of their only daughter, experience together the conviction that the daughter is present with them, communicating to them something of reassurance and of love. They cannot express in words what she has told them; if they could, the mother says,

> They would be such as mediums use to cheat
> Their dupes with, or to make them cheat themselves.[71]

Yet they are mutually convinced of the validity of their experience. Howells returned to the same parents in "The Mother," published in 1902; here the dialogue considers the mystery and the mystical significance of birth, as a young mother and her husband explore it when they are first alone together after their first child, a daughter, has been born. Yet a third scene, published in 1906, shows the same couple alone in their house after their daughter's wedding. They speak of their attitudes when the child was born and recognize their loss of faith since then. The mother says:

> There is no other world, now, as there was
> Then, where the mystery could shape itself—

213

No hitherto, as there is no hereafter.
We have destroyed it for ourselves and her,
And love for all of us is as much a thing
Of earth as death itself.[72]

The three episodes, rearranged so that the first published (that of the daughter's death) stands last, became the verse drama published in book form in 1909 under the title, *The Mother and the Father.* Walter J. Meserve is clearly right in calling this "one of the most meaningful of Howells' dramatic writings," in his commendation of its "frequently strong and moving blank verse," and in his recognition of its Swedenborgian elements.[73]

IX

The tenor of Howells' fiction in the first decade of the twentieth century reflects the degree of his interest in various approaches to the problem of personal immortality. He wrote a series of stories, published serially between 1901 and 1907, and largely collected in *Questionable Shapes* (1903) and *Between the Dark and the Daylight* (1907), which deal with various aspects of the occult and supernatural or at least with extrasensory experience. For several of these stories he employed a uniform method of narration. Three friends meet at their club: the suggestively named Wanhope, a psychologist and author of a book called *Quests of the Occult,* tells a story which involves some aspect or element of the supernatural or extrasensory, and the others question him and make comments. The approach and treatment are always provisional, sometimes mildly satirical. The stories in these volumes attest to Howells' sustained interest during this decade in the possibility of communication with the dead, but they add very little to his total achievement as a writer. The most interesting and effective example of this continuing interest appears, somewhat startlingly, in *The Flight of Pony Baker* (1902), a delightful reworking of the material of

214

William Dean Howells

A Boy's Town in a series of related incidents, some of which appeared serially in *The Youth's Companion*. "The Fourth-of-July Boy," printed in *Harper's Weekly* for July 5, 1902, appeared as Chapter 7 of the book under the title "How Frank Baker Spent the Fourth at Pawpaw Bottom, and Saw the Fourth of July Boy." Frank Baker is an older and more responsible boy than Pony, and in this chapter he and a friend go to the farm of a boy named Dave Black to spend the Fourth. They help haul fence rails, eat mulberries, get caught in a thundershower and take shower baths, build a raft and go swimming.

> It was while they were in the tree that something happened which happened four times in all that day, if it really happened; nobody could say afterwards whether it had or not.[74]

The "something" that may have happened is that the boys have had recurringly the sense that a fourth boy is with them, sharing in their play. As the boys watch the fireworks with their parents from the Bakers' porch that evening, a neighbor, Mrs. Fogle, whose son of their age has died during the preceding year, comes over.

> "It seems pretty hard my Wilford couldn't been having a good time with the rest today. He was always such a Fourth-of-July boy."
> "But he's happy where he is, Mrs. Fogle," said Mrs. Baker, gently.
> "Well, I know he'd give anything to been here with the boys today—I don't care where he is. And he's been here, *too;* I just know he has; I've felt him, all day long, teasing at me to let him go off with your Frank and Jake, here. . . ."[75]

After Frank Baker has told the story of the strange experiences, Pony's father and mother discuss it earnestly:

> ". . . How in the world do you account for it?"
> "I don't account for it," said Pony's father. ". . . if it was *one* boy that saw the fourth boy it might be a simple case of lying. . . . But as they all three saw the boy at different times, why, it's . . . another thing."

215

". . . Do you believe that the child longed so to be back here that—"

"Ah, who knows? There's something very strange about all that. But we can't find our way out, except by the short-cut of supposing that nothing of the kind happened."

. . . Pony's mother drew a long sigh. "Well, I know what *I* shall always think," she said.[76]

This is the end of the story, one which with its wealth of homely detail and its tight yet simple and natural construction has far more impact than any of Howells' other fictions of the supernatural.

Howells' two major novels of the fifth decade of his creative life, *The Kentons* (1902) and *The Son of Royal Langbrith* (1904), offer relatively sparse indication of the active interest in religious problems which is evidenced by his other writings of this period. In *The Kentons,* religious reference is for the most part limited to his mildly derisory treatment of the religious position of Rev. Breckon (the very Howellsian "hero" of the book) and his congregation—"that pied flock, where every shade and dapple of doubt, from heterodox Jew to agnostic Christian, foregathered, as it had been said, in the misgiving of a blessed immortality."[77] Breckon tries to explain his ministerial function to Ellen Kenton:

". . . I'm at the head of a society, you know, ethical or socio-logical, or altruistic, whatever you choose to call it, which hasn't any very definite object of worship, and yet meets every Sunday for a sort of worship; and I have to be in the pulpit. . . ."[78]

The theme of *The Son of Royal Langbrith* is ethical, and in his unpublished preface Howells said that he had consulted a "dear and valued friend," a clergyman, as to "whether it was better or worse for other men that a man's evils should remain unknown when no specific purpose could be served by their discovery." But the story of Royal Langbrith's villainy and cruelty, of his son's infatuated devotion to his memory, and of the effect of these forces on the central character of Dr. Anther and others is consistently held within a moral and ethical this-world field of reference. Even in the portrayal of Rev. Enderby, the clergyman who becomes Anther's confidante, there is little of specific religious meaning in this skillfully executed and largely unrecognized novel.

A single passage in a lesser but fine short work of fiction, *Fennel and Rue,* published in 1908 (after the feeble *Miss Bellard's Inspiration,* 1905, and the previously noted *Through the Eye of the Needle,* 1907), bears testimony to the continuing insistent presence in Howells' mind of the question of personal immortality. This passage appears early in the book, without close connection to its context, and is marked by distinctively solemn and stately structure and cadence:

> Continuity is so much the lesson of experience that in the course of a life by no means long it becomes the instinctive expectation. The event that has happened will happen again; it will prolong itself in a series of recurrences by which each one's episode shares in the unending history of all. The sense of this is so pervasive that humanity refuses to accept death itself as final. In the agonized affections, the shattered hopes, of those who remain, the severed life keeps on unbrokenly, and when time and reason prevail, at least as to the life here, the defeated faith appeals for fulfilment to another world, and the belief of immortality holds against the myriad years in which none of the numberless dead have made an indisputable sign in witness of it.[79]

Roman Holidays, one of the best of Howells' books of travel, also published in 1908, carried abundant evidence of the author's deepening religious feeling during this decade. For large parts of the book Howells was returning to materials treated in the earlier *Italian Journeys* and *Tuscan Cities;* and a striking element in the book as a whole is the author's extensive and often sympathetic observation of aspects of Roman Catholicism. Of the miraculous Bambino in the Church of Ara Coeli he wrote:

> To other eyes than those of faith it has the effect of a life-

size but not life-like doll, piously bedizened and jewelled over, but rather ill-humored looking. . . . To the eyes in which its sickbed visits have dried the tears it must wear an aspect of heavenly pity and beauty; and I am very willing to believe that these are the eyes which see it aright.[80]

On his return journey from Italy Howells stopped at Monte Carlo and visited the casino. His comment is interesting and characteristic:

> The players were of the average of the spectators in dress and carriage, but in the heavy atmosphere of the rooms, which was very hot and very bad, they all alike looked dull. At a psychological moment it suddenly came to me in their presence, that if there were such a place as hell, it must be very dull, like that, and that the finest misery of perdition must be the stupid dulness of it. For some unascertained reason, but probably from a mistaken purpose of ornament, there hung over the centre of each table, almost down to the level of the player's heads, lengths of large-linked chains, and it was imaginable, though not very probable, that if any of the lost souls rose violently up, or made an unseemly outcry, or other rebellious demonstration, those plain, quiet men, the agents of the Administration, would fling themselves upon him or her, and bind them with those chains, and cast them away into such outer darkness as could be symbolized by the shade of the terrace trees. The thing was improbable, as I say, but not impossible, if there is truth in Swedenborg's relation that the hells are vigilantly policed, and from time to time put in order by angels detailed for that purpose. To be sure the plain, quiet men did not look like angels, and the Administration of which they were agents, could not, except in its love of order, be likened to any celestial authority.[81]

As the decade neared its end, Howells gave more active and fuller expression to his interest in the problem of personal immortality. At that time series of related articles—treatments of a single subject by different hands—were favored in popular magazines; and at some time prior to November 16, 1908, Elizabeth Jordan, the editor of *Harper's Bazar*, talked with Howells about the idea of such a series on the future life. On the date mentioned Howells wrote to Miss Jordan to tell her that he had talked with Mr. Duneka, the head of the Harper company, about the suggestion, and that though he "received it grimly at first, he seemed to become more and more interested. . . ." Howells went on:

> The more I think of it the more it interests me, and I believe you can do a great and useful and merciful thing in realizing the notion. It should be a sort of Counsel of Consolation, and people should be asked to write, as far as they will, from their *experiences* as well as their opinions, and to keep in mind that they are addressing those in immediate bereavement. I do not see why a kindly agnostic should not say something comforting to sorrow. But in the hour of grief there is a reviving faith, which has *authority,* and must be respected. . . .[82]

There follows a page of detailed advice on editorial policy and procedure.

Apparently Howells wrote his article for the series immediately, for on December 18, 1908, he sent Miss Jordan "two pages which I will put in their right place when I get the proof of my paper. I hope that will be soon." On January 13, 1909, he asked for revised proof and gave further editorial suggestions. In subsequent letters of January 15, January 27, and May 13, 1909, Howells made a total of seven suggestions for contributors to "our 'Counsel,'" as he called the series in the letter of January 27. Of the seven, Henry Mills Alden and Henry James were among the actual contributors. When Howells' proposed title for the series and ultimate book, "A Counsel of Consolation," was shelved in favor of *In After Days: Thoughts on the Future Life,* Howells used the phrase as the title for his article in the book publication.

The title is apt. Howells' relatively brief article is indeed addressed to the recently bereaved, as he had urged that all the articles should be; and it is quiet, unpretentious, sympathetic. Howells does not argue, expound, or even assert, as the other contributors do in varying degree. His article is "counsel" in the precise sense, very wise and very specific. He says:

> I cannot speak to the stricken from the absolute faith which some others can speak from. I am of those who patiently wait for the fulfilment of the hopes which Christianity has worded from the Greek philosophers rather than from the Hebrew prophets. Once I asked my father, a man whose whole life was informally but deeply religious, whether he kept the vivid interest in his doctrine which he once had. He was an old man, and he answered me, "Youth is the time to believe, age is the time to trust." Now I am myself an old man, and more than ever I feel the wisdom of this saying. There are many things that I doubt, but few that I deny; where I cannot believe, there I often trust; and as all faith is mystical, I would have the bereaved trust their mystical experiences for much truth which they cannot affirm.[83]

It is interesting to note that one of the contributors to the symposium apparently not suggested by Howells, the historian John Bigelow, cites the revelations of Swedenborg as the most positive proof we possess of life after death, and quotes them.

X

On May 6, 1910, Elinor Howells died. To William James, Howells wrote on June 8, 1910: "I wish I could believe in a meeting with her, but she believed in none, and how can I?"[84] On the next day he wrote to his brother Joseph: "I do not know whether I believe that we shall meet again."[85]

Howells was now seventy-three years old. In the final decade of life left to him he was to maintain both the volume and quality of his productive achievement. He was to write three fine novels, two travel books and a fictional "fantasy" with elements of travel experience, and a volume of autobiography, in addition to an undiminishing stream of magazine articles, introductions to books, and miscellaneous writings. A striking general characteristic of these works, from the point of view of religious expression and implication, is a notable increase in emphasis on Swedenborg and in direct reference to his writings. We shall see, too, that from the despair expressed in the letters quoted above, at the time of his wife's death, there is a slow and uncertain return to a hope of immortality. A little more than a year after the letters to James and his brother Joseph, Howells wrote to his friend T. S. Perry: "Well, it is not a bad world; but I wish I could see Mrs. Perry to have her talk to me about the next. Some things that she said did highly hearten me."[86] Early in 1912 he wrote to Sylvester Baxter about Valdes, the Spanish novelist whom he had recently met in Spain: "I said I liked his coming back to the notion of life hereafter. 'Yes,' he said and he touched his gray hairs, 'one *must* do that when he comes to these.' "[87] To his brother Joseph, two years after the letter to him quoted above, he wrote from Kittery Point, Maine, where he and his wife had spent so many summers: "It is terribly strange here without Elinor. I miss her more and more as time passes, and *realize* that I shall never see her again unless I somehow, somewhere, go to her. She will not return to me. Death, which parted us, can alone unite us."[88]

Howells' achievement in his last decade as a novelist began with *New Leaf Mills* (1913): a fictional treatment of the experience Howells had presented in the frankly autobiogaphical *My Year in a Log Cabin* (1893), with sensitive realization of the frontier rural setting and firm establishment of memorable characters. Nearly all of these characters are clearly drawn from life. Howells himself, as the second son of the family, is scarcely developed at all and is known only by his nickname of "the Dreamer"; but his older brother, his father and mother, the miller, and others are readily identifiable with approximate counterparts in the real experience. Portrayal of the father—gentle, sensitive, generous, and incorrigibly hopeful in the face of hardships and reverses—dominates the book. No doubt he is very like Howells' own father, and the book may be in one sense a tribute to the memory of that deeply loved man, who had died twenty years before.

The home at New Leaf Mills is Swedenborgian, like Howells'

own, with the same books and the framed portrait of Swedenborg; the father's treatment of his family and his neighbors is based wholly on the doctrines. Perhaps most prominently stressed are his ideas of harmony and unity with nature, and his confidence in potential goodness in people, no matter how concealed or thwarted. The most effectively dramatized element in the book is the hatred of the miller for the New Leaf family, which the father finally discovers to be rooted in a premonition that he will die within a year after their coming.

Based almost wholly as the book is on the facts of Howells' own early life, it is not surprising to find *New Leaf Mills* saturated with Swedenborgianism. What is surprising is to encounter Swedenborg at Stratford-on-Avon, in Howells' next work of fiction. *The Seen and the Unseen at Stratford-on-Avon* (1914) has the outer integument of a travel book, with detailed descriptions of the Birthplace, the Tomb, and the New House, of Stratford streets and shops, of tourists and teahouses. But the core of the book is straight Swedenborg. Early in his visit to Stratford the anonymous narrator meets Shakespeare and Bacon, who have been permitted to return to the earthly life and to attend the Festival. His conversations with them afford the main "action" of the book, and he learns from them much about the world of spirits, their occupations in it, and their attitudes toward their earthly lives. Shakespeare has forgiven everybody, is able to laugh at those who deny that he wrote plays. Bacon is still suffering remorse for his acceptance of bribes. The tone of the whole work is light and playful; but its fidelity to the letter and spirit of Swedenborg's revelations is striking.

Most careful readers of Howells have recognized *The Leatherwood God* (1916) as a distinguished work of fiction. I agree with Edwin Cady in counting it one of his best novels. But I do not agree with Arnold Fox that this book "can hardly be interpreted as anything but a veiled attack upon the dogmas of revealed religion,"[89] or with his pronouncement that: "When Dylks preaches 'I am God' . . . Howells is protesting against all the bigotry and parochialism of doctrinal religion."[90]

William Dean Howells

The Leatherwood God is strictly a historical novel. It is based upon a real incident of frontier life, that of an impostor who proclaimed himself God, gained adherents, disrupted a community, and eventually led his loyal followers on a fruitless pilgrimage. As a "Publisher's Note" explains, "The details are often invented, and the characters are all invented as to their psychological evolution, though some are based upon those of real persons. . . . Otherwise the story is effectively fiction."[91]

It is also effective fiction. Though the characters are drawn with heavy lines, with little of the delicate shading often found in Howells, they are also drawn with force and vitality; and their relative simplicity of outline is congruous with the crude and violent background of the raw frontier settlement. There is no wasted motion in this novel, no useless material. It is a study of a strange social and psychological phenomenon. But Howells' achievement is to make it the believable experience of real people, and the active vicarious experience of the reader.

It is true that Squire Braile is Howells' spokesman, as Fox suggests; and Squire Braile is a free-thinker. Howells had been saying what he thought about institutional religion for fifty years. He had often been harsh. But the paradigm of Joseph Dylks and his "Little Flock" is not one that Howells ever applied to the ministers and believers of his time, or ever would have. If the novel had been written by Twain—as it almost could have been with its vigorous and colorful portrayal of a primitive backwoods community—Fox's reading might be defensible. But for Howells it is grossly inaccurate; and to characterize *The Leatherwood God* as primarily a polemic, a work intended as propaganda, is gravely to underrate its integrity as a work of art.

In common with other works of Howells in this final decade, however, *The Leatherwood God* has obvious elements of Swedenborgianism. An interesting example is in what Squire Braile says to Nancy Billings, whom the impostor Dylks had married and deserted and now returns to tempt her to share in his

223

imposture. She appeals to Squire Braile, who has recently lost a beloved only son:

"Squire Braile, do you believe that God is good?"

"Ah, now, I'm more at home in a question like that. You might say that if He lets evil prevail, it's either because He can't help it, or because He don't care, or even because He thinks it's best for mankind to let them have their swing when they choose to do evil. I incline to think that's my idea. He's made man, we'll say, made him in His own image, and He's put him here in a world of his own, to do the best or the worst with it. The way I look at it, He doesn't want to keep interfering with man, but lets him play the fool or play the devil just as he's a mind to. But every now and then He sends him word. If we're going to take what the Book says, He sent him Word made flesh, once, and I reckon he sends him Word made Spirit whenever there's a human creature comes into the world, all loving and all unselfish—like your Joey, or—my—my Jimmy—"

The old man's voice died in his throat, and the woman laid her hand on his knee. He trembled to his feet, now. "When I think of such Spirits coming into this world, I'm not afraid of all the devils out of hell Dylksing around."[92]

Lionel Trilling is clearly right in his comment on Howells' last novel:

And the man is not easily done with who at eighty-three, in the year of his death, wrote that strange "realistic" idyl, The Vacation of the Kelwyns, with its paraphernalia of gypsies and dancing bears and its infinitely touching impulse to speak out against the negation and repression of emotion, its passionate wish to speak out for the benign relaxation of the will, for the reservation of moral judgment, for the charm of the mysterious, precarious little flame that lies at the heart of the commonplace. No one since Schiller has treated the genre of the idyl with the seriousness it deserves, yet even without a standard of criticism the contemporary reader will, I think, reach beyond the quaintness of the book to a sense of its profundity, or at least of its near approach to profundity. It will put him in mind of the early novels of E. M. Forster, and he will even be drawn to think of The

224

Tempest, with which it shares the theme of the need for general pardon and the irony of the brave new world: Howells, setting his story in the year of the centennial of the Declaration of Independence, is explicit in his belief that the brave newness of the world is all behind his young lovers.[93]

For the substance of this final work of fiction, not published until after his death, Howells returned to the Shaker community of *The Undiscovered Country* and his experience in spending a summer there with his family. Though a mildly interesting love story is interwoven, the chief line of interest in the book lies in the conflict between the Kelwyns (i.e. the Marches, i.e. the Howellses) and a local family, the Kites, to whom they have granted the use of the house and land they have bought from the Shakers in exchange for food and other services which the Kites prove unable or unwilling to provide. The theme of the novel is ethical rather than religious. It parallels the theme of complicity as developed most clearly in Howells' work of the 1880's and 1890's, and is summed up by Kelwyn, whose conscience is bothering him about the Kites, in a speech to his wife at the end of the book:

> "It doesn't seem my private debt that troubles me, but my private portion of the public debt which we all somehow owe to the incapable, the inadequate, the—the—shiftless."[94]

During the last decade of his life, Howells repeatedly voiced his thinking about religious matters in his magazine articles. One of his lighter approaches to the idea of the other world occurs in the "Easy Chair" essay in *Harper's Monthly* for November, 1912. The sketch purports to present the conversation of a group of intelligent people concerning current reports of the activity of mischievous spirits in the homes of a perfervid Methodist preacher and a Catholic priest. One speaker suggests: "Ghosts we have always with us, though from time to time we gather heart to condemn them, to ignore them; but now they begin to insist upon themselves, to demand recognition." On this suggestion Howells comments in the first person plural:

> Of course, we immediately, all of us, disabled our friend's judgment, and measureably his sanity. When a man so much as hints at the unity of life in this world and some world beyond it, at the idea in which the Christian religion began and has persisted for two thousand years, we cannot do less than think him some sort of fool.[95]

In January, 1915, the "Easy Chair" was devoted to an interview between "two lively sages, one in his last seventies, and the other in his first eighties," which arrives at this conclusion:

> When we all seemed to go down before agnosticism, we really didn't all go down, and even those who did held fast to the greatest of the virtues, Charity. Your central doctrine of the survival of the fittest interpreted itself at last as the survival of the kindest, of the truest to the claim of the humanity which had once seemed to deny itself in the interest of the missing link. Those patient poor who had the habit of enduring began for the first time to be considered scientifically as part of every other part of society. Faith came back with Charity and Hope for life hereafter, till now we seem to be in a way again of going forward in the old way, the religious way.[96]

In 1917 Howells wrote for the "Easy Chair" a review of Sir Oliver Lodge's *Raymond: or, Life After Death,* in which the author had described his communication with his dead son, killed in the war. While dealing gently with the father's grief, Howells asserted that the spirit world had been explored much more satisfactorily by Swedenborg. The article expressed an affirmative view of Swedenborg's revelations to such a degree that after Howells' death a group of New Church ministers procured the reprinting of the article as a pamphlet under the title *Immortality and Sir Oliver Lodge* and circulated it in their churches.

For Howells' final words on his religious position we must turn to the autobiographical volume published in 1916, *Years of My Youth,* and to an especially important magazine article.

William Dean Howells

For some one hundred pages of *Years of My Youth* Howells used material previously printed; the remaining 140 pages were new writing, and among these are the passages of specifically religious character. The grace, the humor, and the modesty (at one point he says, "I still have my masterpiece before me,"[97]) which mark Howells' writing throughout his life are richly present in this highly personal book. The references to his mother and father, his brothers and sisters, are warm and tender. Following a recollection of an incident of childhood, when he and his older brother—returning from an errand—stopped to rest and to enjoy the beauty of the summer night, Howells wrote a passage of positive affirmation:

> Such moments never pass; they are ineffaceable; their rapture immortalizes; from them we know that, whatever perishes, there is something in us that cannot die, that divinely regrets, divinely hopes.[98]

The book ends, however, on a note of wistful uncertainty, in a tribute to the memory of a long-dead friend of the Columbus days:

> If we somewhere should somewhen meet, perhaps it will be with a fond smile for the time when we were young and so glad together, with so little reason.[99]

In December, 1919, *Harper's Monthly* published an article by Howells entitled "Eighty Years and After." He died in May, 1920. Clearly this article had for Howells the nature and intention of a valedictory, a parting message. In it he says of God:

> The fear of His judgment has passed from me more and more as I have grown older; but at no time have I thought irreverently of Him or spoken so of Him. . . .[100]

He recalls the great blessing of his marriage:

> Love at its best means marriage, and is altogether the most beautiful thing in life. . . . Its perversion is the ugliest thing in life and the shamefulest.[101]

227

He draws once more a potent reflection from Swedenborg, in Swedenborgian terms:

> . . . nothing can be more terrible than remembering every-thing, as those newly arrived spirits do in the life to come, when their inner memories are explored for the things which have been dropped into their outer memories and comfort-ably forgotten.[102]

Finally he expresses the hope (rather than faith) in which we may believe he died and the best ground he has found for it:

> . . . the merciless morrow of death is coming. But why call it merciless? No one knows whether it is merciless or not. We know that somewhere there is love, the love that wel-comed us here, the love that draws us together in our pair-ing, that our children may live, the love in our children which shall see that their fathers and mothers do not die before their time, even if their time shall be delayed till eighty and after.[103]

6

Henry James

THIS CHAPTER CAN BE MUCH BRIEFER THAN THOSE THAT HAVE preceded it, for Henry James escaped the major impact of the forces which marked the religious dilemma of the nineteenth century and burdened the lives of his predecessors in American fiction. The primary reason for his escape was that his father had undergone that experience in extreme measure and passed beyond it before his second son was born. Overt or implicit treatment of religious controversy, religious doubt, or even religious faith as ordinarily defined is minimal in all James's thousands of pages of fiction.

Yet if we make our definition of religion broad enough, Henry James is the most religious of our six writers. In all but a handful of his stories and in all of his major novels, character and conduct are viewed and evaluated ultimately in relation to positive moral and ethical principles. These constitute an operative set of values hard to define in terms other than religious. The fragmentation of sects and the higher criticism of the Bible were irrelevant matters for James from his earliest experience. He rejected the claims of science insofar as these conflicted with his view of life, though he did finally come to grips with the problem of personal immortality, and emerged with a positive conviction.

THE DARKENED SKY

I find evidence of a sustained crisis, of recognition rather than redirection, in the religious life of James, and it centers in the year 1882, when both his mother and his father died. Before this time he had reviewed many books pertinent to religion, often rather frankly expressing his own views; and his records of travel experiences are rich in religious reference. After this time his commentary on the religious aspects of literature is guarded or nonexistent, and allusions to religious matters disappear from his travel records—except for *The American Scene,* written very late in his life. At the same time, clergymen and the professionally religious nearly vanish from his fiction. I believe that in his late thirties, James recognized more fully what was already implicit in the profound ethico-religious significance of *Washington Square* and *The Portrait of a Lady,* and thenceforth he consciously made his art the expression and evidence of his religion, and his religion his art.

Though I feel it unprofitable to try to discover in James's fiction specific details drawn from the writings of Swedenborg, or from his father's applications of these writings, it is clear that the basis of the religion Henry James expressed in his fiction is Swedenborgian, resting on conviction of the absolute reality of evil and of the essence of evil as selfishness. The range, the intensity, and the power of his dramatizations of these convictions constitute the ground for my assertion that Henry James can be viewed as the most religious of our writers. None of his major fictions, and very few of the minor ones, lack implicit or explicit statement of these beliefs concerning evil.

Henry James, Sr., the father of the novelist, was born to what was considered great wealth for that time and place. His father's estate of three million dollars, built largely by land speculation, was second only to that of John Jacob Astor. In early youth he was involved in an accident which resulted in the loss of a leg. His upbringing was very rigidly Calvinistic. He graduated with scholastic and social distinction from Union College, which his father had helped to found, and after a lapse of five years he entered the Princeton Theological Seminary, then a stronghold of Calvinism. But he withdrew after two years, became interested in social and religious controversy and a friend and critic of Emerson, and devoted himself for the rest of his life to writing and lecturing. While the family was living in England and when his son William was a little over two and Henry just past his first birthday, Henry James, Sr., underwent a sudden and intense experience of acute fear and mental pain involving the loss of all self-confidence and all sense of meaning in life. At a friend's suggestion he undertook reading of the works of Swedenborg and came to call this crucial experience, in Swedenborg's term, a "vastation." He did not adopt or accept all of Swedenborg's ideas, but the system of beliefs which he elaborated in successive books was strongly influenced by them. Major among these were the conception of self-assertion or selfishness as the major sin and the conviction of the reality of evil.

Their common inheritance of interest in Swedenborg may have been a minor factor in the mutual attraction between Henry James, Jr., and William Dean Howells in their early lives, and in their lifelong friendship. The interest of their respective fathers in Swedenborg was widely different, however. In the boyhood of Howells, as we have noted, Swedenborgian faith and study of Swedenborg's works was a consistent and important part of family life; for Henry James, Swedenborgianism was in early years merely an element of what the family called "father's ideas." Henry James, Sr., never was actually a Swedenborgian in the sense in which the term applies to William Cooper Howells.

It seems to me a mistake, or at least irrelevant to the major effect and meaning of the work, to attempt to apply to the fiction of Henry James in elaborate detail the symbology of his father, as Quentin Anderson has done in *The American Henry James*. After the elder James's death, Henry wrote to his brother William, concerning their father's religious system:

> I can't enter into it (much) myself—I can't be so theological, nor grant his extraordinary premises, nor throw myself

into conceptions of heavens and hells, nor be sure that the keynote of nature is humanity. . . .[1]

But I am convinced that the basis of the religious experience and position of the novelist, as defined in the general terms I have used above, is in harmony with his father's convictions and owes much to his influence.

According to the view of the senior Henry James, all churches and religious organizations of any kind were evil, deterring rather than contributing to the individual's true religious development. In accordance with his view of education, however, his children were encouraged to attend religious services of various denominations. To William and Henry as boys this breadth of privilege was not always pleasant. In *Notes of a Son and Brother* Henry wrote of his frequent embarrassment as a child on being asked "What church do you go to?" and of his sense of frustration, when he referred the question to his father, on being told that

> we could plead nothing less than the whole privilege of Christendom and that there was no communion, even that of the Catholics, even that of the Jews, even that of the Swedenborgians, from which we need find ourselves excluded.[2]

Later he relates, in the course of a most thoughtful and appreciative consideration of his father's influence:

> My father liked in our quite younger period to read us chapters from the New Testament and the Old, and I hope we liked to listen to them—though I recall their seeming dreary from their association with school practice; but that was the sole approach to a challenge of our complete freedom of inward, not less than our natural ingenuity of outward, experience. No other explicit address to us in the name of the Divine could, I see, have been made with any congruity—in face of the fact that invitations issued in all the vividest social terms, terms of living appreciation, of spiritual perception, of "human fellowship," to use the expression that was perhaps oftenest on his lips and his pen alike, were the very substance of the food supplied in the parental nest.[3]

Henry James

In his earlier manhood Henry James was a frequent churchgoer.

> At twenty he wrote from New York to T. S. Perry that he had
> filled two Sundays with the sermon of a Presbyterian preacher
> and visits to a revival meeting and to a "congregation of the
> new dispensation."[4]

But as a child he had been aware that the friends who frequented his father's home for conversation included few or no
clergymen. It is perhaps the effect of his father's condemnation
of churches in general and his low opinion of organized religion that men of the cloth appear but rarely in Henry James's
early fiction, and then in less than favorable light. In a very
early story, "Gisborne's Revenge," published in *The Galaxy* in
1868, a clergyman appears as a minor character, and a somewhat deprecatory comment is made upon him. In James's first
novel, *Watch and Ward,* serialized in *The Atlantic Monthly*
in 1871 though not published in book form until 1878, one of
the major characters is a clergyman: Hubert Lawrence, a cousin
of the novel's central character, Roger Lawrence. In this portrayal James records vividly his antagonism toward the superficial, fashionable, and worldly type of clergyman. Hubert is
passionate, eloquent—and utterly selfish. Though he is engaged
to another young woman, he makes love to Nora, the "ward" of
the punning title and is "cornered" and exposed. On his ministerial practice and pretensions James editorializes caustically:

> He fought the Devil as an irresponsible skirmisher, not as a
> sturdy gunsman planted beside a booming sixty-pounder.
> The clerical cloth, as Hubert wore it, was not unmitigated
> sable; and in spite of his cloth, such as it was, humanity
> rather than divinity got the lion's share of his attentions. . . .
> He was rather an idler in the walks of theology, and he was
> uncommitted to any very rigid convictions. He thought the
> old theological positions in very bad taste, but he thought the
> new theological negations in no taste at all. In fact, Hubert
> believed so vaguely and languidly in the Devil that there was
> but slender logic in his having undertaken the cure of souls.
> He administered his spiritual medicines in homeopathic doses.
> It had been maliciously said that he had turned parson be-

cause parsons enjoy peculiar advantages in approaching the fair sex.[5]

There is also a suggestion of the attitude of James (and his father) toward institutional religion in a minor element of this early and imperfect novel. A Mrs. Keith, who has rejected the marriage proposal of the major character, Roger Lawrence, becomes the friend of the ward, Nora, and takes her to Rome, where Mrs. Keith becomes a Catholic and tries to induce Nora to follow her example. Nora—like James himself—finds attractiveness in some aspects of Catholicism, but concludes that the attraction is superficial.

It is a very striking fact that after these early efforts, the problem of specific religious affiliation is not again raised in James's writing, and the species clergyman all but disappears from his pages. In the great multitude and variety of characters treated by James, men of the cloth are a tiny minority. The Reverend Mr. Brand of *The Europeans* is treated much less unkindly than is the clergyman in *Watch and Ward,* but he is far from being either likable or brilliant. A bishop is one of the company at Mrs. Lowder's dinner for Millie Theale in *The Wings of the Dove;* but his presence is not accounted for except as exemplary of Mrs. Lowder's pretentiousness, and he plays no active role. In all the themes and dramatic situations of James's many volumes of fiction, a definite issue related to church affiliation or public profession of faith is never raised. A major character in the ill-fated play *Guy Domville* is a priest who is persuaded to renounce his vocation in order to marry and perpetuate the family name, but who later returns to the priesthood. He is treated sympathetically. James ascribed the failure of the drama in part to the prejudice of the British public. Concerning his problem in this play James wrote to his friend John Hay on February 9, 1895:

> The subject of my little play demanded that I should put Catholics *en scene,* & the British public won't stand Papists. I thrust them back into the last century & toned them down with the mellowest old-world atmosphere and grace, of an ingenious & human little story—but it was no go.[6]

Henry James

James does occasionally use characters of avowed religious faith or pretension—Kate Croy's sister and the obnoxious Miss Condrips in *The Wings of the Dove,* and Mrs. Mark Ambient in "The Author of Beltraffio" suggest themselves—but the implications associated with these characters are almost invariably and often strongly unfavorable. It seems that in his writing Henry James applied stringently his father's distrust and dislike of organized religion.

II

Yet Henry James was a man marked by religious sensibility in extreme degree. For positive documentation of this fact in terms of his own responsive interest we must turn to his reviews of religious books and to his thoughts on the religious aspects of art, especially architecture, in his early years as a writer.

James included a number of books of primarily religious content or implication among the many he reviewed during the years of his literary apprenticeship and thereafter. Again and again we may discover in these reviews implicit or acknowledged revelation of his own religious stance. One of the earliest and most interesting of these comments is in a review of *The Journal of Eugenie de Guerin,* in *The Nation* for December 14, 1865. James wrote:

> Religion without imagination is piety; and such is Mlle. de Guerin's religion. Her journal, taken as a whole, seems to us to express a profound contentment. . . . Her peculiar merit is that, with exaltation, enthusiasm, or ecstasy, quietly, steadily, and naturally, she entertained the idea of the Divine goodness. The truth is that she was strong. She was a woman of character. Thoroughly dependent on the church, she was independent of everything else.[7]

When in *The Nation* for September 13, 1866, James reviewed *Eugenie de Guerin's Letters,* he did not hesitate to call her a saint:

> . . . it seems almost illogical to imply that saintship is possible

among our contemporaries. Yet it is equally certain that men and women of extraordinary purity of character constantly attain to a familiarity with divine things as deep and undisturbed as Mlle. de Guerin's.[8]

In a review of Francis Parkman's *The Jesuits in North America in the Seventeenth Century*, in *The Nation* of June 6, 1867, James commented:

> Mr. Parkman's pages . . . furnish us . . . with a second inference, more gratifying to human vanity than the first, and that is, that religion, in spite of the commonplace, intellectual form which it has recently grown to assume in many quarters, is essentially bound up with miracles. Only the miracles are a tribute of man to God, and not of God to man. It may be fairly said of the Jesuit missionaries that, in the firmness of their endurance of horrible sufferings, they fairly broke the law of nature. They broke at least those of their own temperaments. The timid man hourly outfaced impending torture, and the weak outlasted it. When one can boast of such miracles as these, what is the use of insisting on diseases cured by the touch of saintly bones, or . . . enthusiasts visibly transported in the arms of angels?[9]

In 1868, reviewing George Sand's *Mademoiselle de Merquem* in *The Nation* for July 16, young Henry James administers a vigorous rebuke to Thackeray:

> We can perfectly well understand that Thackeray should not have liked "Spiridion"—to ourselves it is not an agreeable book—but there can be no better instance of that superficial and materialistic quality of mind which constantly chafes the reader of his novels, than his gross failure to appreciate the relative dignity of Madame Sand's religious attitude and of his own artificial posture.[10]

Comments on religious concerns are less frequent in James's critical writings after the first few years. This change is even more noticeable in his books of travel. The only expression I have found of a response to nature—as distinguished from human achievement in art or architecture—in which a religious element is clearly present is, appropriately, in a comment on

236

Niagara Falls which appeared in a very early travel sketch published in 1871. The sketch was included in the book *Portraits of Places* in 1884. There is something of genuine personal religious attitude and experience in these sentences:

> If the line of beauty had vanished from the earth elsewhere, it would survive in the brow of Niagara. It is impossible to insist too strongly on the grace of the thing, as seen from the Canada cliff. The genius who invented it was certainly the first author of the idea that order, proportion and symmetry are the conditions of perfect beauty. He applied his faith among the watching and listening forests, long before the Greeks proclaimed theirs in the measurements of the Parthenon. Even the roll of the white batteries at the base seems fixed and poised and ordered, and in the vague middle zone of difference between the flood as it falls and the mist as it rises you imagine a mystical meaning—the passage of body to soul, of matter to spirit, of human to divine.[11]

The *Transatlantic Sketches* of 1875, James's first book of travel, reflects chiefly the eager delight of his first full years of maturity in Europe (1872–74). It is rich in detail and incident which express the young writer's lively responses to new places, with many which reveal his religious sensibility. These range from the overtly satirical and the quietly humorous to an unmistakable seriousness. In England, James is amused by the contrast between conservatism (embodied in the Church of England) and dissent. At Chester, in May, 1872, he wrote:

> Conservatism has the cathedrals, the colleges, the castles, the gardens, the traditions, the associations, the fine names, the better manners, the poetry. Dissent has the dusky brick chapels in provincial by-streets, the names out of Dickens, the uncertain tenure of the *h,* and the poor *mens sibi conscia recti.* Differences which in other countries are slight and varying, almost metaphysical, as one may say, are marked in England by a gulf.[12]

Elsewhere in England, too, James is keenly aware of the this-wordly aspect of institutional religion. At Wells Cathedral he is moved to comment:

. . . you may fancy it less a temple for man's needs than a monument of his pride,—less a fold for the flock than for the shepherds,—a visible sign that, besides the actual assortment of heavenly thrones, there is constantly on hand a choice lot of cushioned cathedral stalls.[13]

There is a hint of James's personal dislike of Calvinism in a passage written at Berne:

I doubt whether we can twist the Rhone into a channel for even the most diluted Calvinism. It must have seemed to the grim Doctor as one of the streams of the paradise he was making it so hard to enter. For ourselves, as it hurries undarkened past the gray theological city, we may liken it to the impetus of faith shooting in deep indifference past the doctrine of election.[14]

A possibly more serious note enters a comment at Milan:

. . . that solid old basilica of St. Ambrose, with its spacious atrium and its crudely solemn mosaics, in which it is surely your own fault if you do not forget Dr. Strauss and M. Renan and worship as simply as a Christian of the ninth century.[15]

Clearly serious, and personal indeed, is the writer's response to certain paintings which most deeply moved him:

You may be as little of a formal Christian as Fra Angelico was much of one; yet it seems a kind of intellectual duty to let so sincere a presentment of the Christian story [as the *Crucifixion*] work its utmost purpose on your mind.[16]

At Rome the traveler is startled by the impression, as he looks at the equestrian statue of Marcus Aurelius, "that in the capital of Christendom the portrait most suggestive of a Christian will is that of a pagan emperor,"[17] and he records a thoughtful and not wholly consistent experience of St. Peter's:

A good Catholic, I suppose, is a Catholic anywhere, in the grandest as well as the humblest churches; but to a traveller not especially pledged to be devout, St. Peter's speaks more of contentment than of aspiration. The mind seems to expand there immensely, but on its own level, as we may say. It marvels at the reach of the human imagination and the vastness of our earthly means. This is heaven enough, we say; what it lacks in beauty it makes up in certainty. And yet if one's half-hours at St. Peter's are not actually spent on one's knees, the mind reverts to its tremendous presence with an ardor deeply akin to a passionate effusion of faith. When you are weary of the swarming democracy of your fellow-tourists . . . of addled brains and lacquered boots, of ruin and dirt and decay . . . the image of the great temple depresses the balance of your doubts and seems to refute the invasive vulgarity of things and assure you that nothing great is impossible.[18]

Of the numerous references to monasticism in the account of his experiences in Italy in *Transatlantic Sketches,* most are obviously playful. An example is his comment on the judgment of a popular guidebook on a matter of artistic merit:

It is surely an unkind stroke of fate for him [Domenichino] to have Murray assuring ten thousand Britons every winter . . . that his Communion of St. Jerome is the "second finest picture in the world." If this were so, I should certainly, here in Rome, where such institutions are convenient, retire into the nearest convent; with such a world I should have a standing quarrel.[19]

But James is again serious when he speaks of a young priest whom he observed at solitary prayer in an obscure shrine, just after the young writer had been attending the Carnival:

It was my late impression of these frivolous people, I suppose, joined with the extraordinary gravity of the young priest's face—his pious fatigue, his droning prayer, and his isolation—which gave me just then and there a supreme vision of the religious passion—its privations and resignations and exhaustions, and its terribly small share of amusement. He was young and strong and evidently of not too refined a fibre to enjoy the Carnival; but planted there with his face pale with fasting and his knees stiff with praying, he seemed so stern a satire on it and on the crazy thousands who were preferring it to *his* way, that I half expected to

239

see some heavenly portent out of a monastic legend come down and confirm his choice. . . .[20]

It is a curious and noteworthy fact that comments on places and impressions which carried religious significance for James are lacking in the records of foreign travel which he published in the thirty-five years following the appearance of *Transatlantic Sketches* in 1872. None of these—*A Little Tour in France* (1884), *Essays in London and Elsewhere* (1893), *English Hours* (1905), and the later *Italian Hours* (1909)—afford any personal revelation as to religious concern and interest that is at all comparable to what is found in the early volume. This marked change roughly parallels his diminished attention to books of religious import in his reviewing. It also parallels the disappearance of clergymen as well as conventionally defined religious issues from his fiction which we have previously noted.

Not until *The American Scene* (1907), the record of James's trip to America in the last decade of his life, is there much commentary on religious architecture or religious values. Here it is demanded by his purpose. James sees the church architecture—or its absence—in America as clearly expressive of the major fault he finds in American culture as a whole: its materialism, its lack of recognition of the arts, its worship of money. He finds the meetinghouses of New England immediately unpleasing:

> Here was no church, to begin with; and the shrill effect of the New England meetinghouse, in general so merely continuous and congruous, as to type and tone, with the common objects about it, the single straight breath with which it seems to blow the ground clear of the seated solidity of religion, is an impression that responds to the renewed sight of one of these structures as promptly as the sharp ring to the pressure of the electric button. One lives among English ancientries, for instance, as in a world towards the furnishing of which religion has done a large part. And here, immediately, was a room vast and vacant, with a vacancy especially reducible, for most of the senses, to the fact of that elimination.[21]

In New York, James is, predictably, impressed by the skyscrapers but not favorably. He sees them as "impudently new and still more impudently 'novel'—this in common with so many other terrible things in America—and they are triumphant payers of dividends."[22] James judges the skyscrapers—prophetically, for those of 1907—as provisional merely, lacking "the authority of things of permanence or even of things of long duration. One story is good only until another is told, and skyscrapers are the last word of economic ingenuity only till another word be written."[23] He laments for the beauty of the spire of Trinity Church, "so cruelly overtopped and so barely distinguishable, from your train-bearing barge, as you stand off, in its abject helpless humility."[24] The modern reader can understand the feeling James expresses if he looks down on Trinity Church from the windows of 40 Wall Street, or on St. Patrick's Cathedral from the roof of Rockefeller Center.

In Washington, James is profoundly struck by the absence of any spiritual symbol or other suggestion of religious faith in the establishment of the national government. He finds only one church in America that he likes, only one that seems to him an appropriate expression of religious faith and aspiration. It is St. Michael's, at Charleston:

> The high, complicated, inflated spire has the sincerity, approved of time, that is so rare, over the land, in the work of man's hands, laden though these be with the millions he offers as a vain bribe to it; and in the sweet old churchyard ancient authority seemed to me, on the occasion of my visit, to sit, among the sun-warmed tombs and the inter-related slabs and the extravagant flowers, as on the sole cushion the general American bareness in such connections had left it. . . . the place feels itself, in the fine old dusky archaic way, the constituted temple of a faith—achieves, in a word, the air of reality that one had seen in every other such case, from town to town and from village to village, missed with an unconsciousness that had to do duty for success.[25]

One feels reasonably sure that the elder Henry James would not have approved of his son's acute concern over the meager architectural expression of religious devotion in American life. To the elder Henry James, as I have noted, religious institutions were by nature anathema, and a church—under any name and of any denomination—was an agency of the Devil. The attitude of the younger Henry as revealed in the *Transatlantic Sketches* was far different, as we have seen. The long interval in which no comparable experience was disclosed suggests that in middle life the novelist in some measure conformed to his father's views. But in these revealing comments of his later years there is manifest a response to religious institutions—at least in their material expression—which is clearly at variance with his father's; for though the passages from *The American Scene* quoted above are immediately concerned with the church as material symbol, the architectural reference is always linked with human significance.

III

If the suggestion of religious attitude and experience diminishes in Henry James's comments on books and on places as he reaches maturity, it seems to me to become increasingly powerful and explicit in his fiction from 1880 on. It is necessary to try to define distinctly our use of the term "religious" in this application. To Henry James, religion was a matter of conduct, not of church membership or acceptance of a stated creed. Further, it was less a matter of external action than of internal attitude and motive, though these are unmistakably demonstrated through specific action. Evil, sin, he equated with selfishness—the acquisitive and/or domineering assertion of selfhood at the expense of others. Good, then—the opposite of evil—lay in the subjugation or abnegation of self, the use of life for the good and growth and happiness of other human beings. The vital central conflict in all of James's mature fiction is that between the impulse to dominate, to exploit or control others—whether it be conscious or unconscious—and the will and power to give, to renounce, to live and love unselfishly. This appears to have been the essential core of the religious system of the elder Henry James, beneath all the complex theological and metaphysical elaboration he gave it. It is also the heart of Christianity. "Thou shalt love thy God. . . . Thou shalt love thy neighbor as thyself." If we accept this formulation and apply it thoughtfully to the fiction of Henry James, we can see that it is indeed possible to view him as the most positively religious of our American novelists of the nineteenth century.

Dramatization of this central theme seems to me to begin with *Washington Square* of 1880 and to mark every major achievement in James' fiction thereafter. The irony implicit in Dr. Sloper's determination to dominate his daughter's life—for her own good—does not extenuate his sin, in James's eyes or the reader's; and the purely selfish and hence destructive motivation of Morris Townsend and Mrs. Penniman is all too obvious.

In *The American* (1877) the issue has been less clearly defined. Christopher Newman's quest for a wife is essentially acquisitive in motivation, though far less basely so than Townsend's. The real villains of the story, the elder Bellegardes, are much less firmly accounted for in their cruelty than is Dr. Sloper and hence are less capable of gaining the reader's comprehension and even pity. Claire de Cintre—the woman as victim, so prevalent in James's fiction—is a person actually less accessible to the reader's full understanding and sympathy than is poor Catherine Sloper with all her limitations. The ethico-religious crisis of the novel is of course Newman's decision to refrain from revenge, the means for which he has been at such pains to acquire; but this has almost the effect of anticlimax. It may be noted that in this early novel, Claire de Cintre's decision to enter a convent and devote herself to a life of religious contemplation is treated by James with less understanding than some of the travel notes cited above might lead us to expect, though his use of Newman's point of view sufficiently accounts for this impression.

In our attempt to trace the ethico-religious principle as fun-

damental in James's fiction, *The Portrait of a Lady* presents
another less than unequivocal pattern. Isabel Archer's own initial attitude toward life is in part that of the exploiter, the
willing user of others, the asserter of self. Madame Merle and
Gilbert Osmond are of course unmistakable and powerful dramatic embodiments of ruthless selfishness, and Pansy and Isabel
in widely different ways and degrees are their victims. But even
Ralph's generous motivation has an element of self-gratifica-
tion in it; the motives of both Casper Goodwood and Lord
Warburton are fundamentally selfish; and the figure of Mrs.
Touchett is one of almost total self-indulgence and self-
immurement. It is only in relation to the theme of self-assertion versus self-surrender that Isabel's return to Rome at the
end of the novel can be recognized in its full significance.

In *The Bostonians* the cardinal sins of appropriation and
exploitation of a human personality by selfish human beings are
dramatized in the attempt of Olive Chancellor (unconsciously
motivated by homosexual attraction) to dominate Verena Tal-
lant and in the opposing aggressiveness of Basil Ransom. In
The Princess Casamassima the conflict is more complex, the
would-be exploiters and dominators of Hyacinth Robinson are
more varied: the Princess on the one hand, the Muniments (the
marvelously achieved Rosie no less than her brother) on the
other. In this novel (never fully appreciated) we have as frustrated countering figures Miss Pynsent, Mr. Vetch, and Millicent
Henning: each in a markedly individual way motivated by
unselfish love.

Many of the shorter fictions of the 1880's express James's
ethico-religious evaluation of conduct with especial power.
"Four Meetings" illustrates selfish appropriation and exploitation with great poignancy. "The Author of Beltraffio" dramatizes the conflict between contrarily directed attitudes of selfishness almost to the point of melodrama. A more candid and
violent portrayal of destructive evil than is usually encountered
in James's depiction of selfishness is found in "A London Life."
The Aspern Papers is one of his most completely achieved ren-